THE WAR IN THE AIR

MAP CASE 3

THE WAR IN THE AIR

Being the story of the part played
in the Great War by the Royal Air Force

MAP CASE 3

Airship Raids from
19-20 January 1915 to 27-28 November 1916

www.naval-military-press.com

Published by

The Naval & Military Press Ltd
Unit 5 Riverside, Brambleside
Bellbrook Industrial Estate
Uckfield, East Sussex
TN22 1QQ England

Tel: +44 (0)1825 749494

www.naval-military-press.com
www.nmarchive.com

In reprinting in facsimile from the original, any imperfections are inevitably reproduced and the quality may fall short of modern type and cartographic standards.

LIST OF MAPS

1. Typical Aeroplane Raids, 1914-1916 1

Airship Raids

2. 19-20 January 1915 7
3. 14 April 1915 9
   15 June 1915
4. 15-16 April 1915 13
5. 29-30 April 1915 17
   10 May 1915
6. 7 May 1915 19
   26 May 1915
   31 May - 1 June 1915
7. 4-5 June 1915 23
8. 4-5 June 1915 27
   6-7 June 1915
9. 9-10 August 1915 31
10. 9-10 August 1915 35
11. 12-13 August 1915 37
12. 17-18 August 1915 41
13. 7-8 September 1915 47
14. 8-9 September 1915 53
15. 8-9 September 1915 59
16. 11-12 September 1915 61
    12-13 September 1915
17. 13-14 September 1915 65
18. 13-14 October 1915 67
19. 31 January - 1 February 1916 73
20. 5-6 March 1916 79

21.	31 March - 1 April 1916	87
22.	1-2 April 1916	93
23.	2-3 April 1916	97
24.	2-3 April 1916	101
25.	3-4 April 1916	103
26.	5-6 April 1916	105
27.	24-25 April 1916	109
28.	25-26 April 1916	113
29.	26 April 1916	117
30.	2-2 May 1916	119
31.	2-3 May 1916	123
32.	28-29 July 1916	129
33.	31 July - 1 August 1916	135
34.	2-3 August 1916	141
35.	8-9 August 1916	145
36.	23-24 August 1916	151
37.	24-25 August 1916	153
38.	2-3 September 1916	157
39.	23-24 September 1916	163
40.	25-26 September 1916	169
41.	1-2 October 1916	183
42.	27-28 November 1916	189

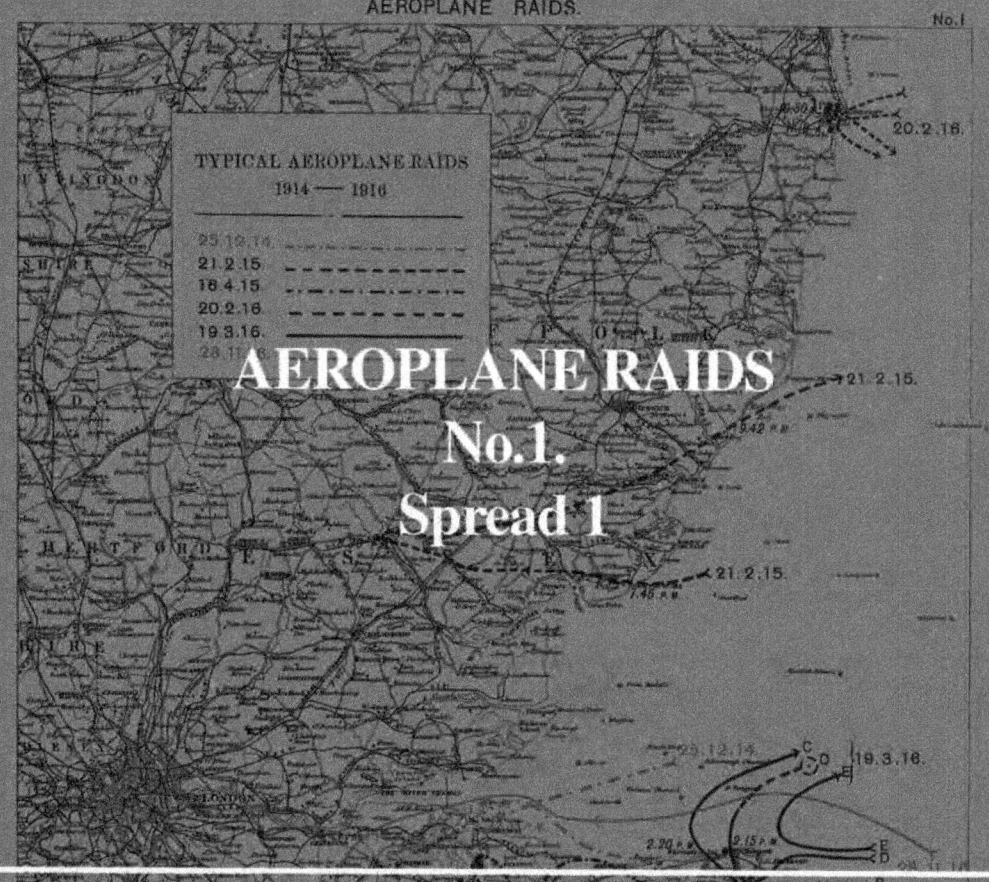

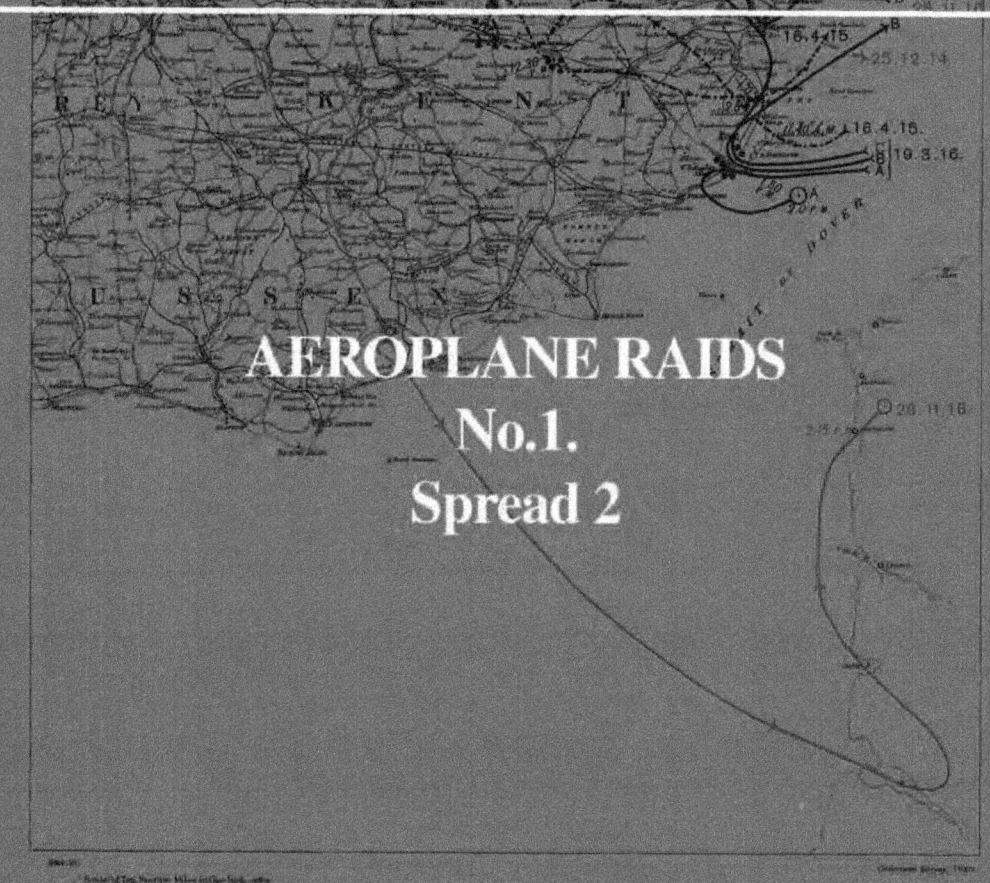

Spread 1

AEROPLANE

TYPICAL AEROPLANE RAIDS
1914 — 1916

- 25.12.14.
- 21.2.15.
- 16.4.15.
- 20.2.16.
- 19.3.16.
- 28.11.16.

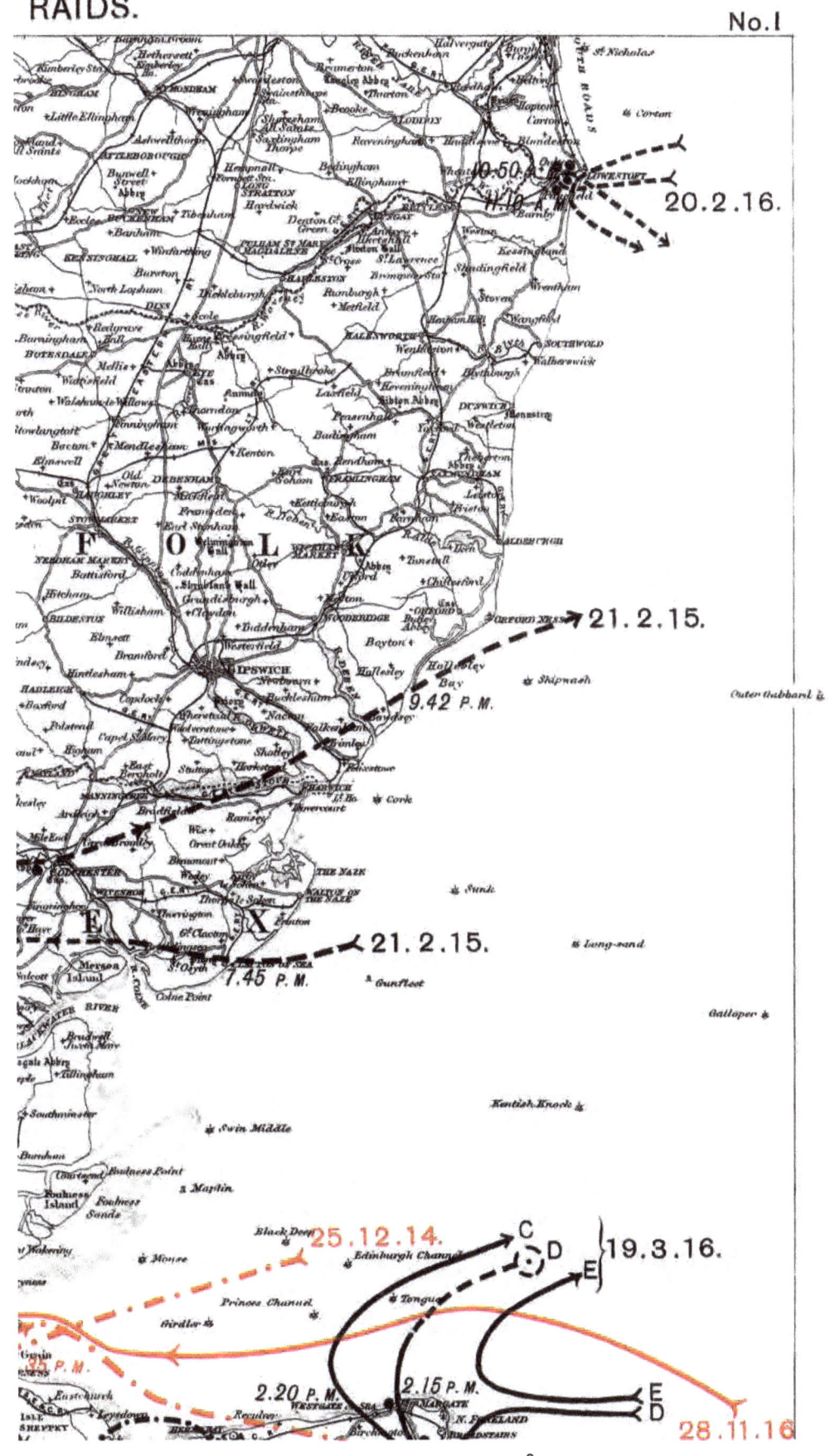

Spread 2

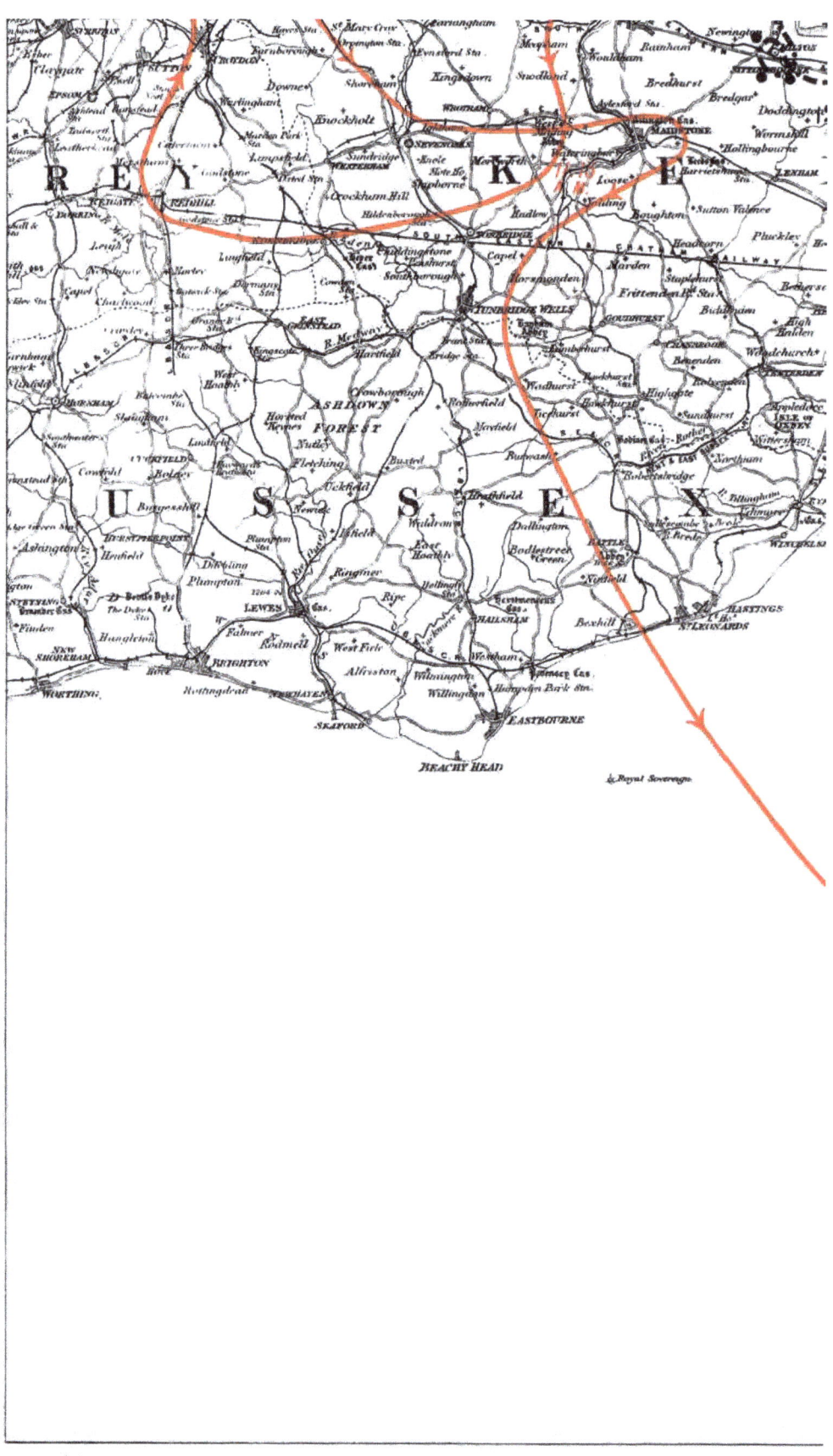

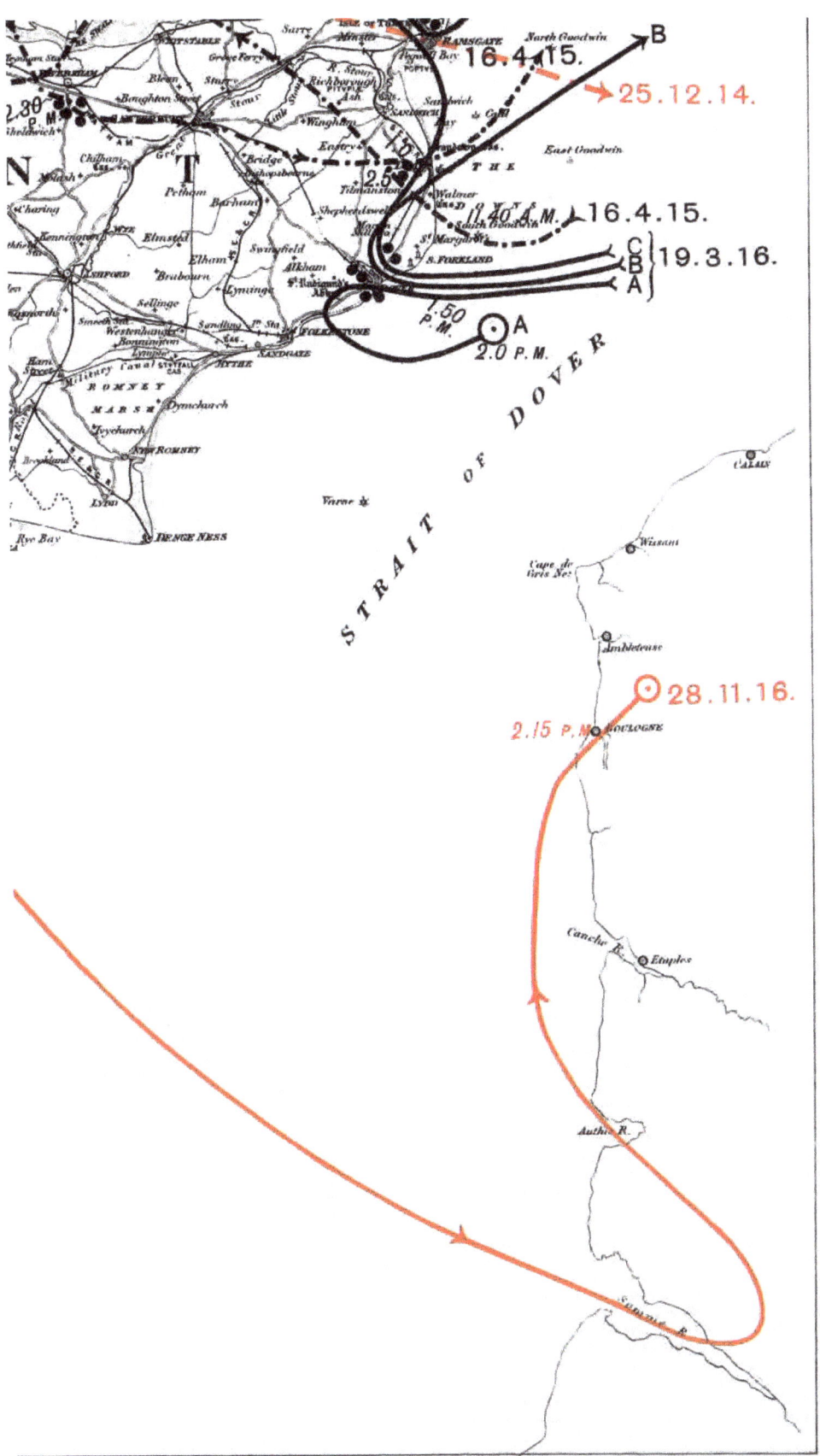

AIRSHIP RAID, 19-20 JANUARY, 1915.   No. 2.

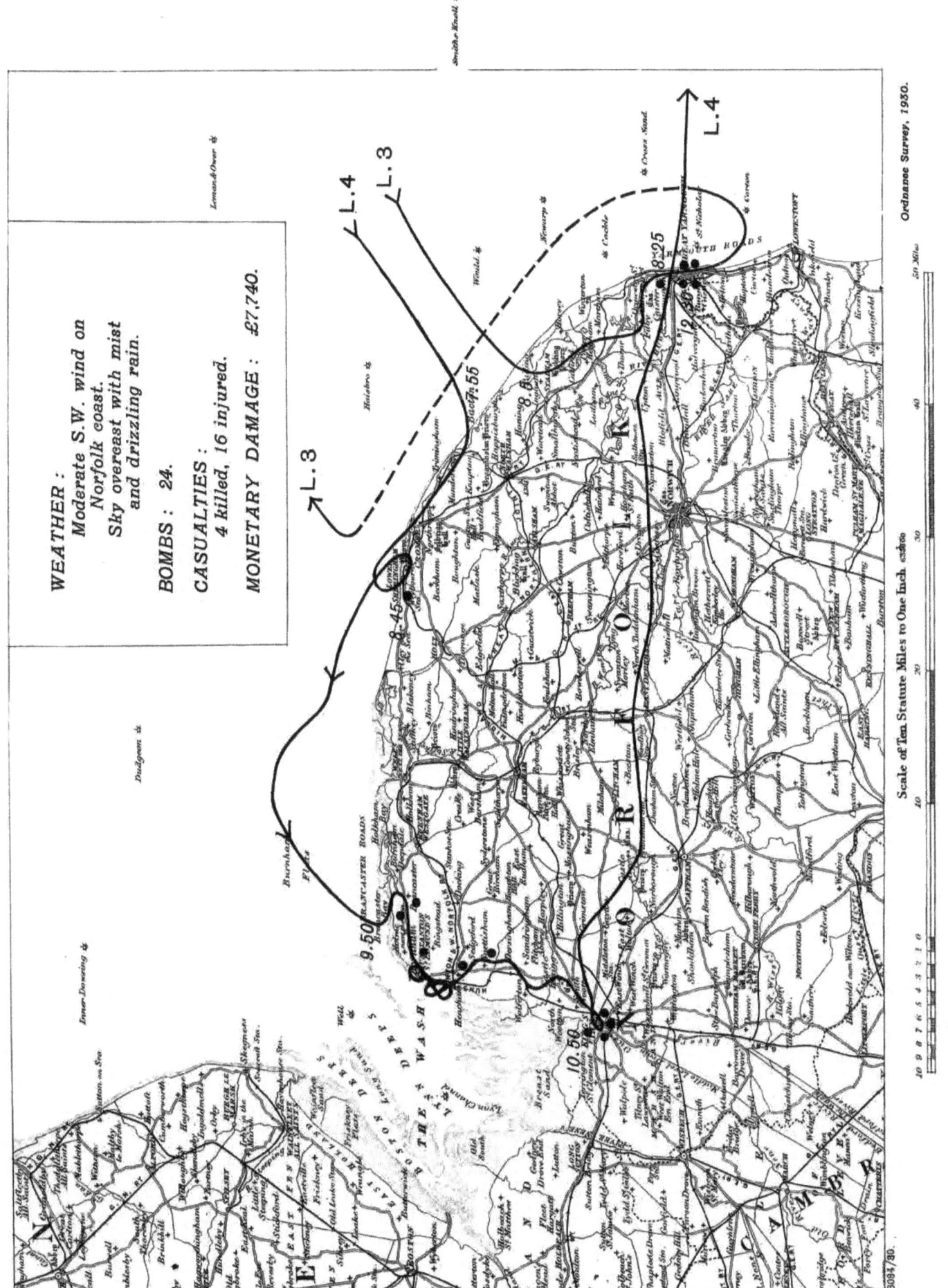

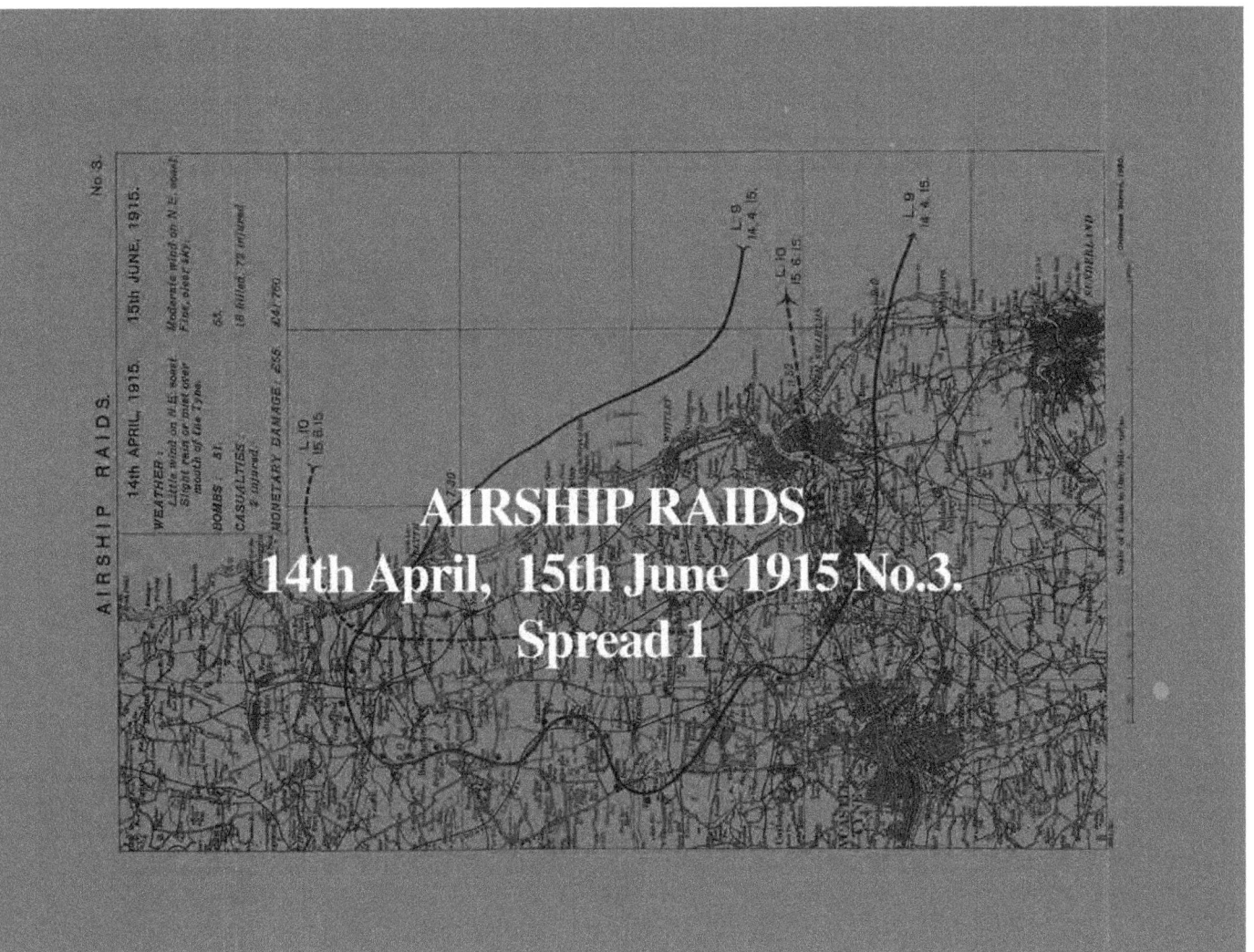

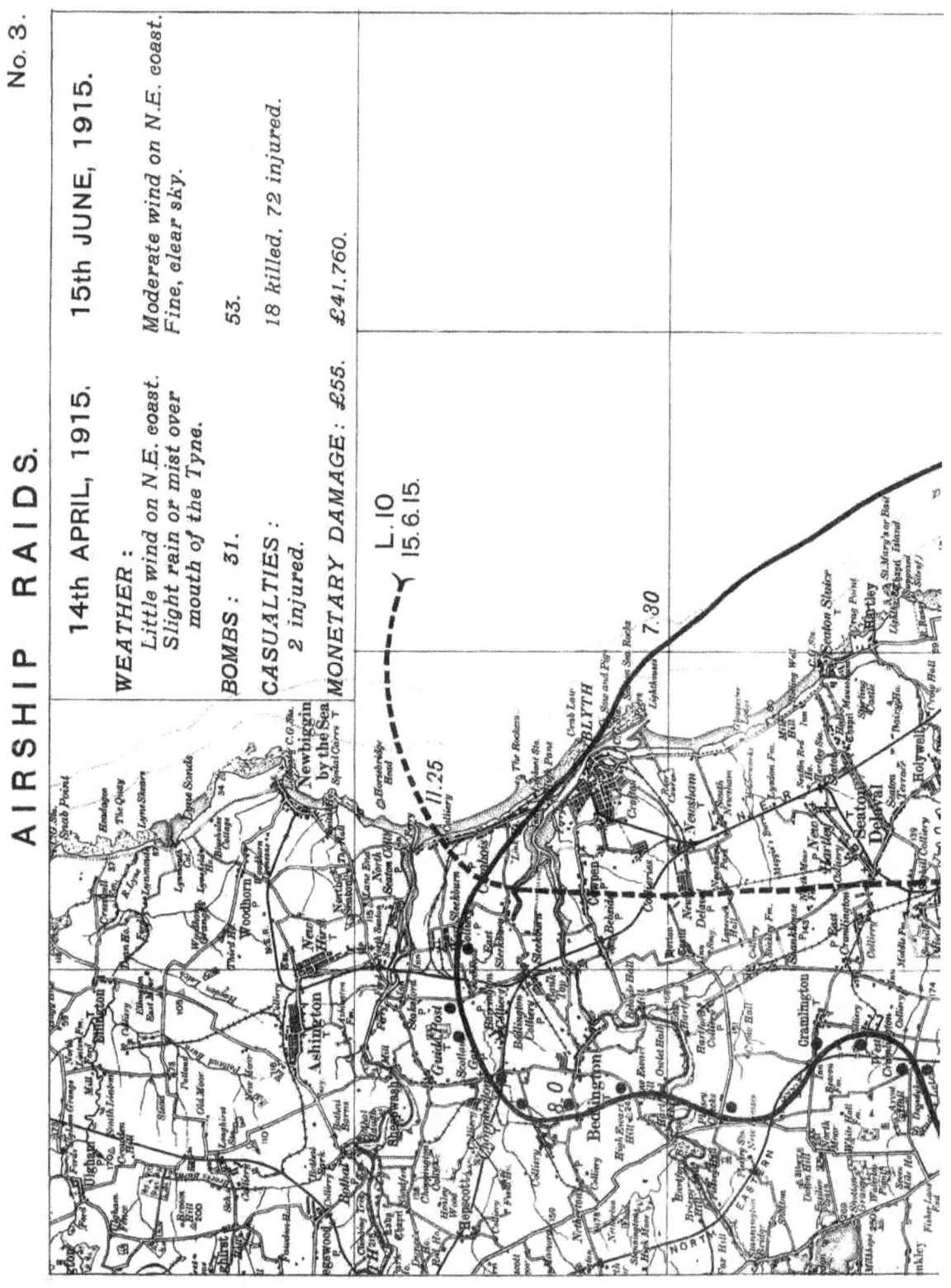

AIRSHIP RAIDS. No. 3.

14th APRIL, 1915.

WEATHER: Little wind on N.E. coast. Slight rain or mist over mouth of the Tyne.

BOMBS: 31.

CASUALTIES: 2 injured.

MONETARY DAMAGE: £55.

15th JUNE, 1915.

Moderate wind on N.E. coast. Fine, clear sky.

53.

18 killed, 72 injured.

£41,760.

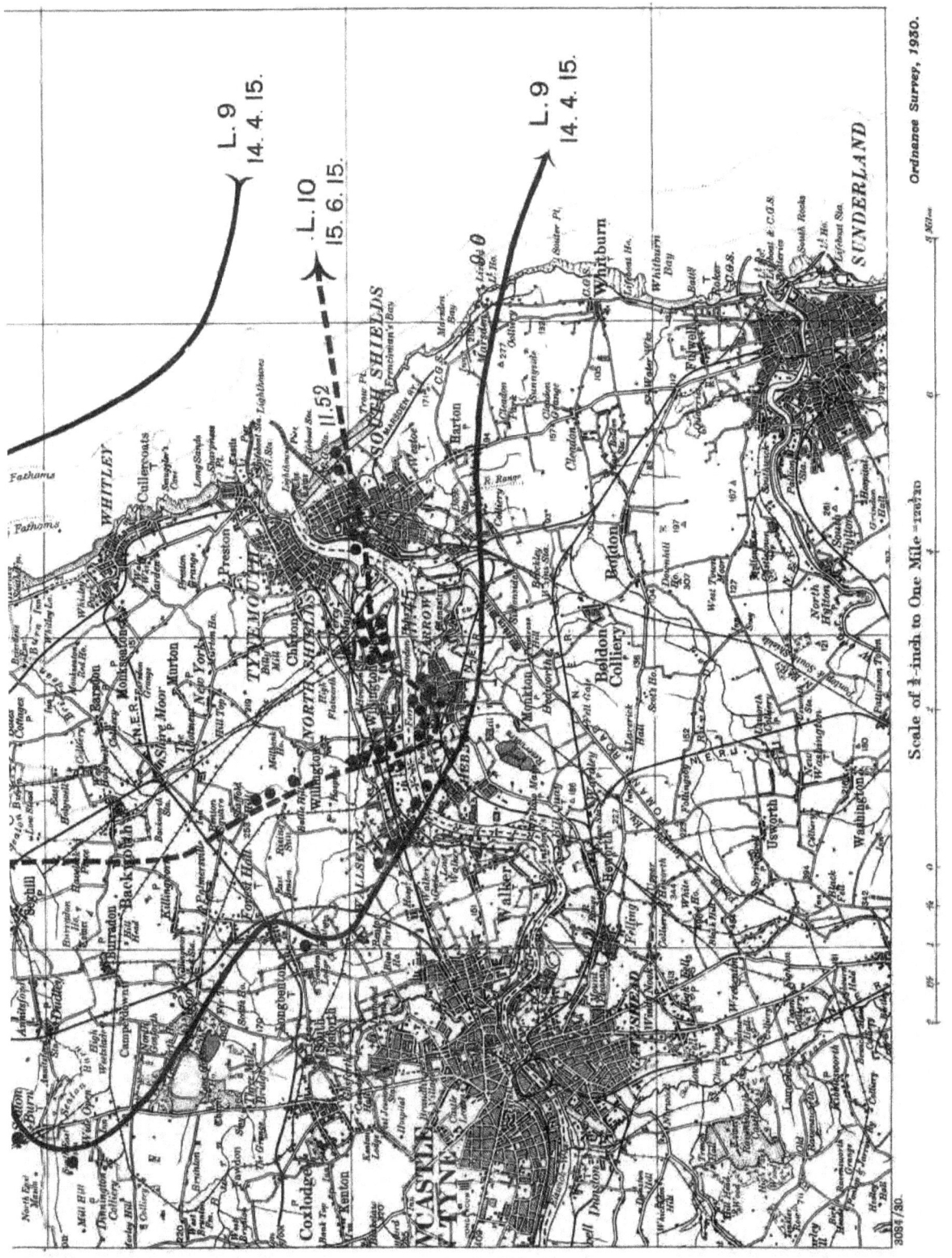

Spread 1

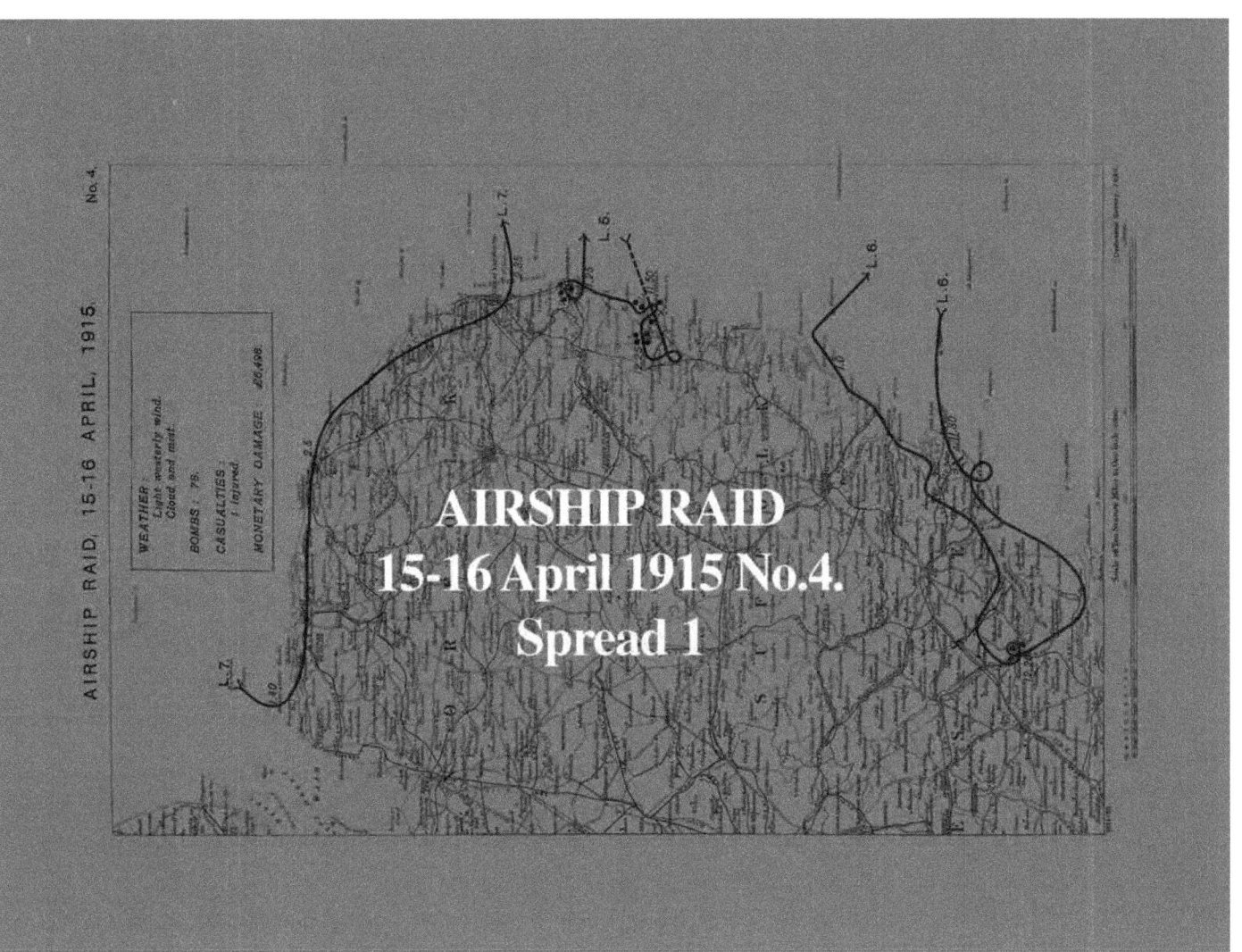

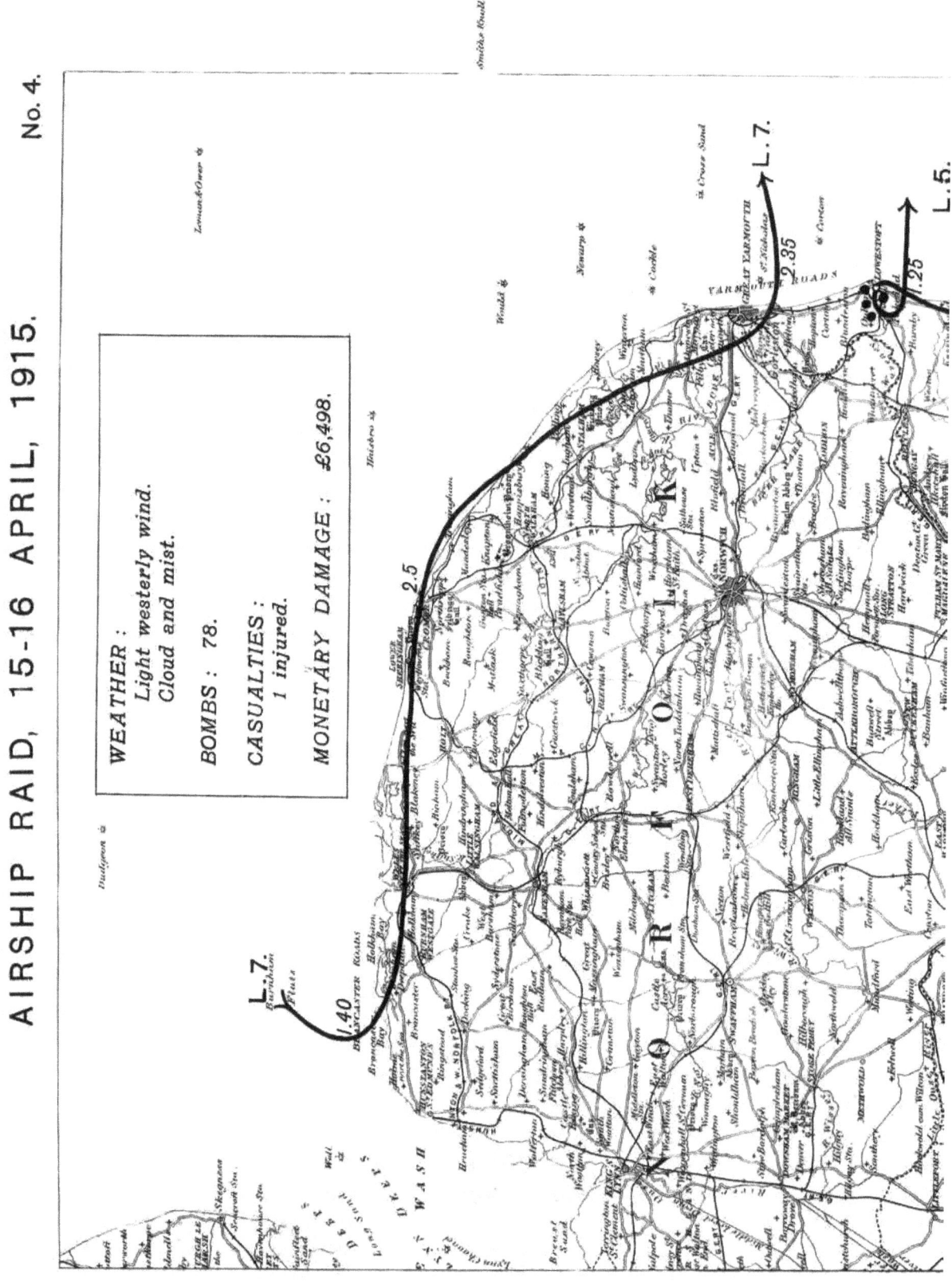

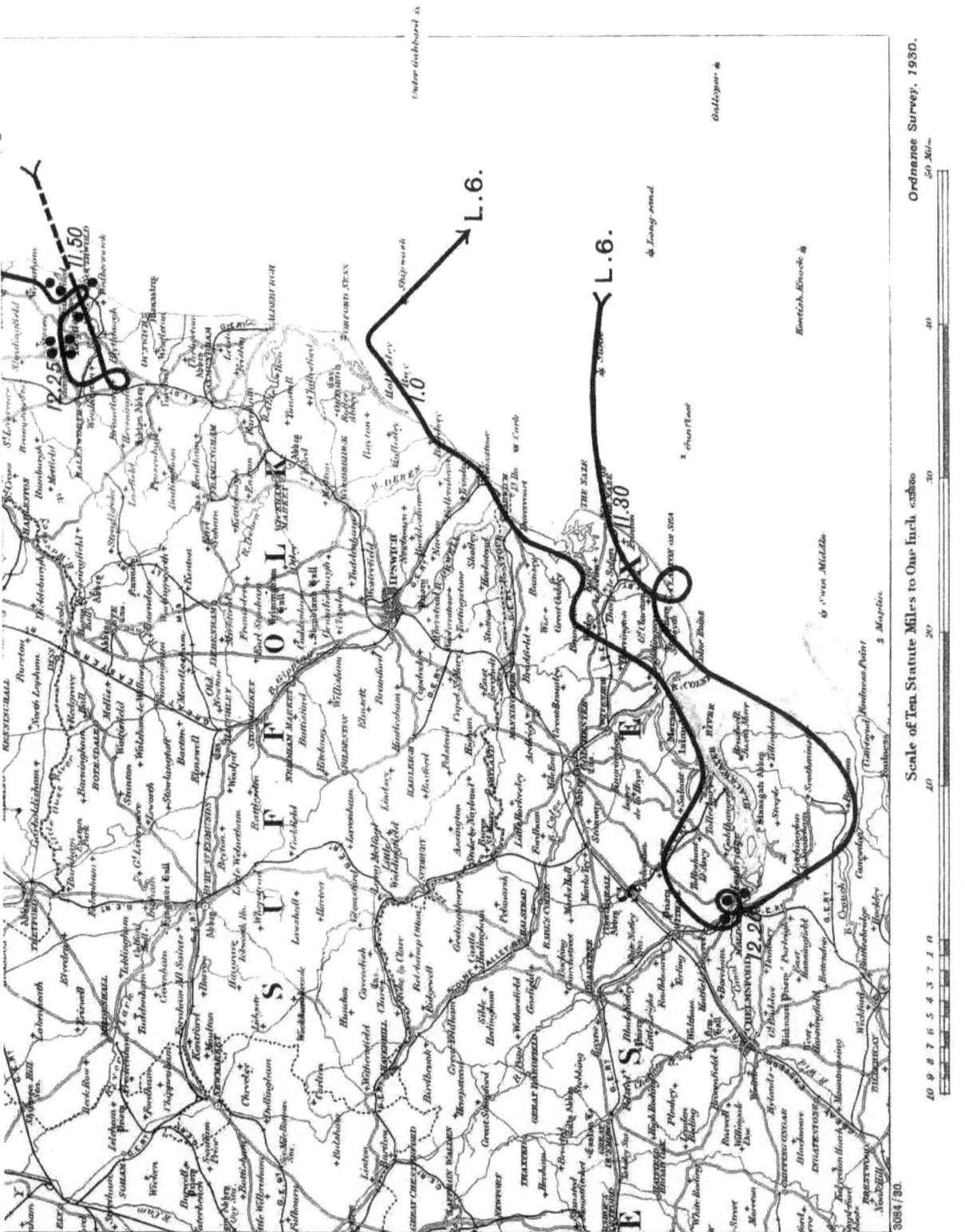

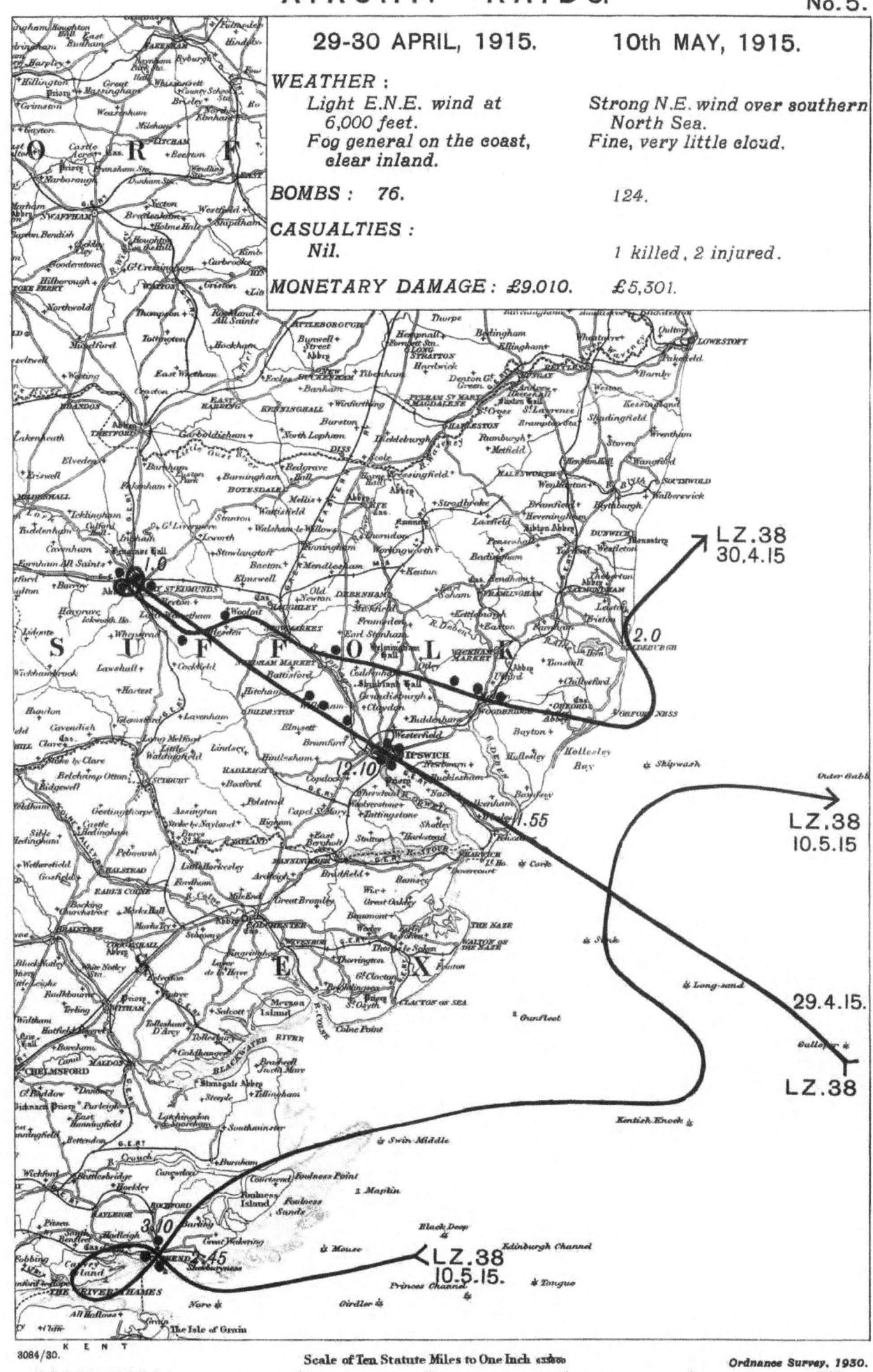

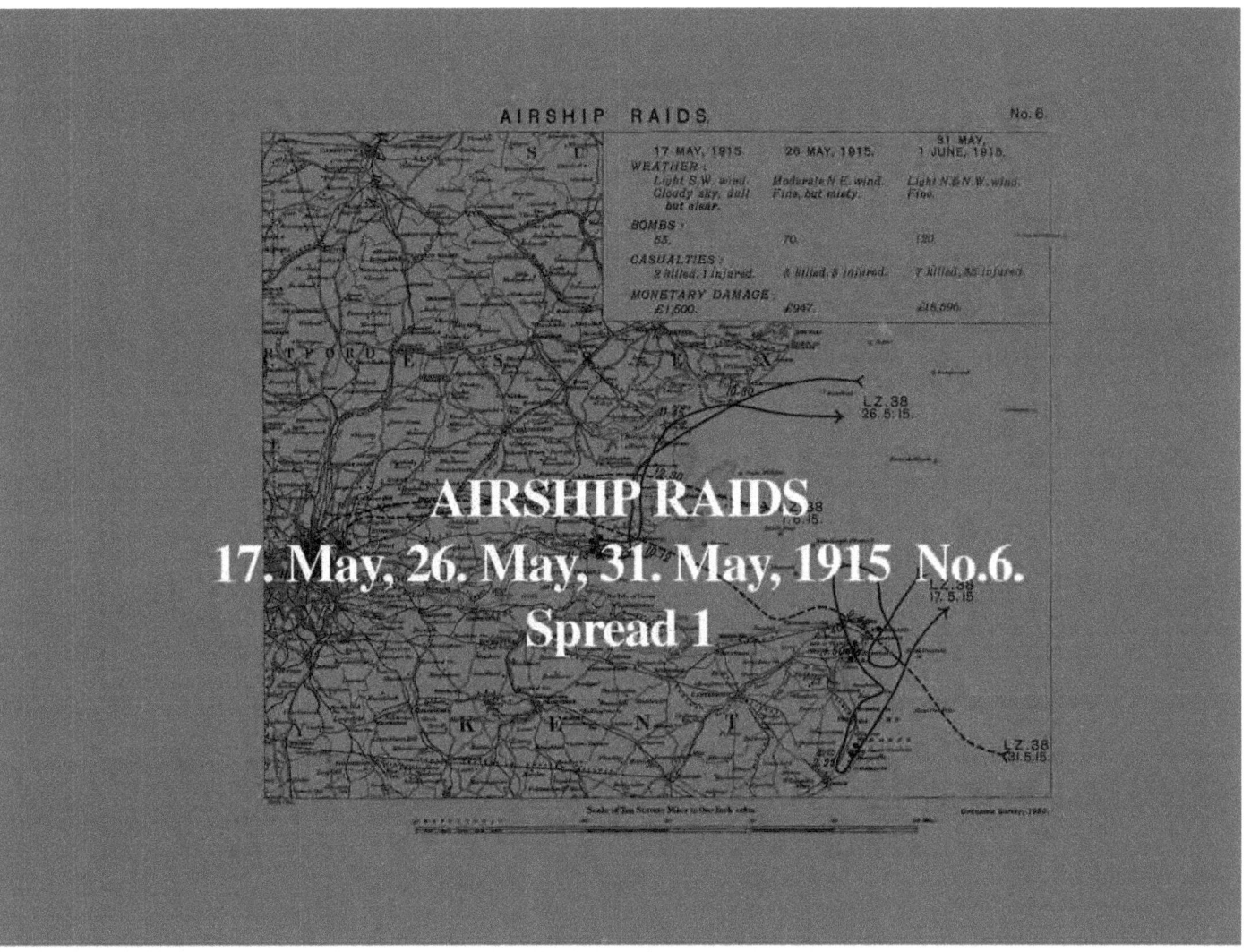

AIRSHIP

RAIDS. No. 6.

17 MAY, 1915.	26 MAY, 1915.	31 MAY, 1 JUNE, 1915.
WEATHER:		
Light S.W. wind. Cloudy sky, dull but clear.	Moderate N.E. wind. Fine, but misty.	Light N.&N.W. wind. Fine.
BOMBS:		
53.	70.	120.
CASUALTIES:		
2 killed, 1 injured.	3 killed, 3 injured.	7 killed, 35 injured.
MONETARY DAMAGE:		
£1,600.	£947.	£18,596.

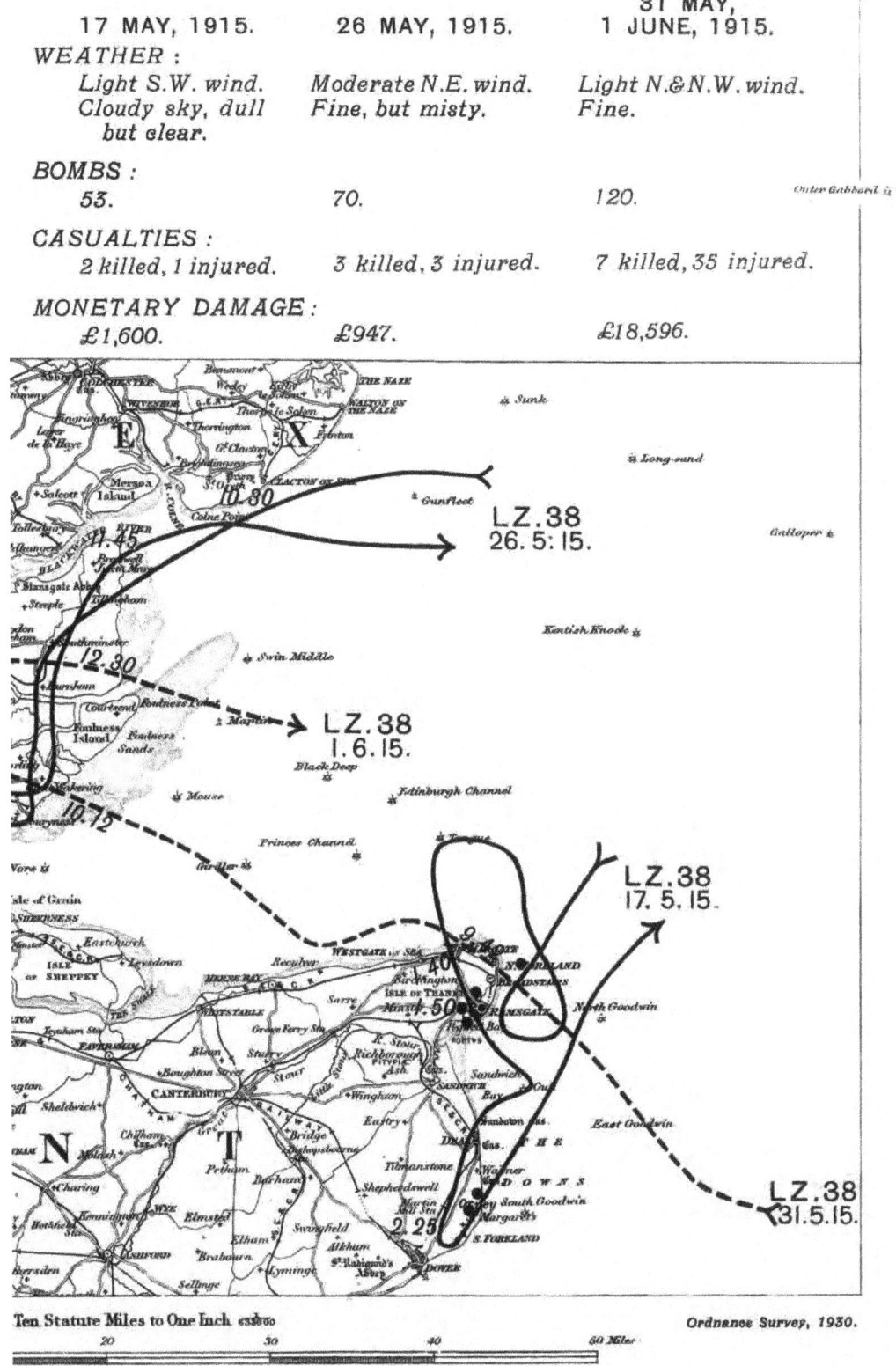

Spread 1

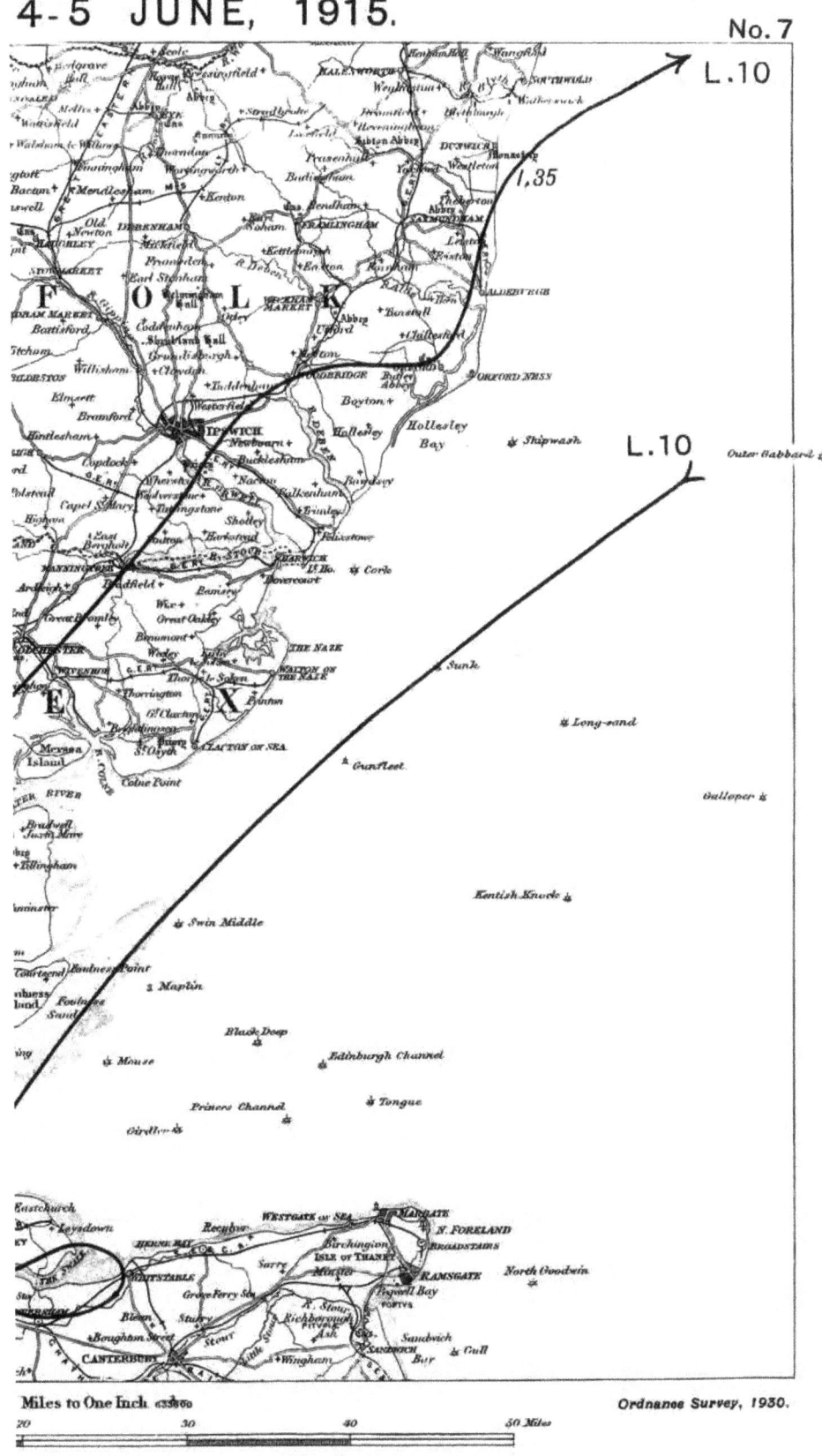

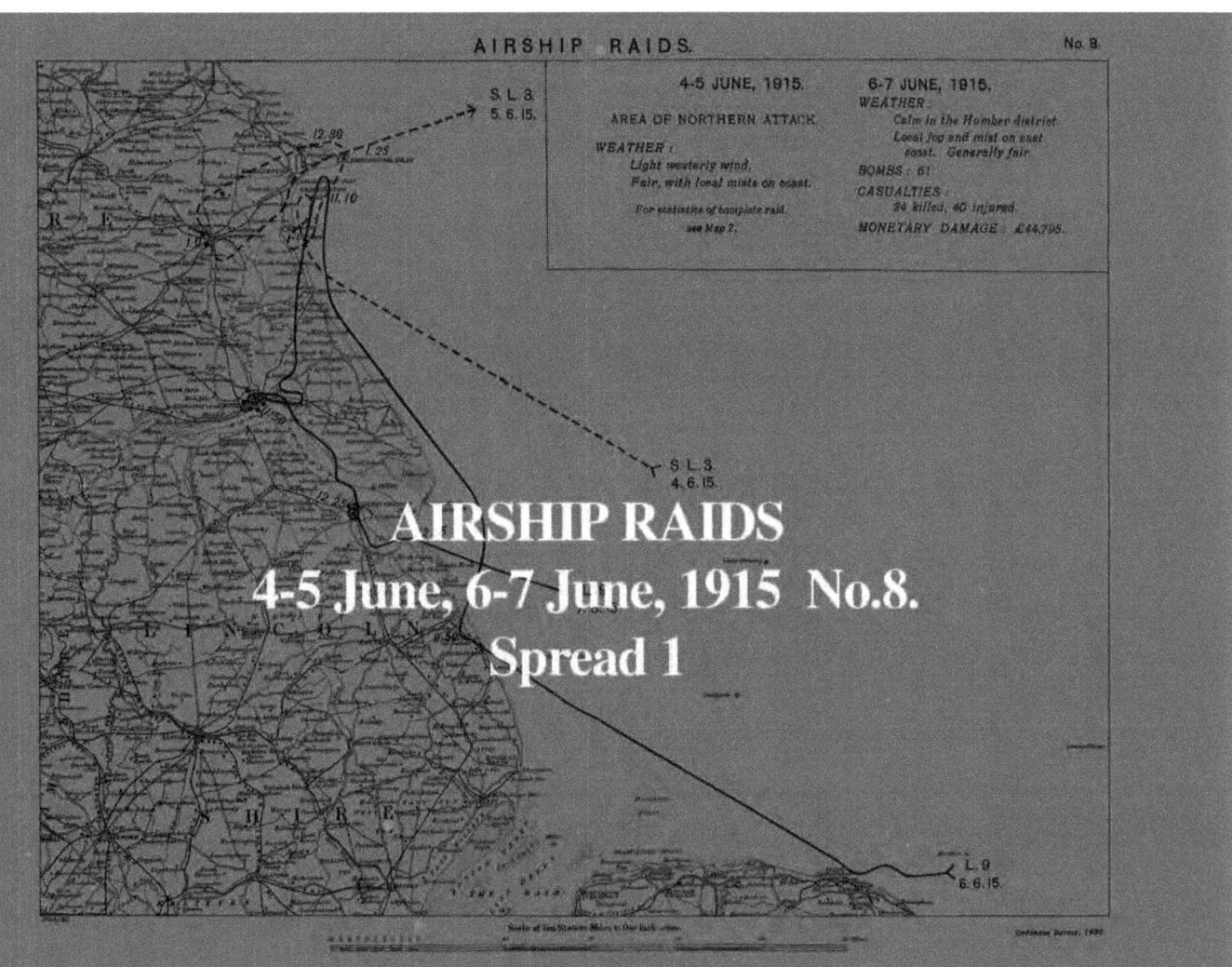

Spread 1

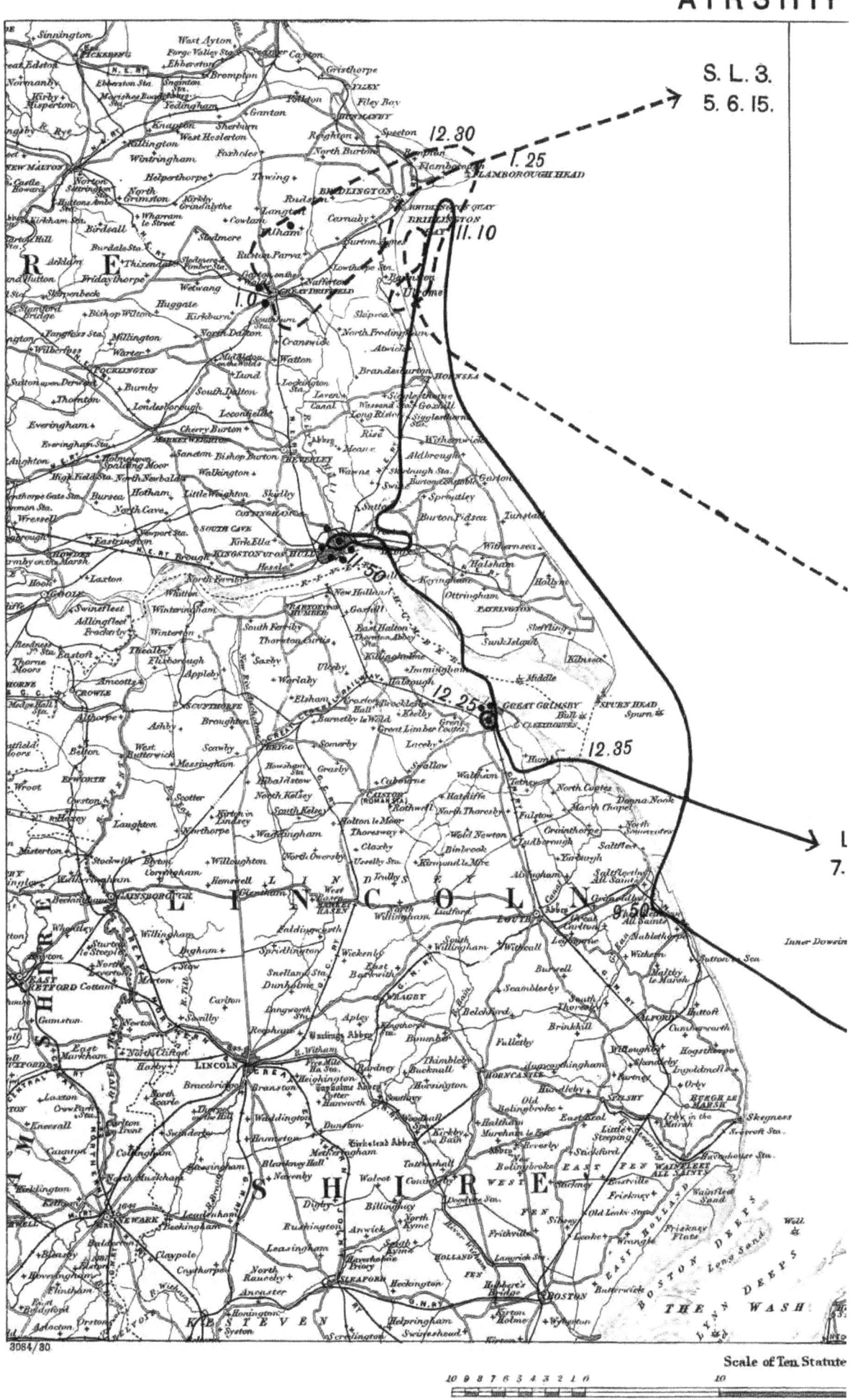

RAIDS.

No. 8.

4-5 JUNE, 1915.

AREA OF NORTHERN ATTACK.

WEATHER :
   Light westerly wind.
   Fair, with local mists on coast.

For statistics of complete raid,
   see Map 7.

6-7 JUNE, 1915.

WEATHER :
   Calm in the Humber district.
   Local fog and mist on east
      coast. Generally fair.
BOMBS : 61.
CASUALTIES :
   24 killed, 40 injured.
MONETARY DAMAGE : £44,795.

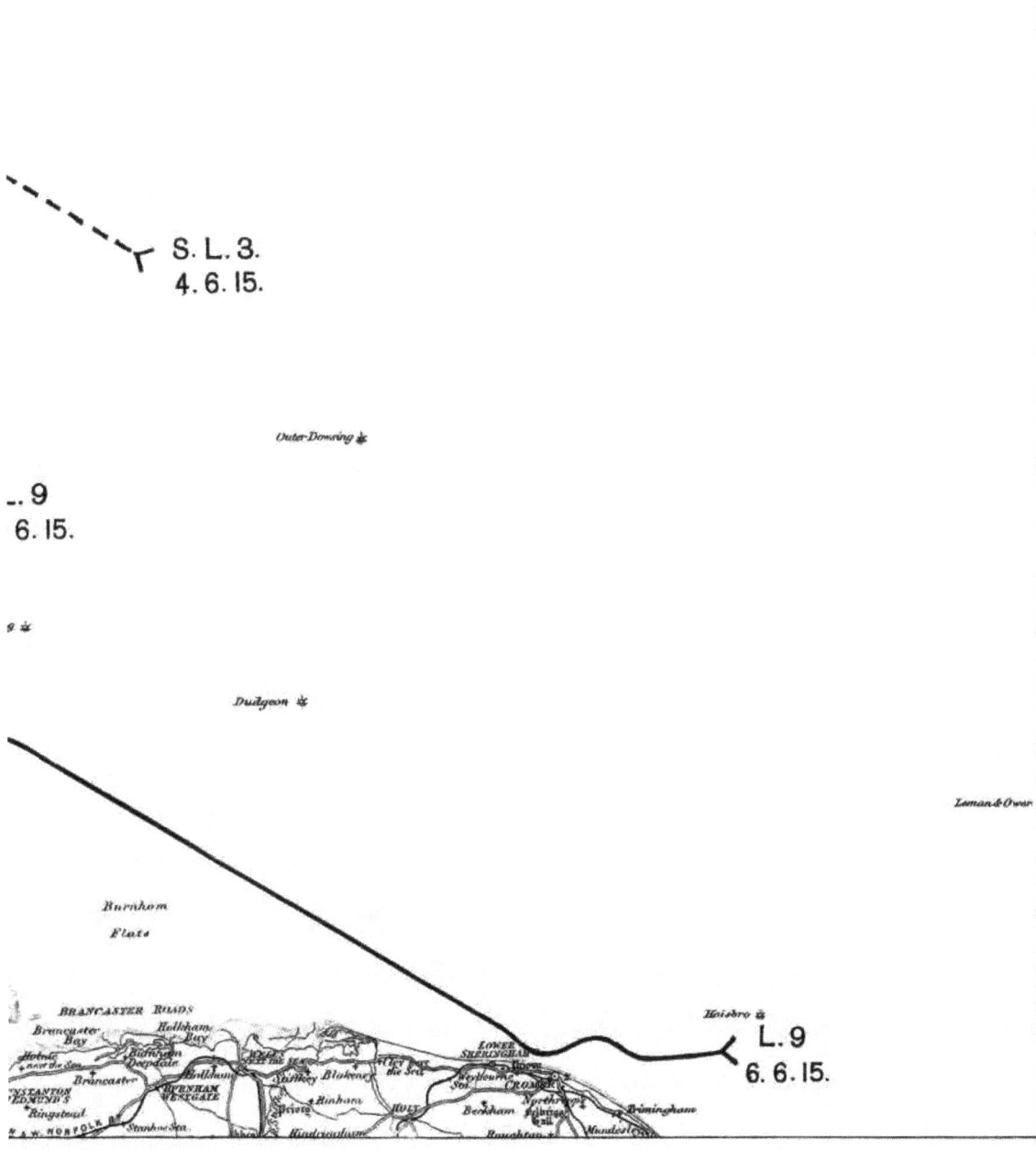

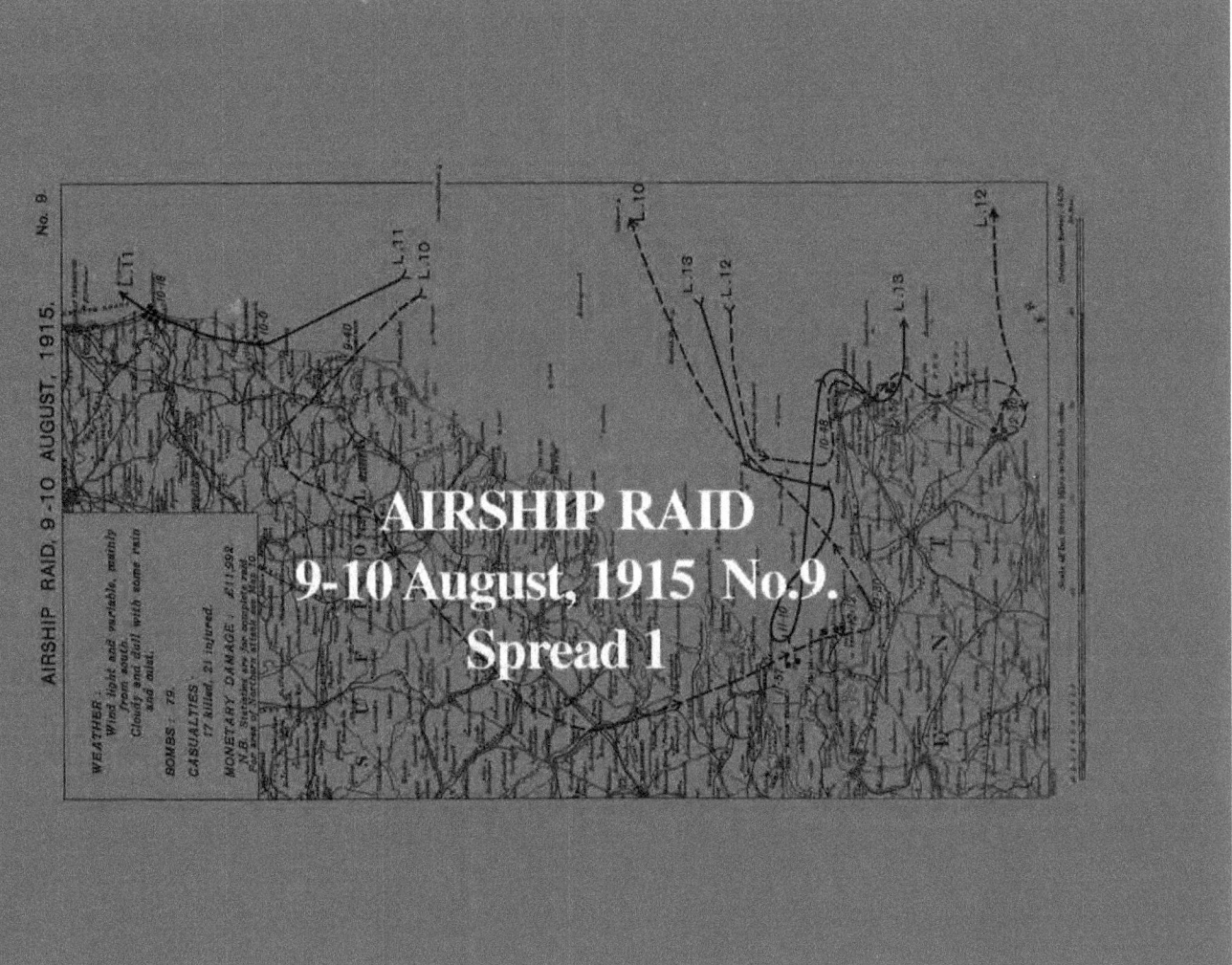

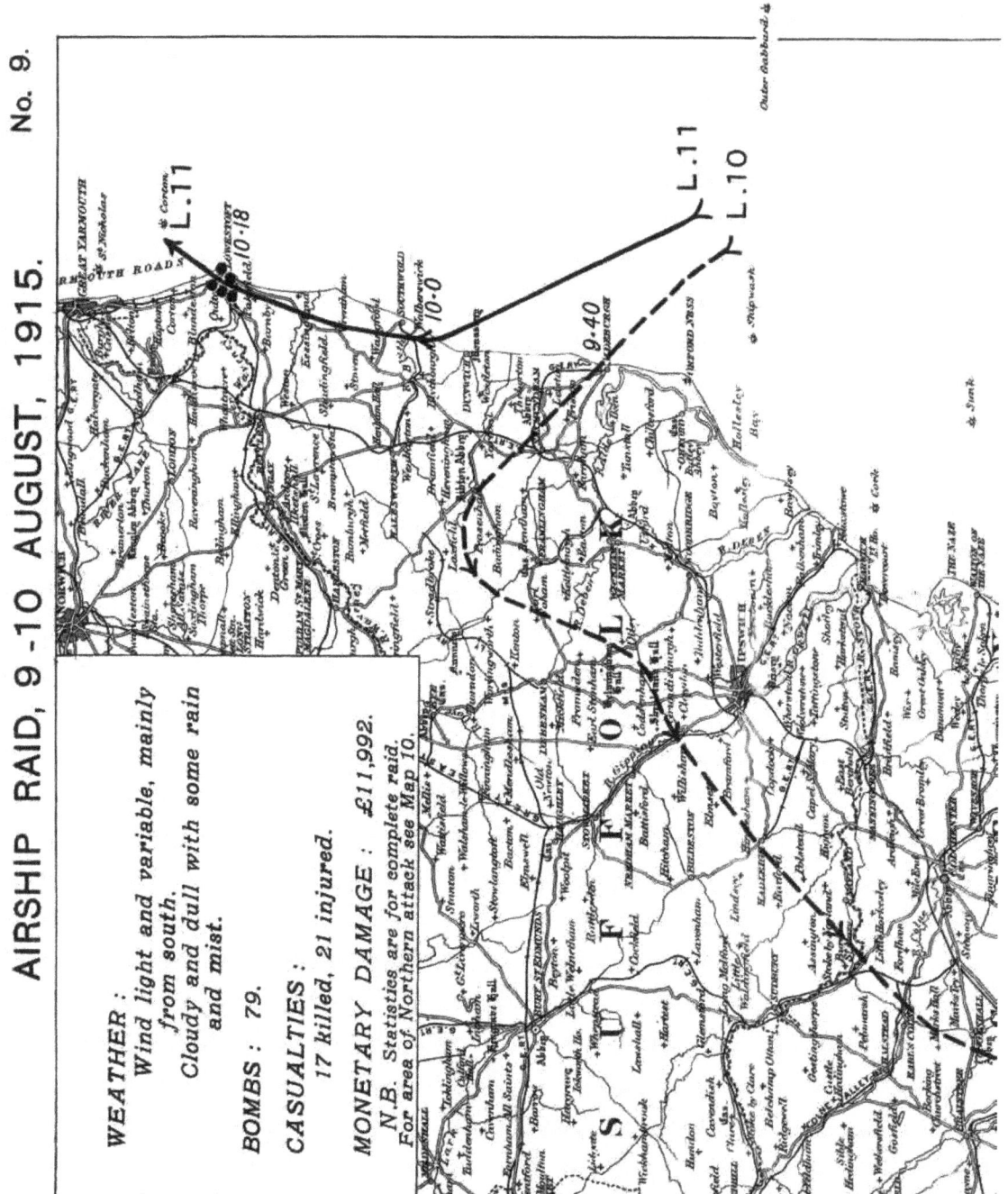

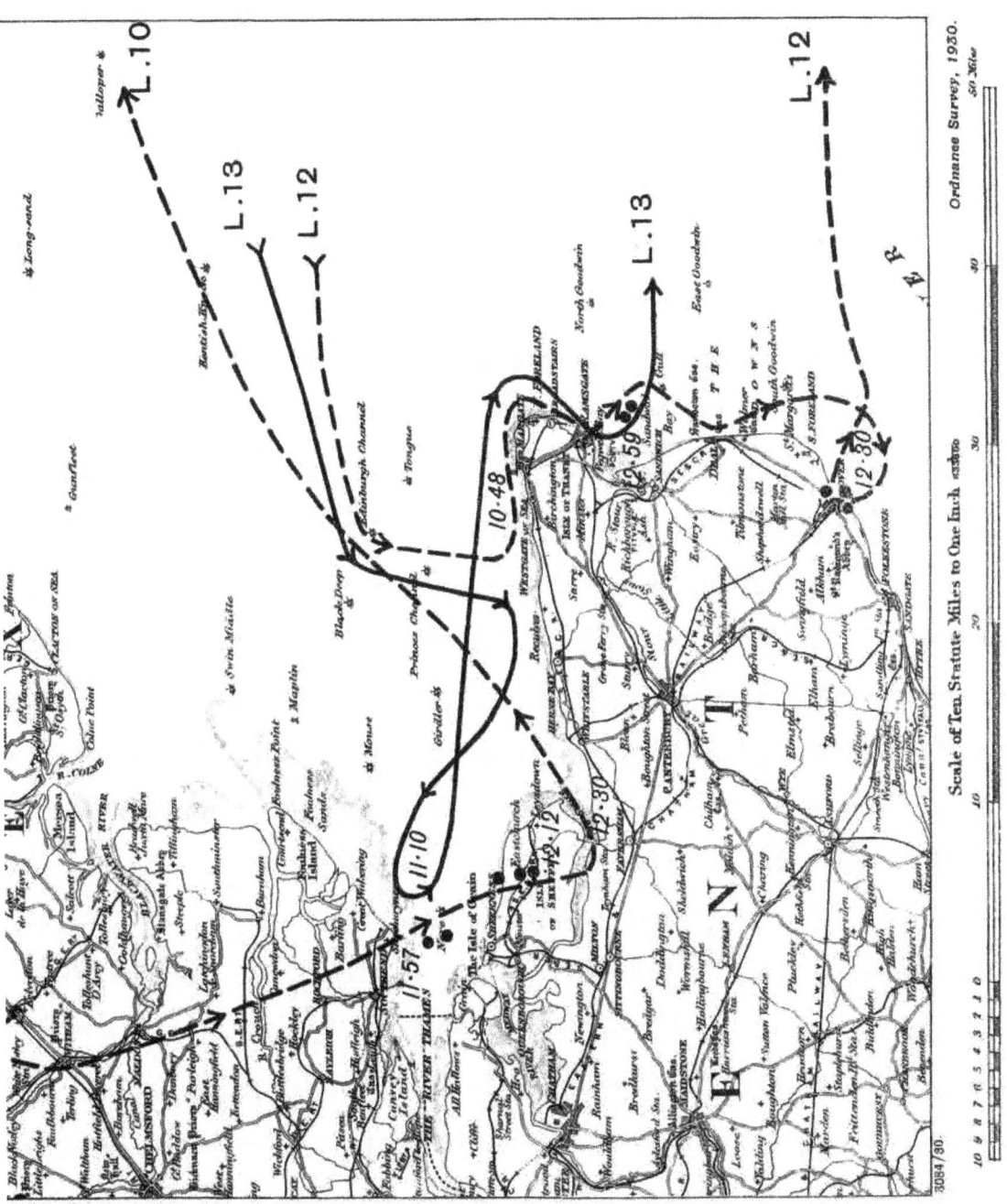

AIRSHIP RAID, 9-10 AUGUST, 1915. No. 10.

AREA OF NORTHERN ATTACK.

WEATHER:

Wind light and variable, mainly from south.

Cloudy and dull with some rain and mist.

For statistics of complete raid, see Map 9.

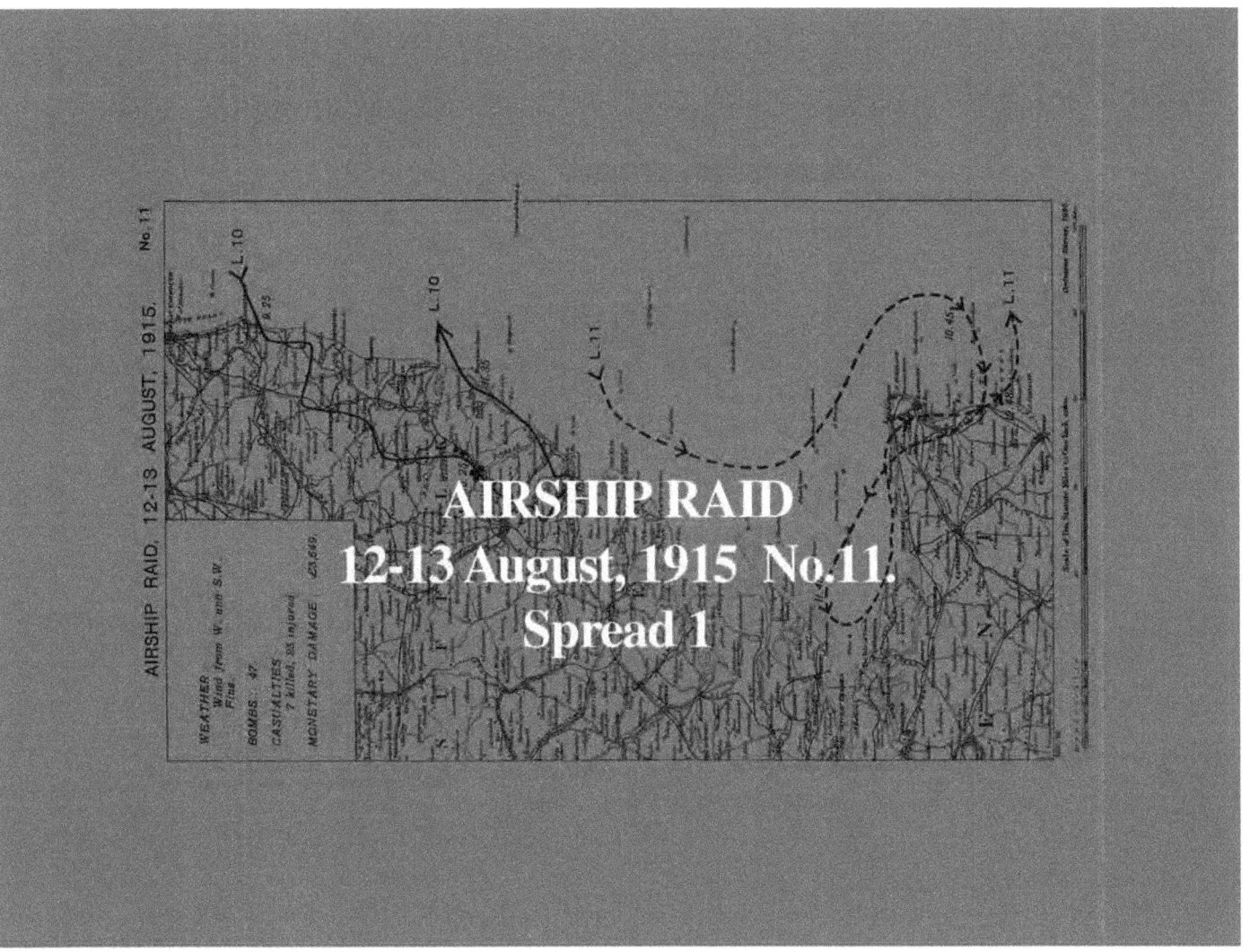

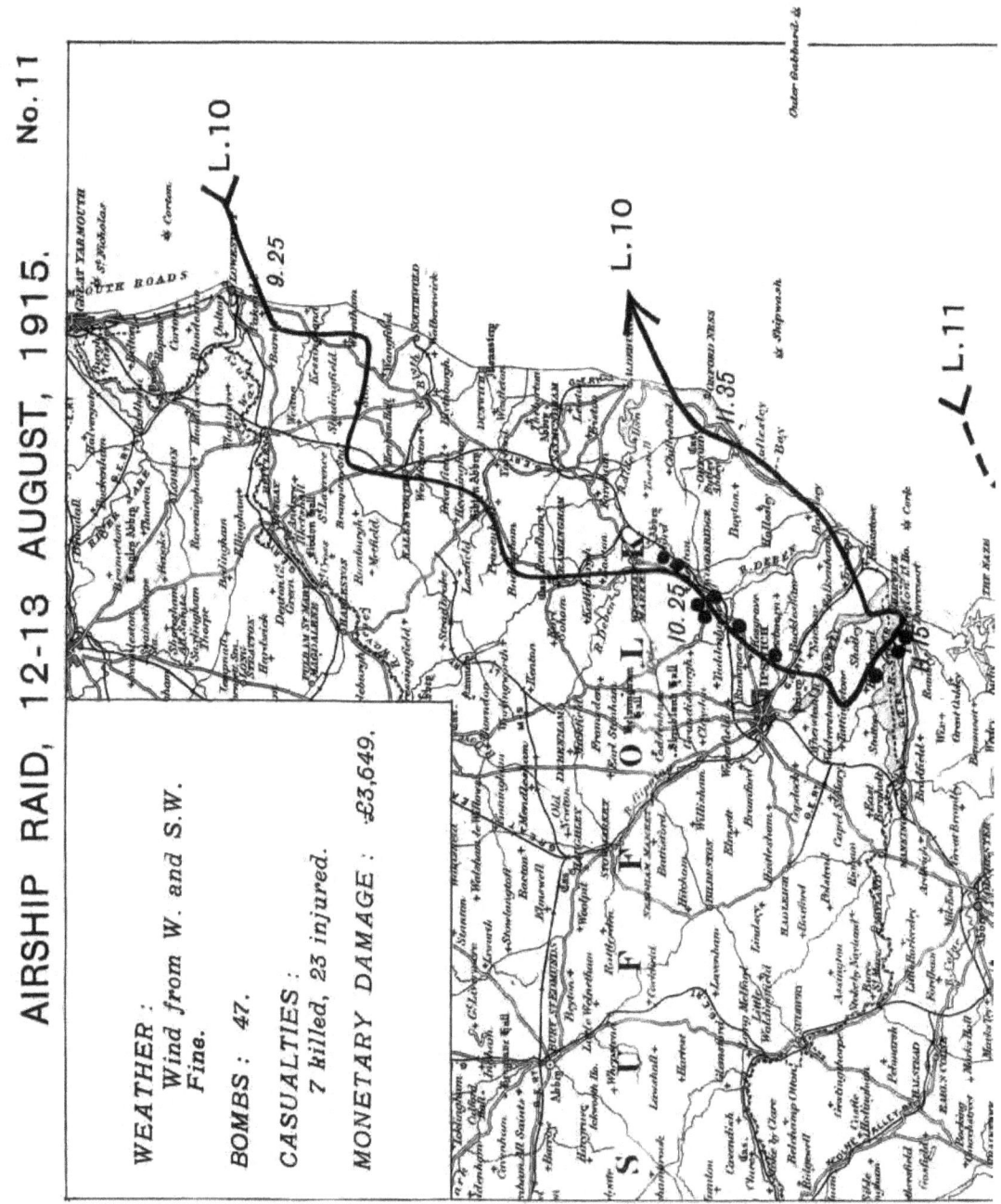

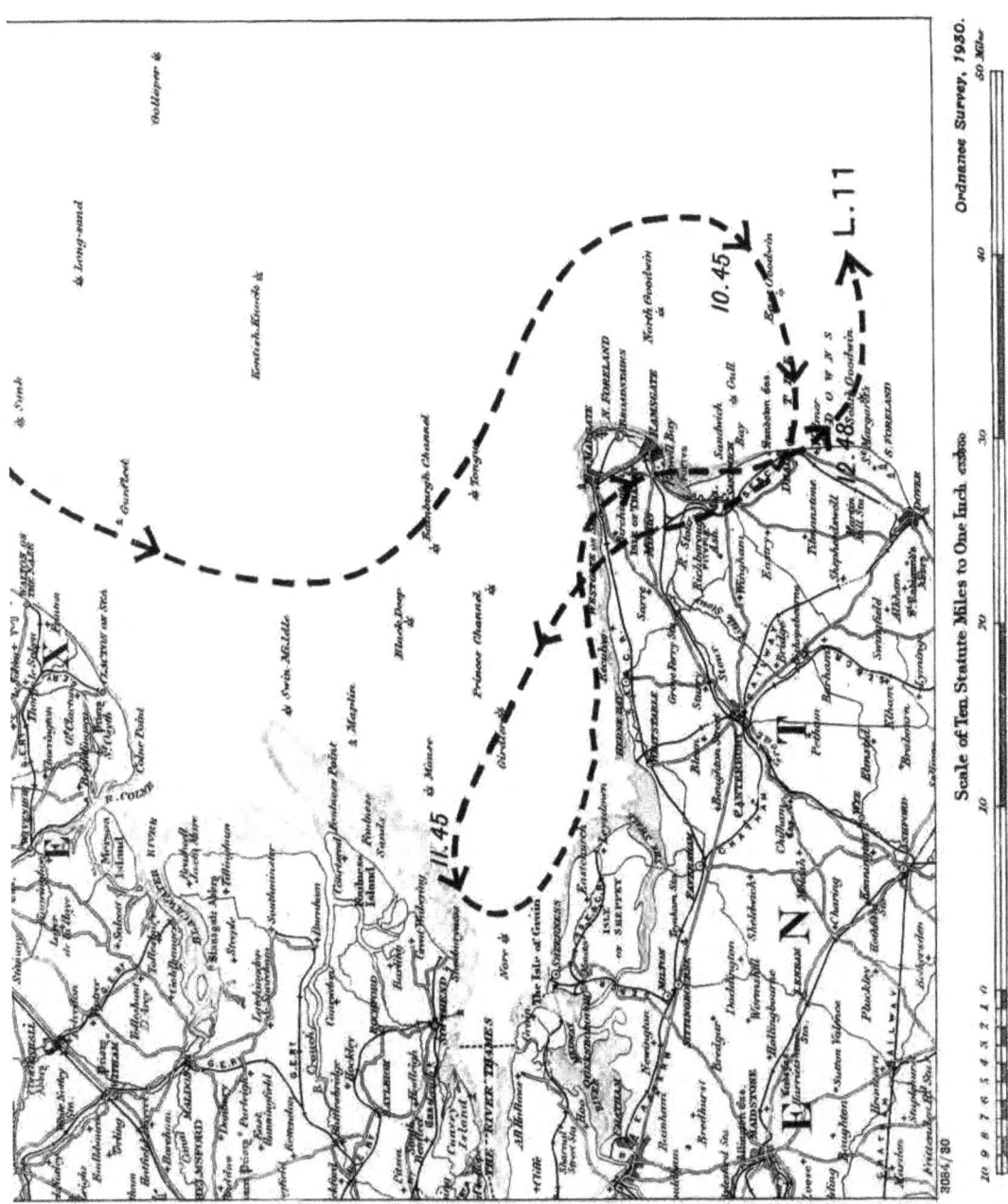

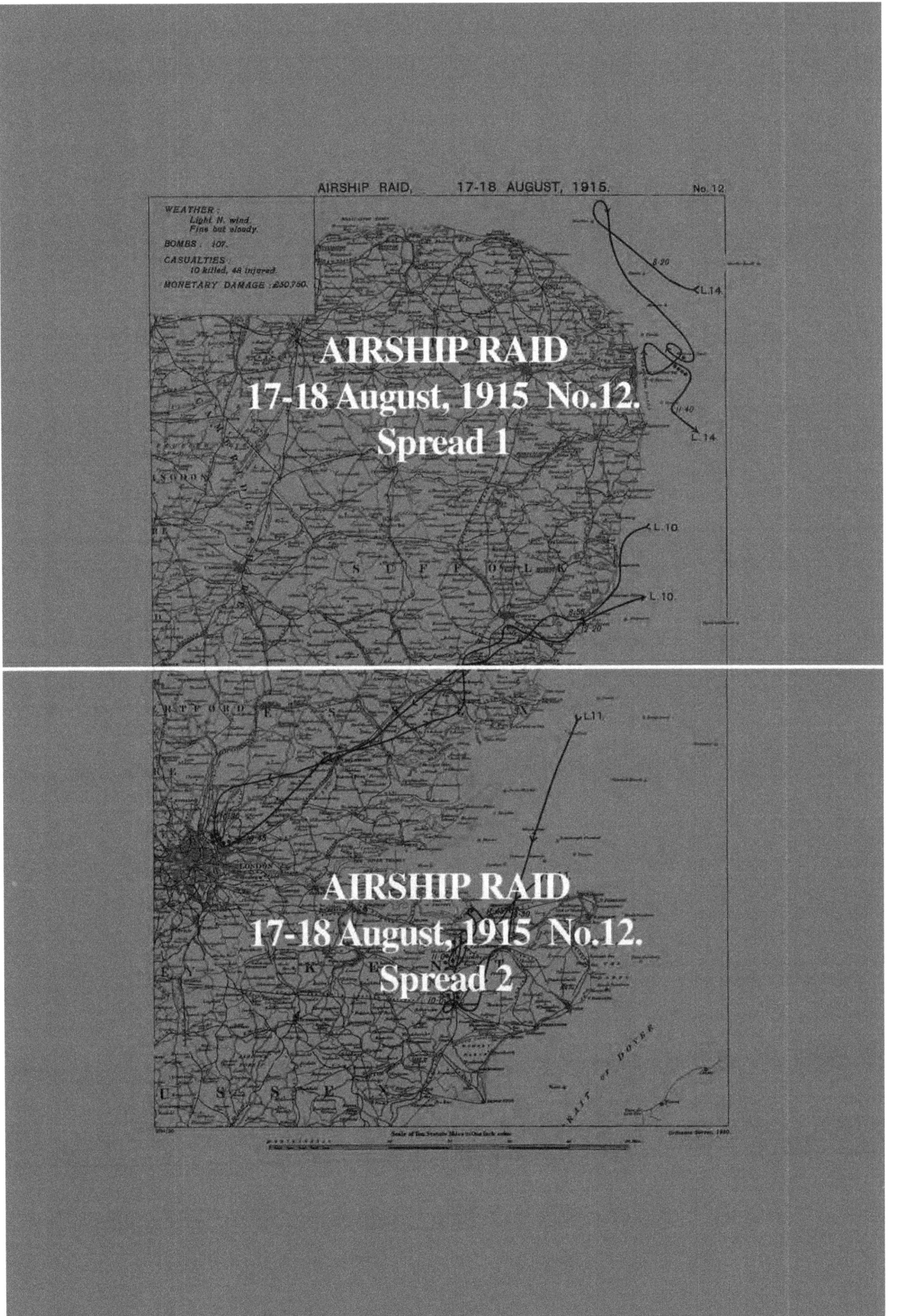

Spread 1

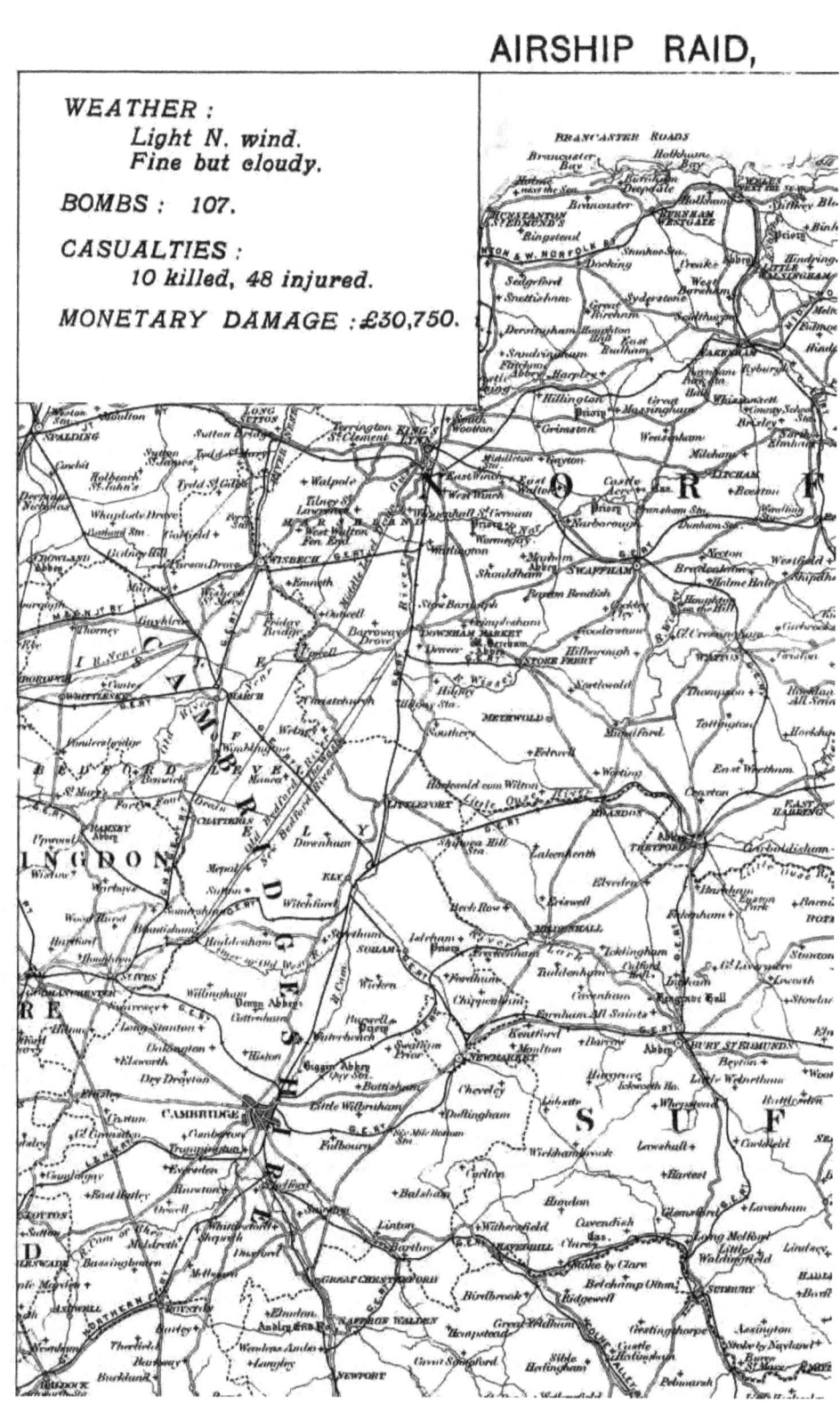

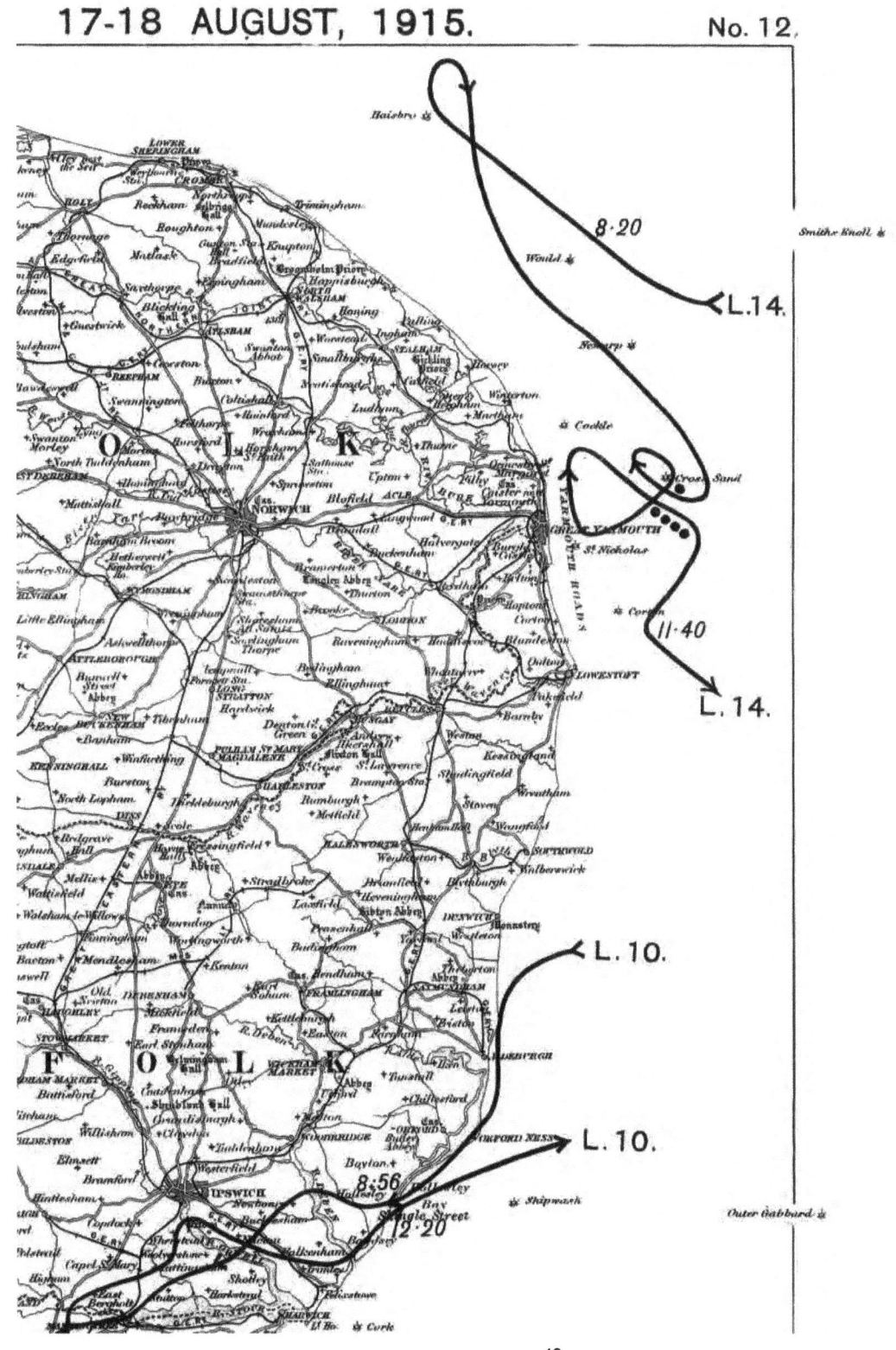

Spread 2

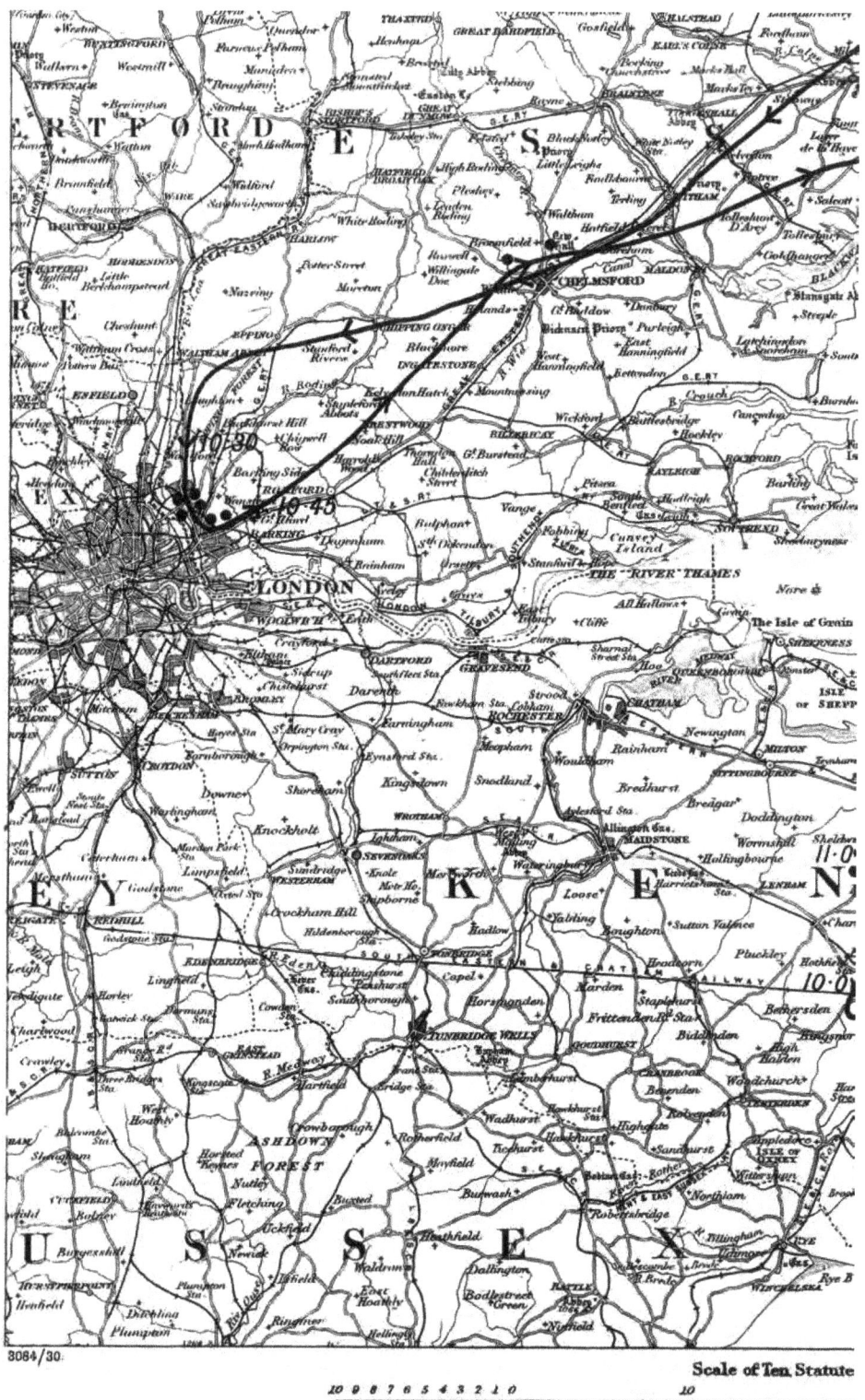

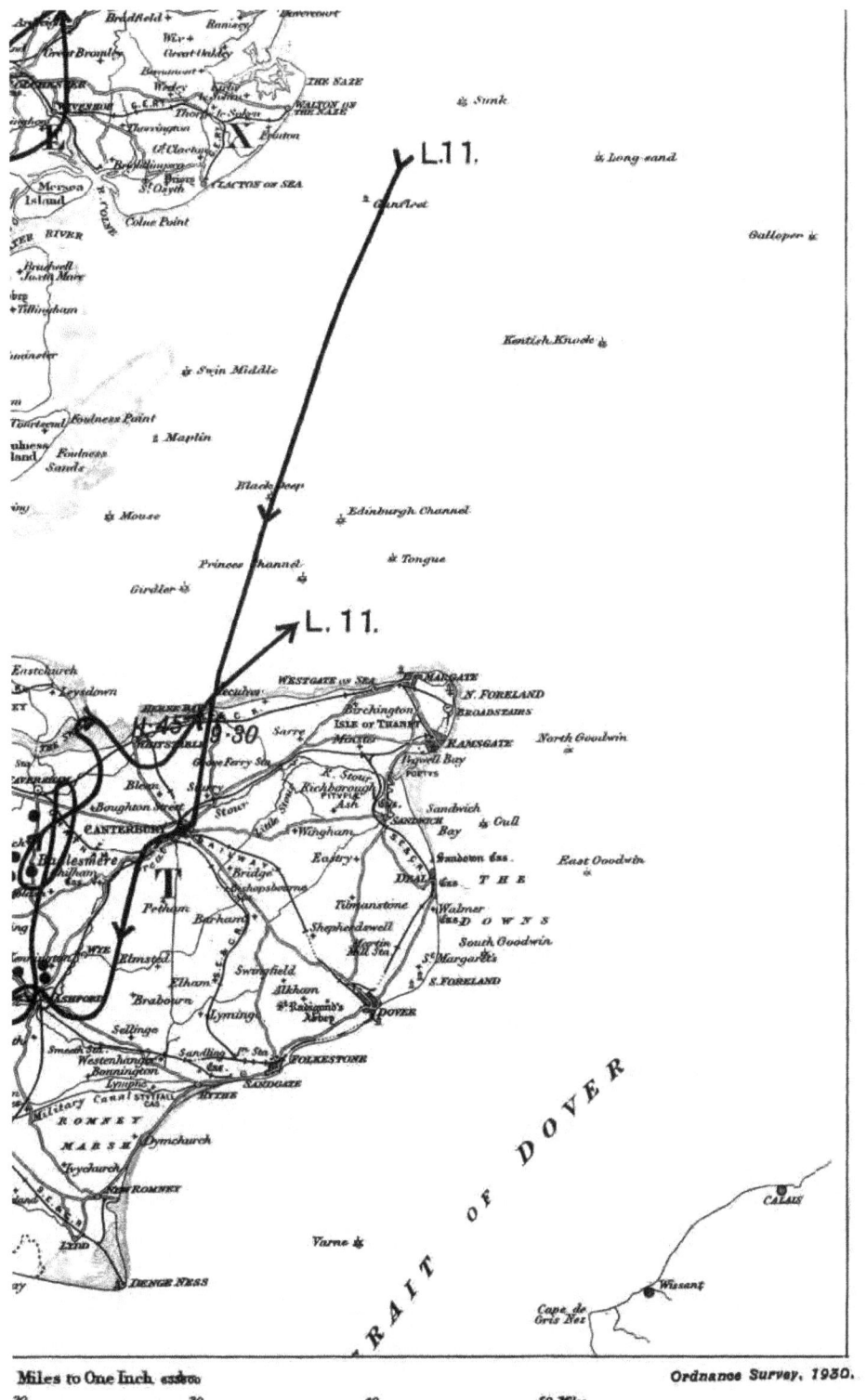

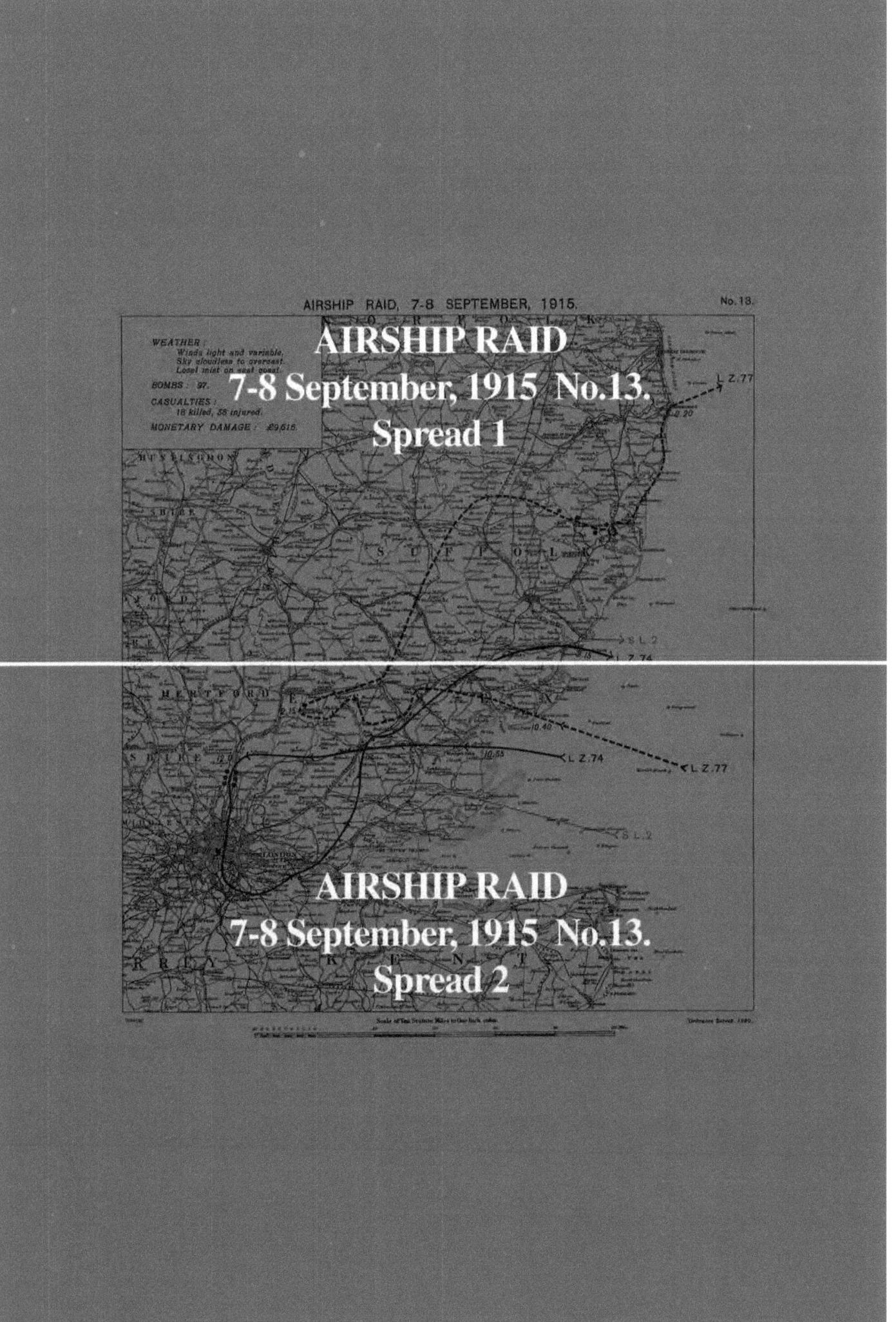

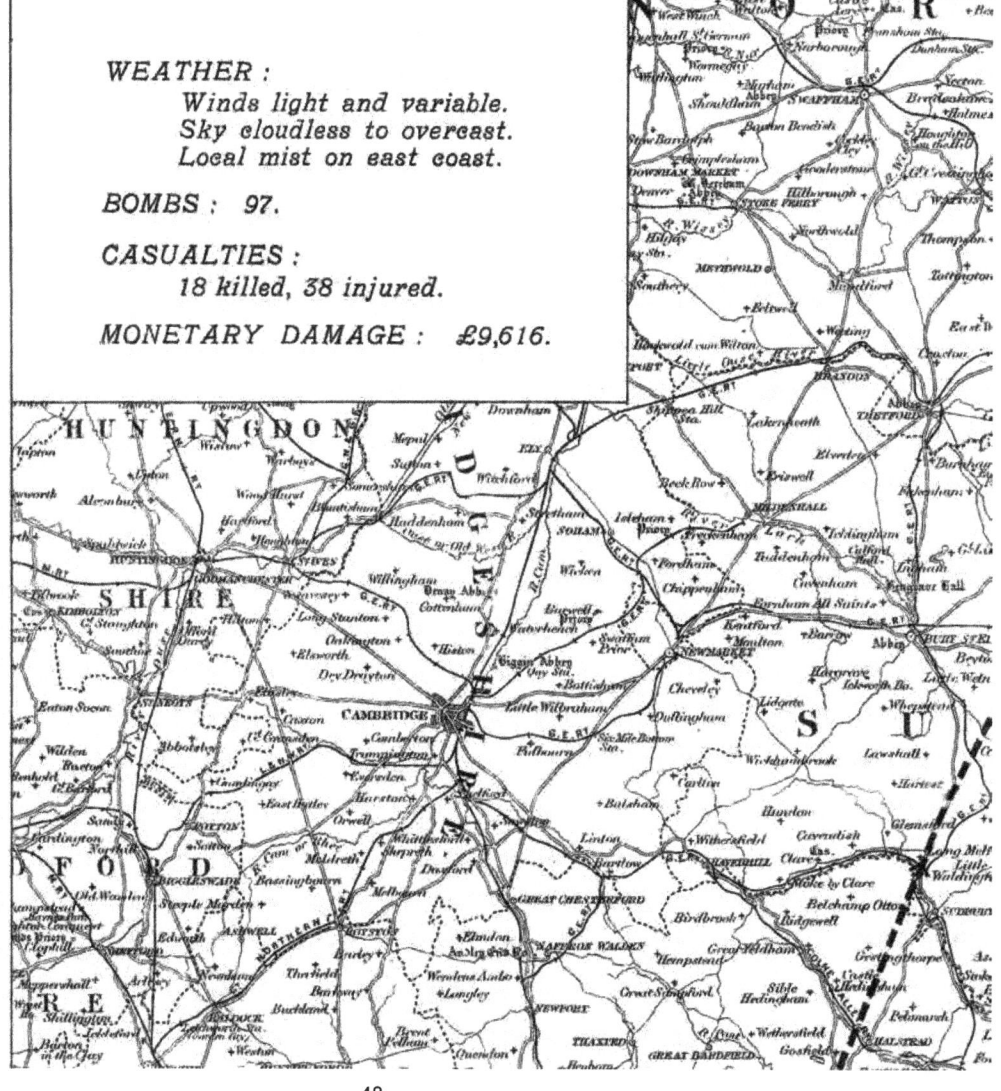

AIRSHIP RAID, 7-8

WEATHER:
  Winds light and variable.
  Sky cloudless to overcast.
  Local mist on east coast.

BOMBS: 97.

CASUALTIES:
  18 killed, 38 injured.

MONETARY DAMAGE: £9,616.

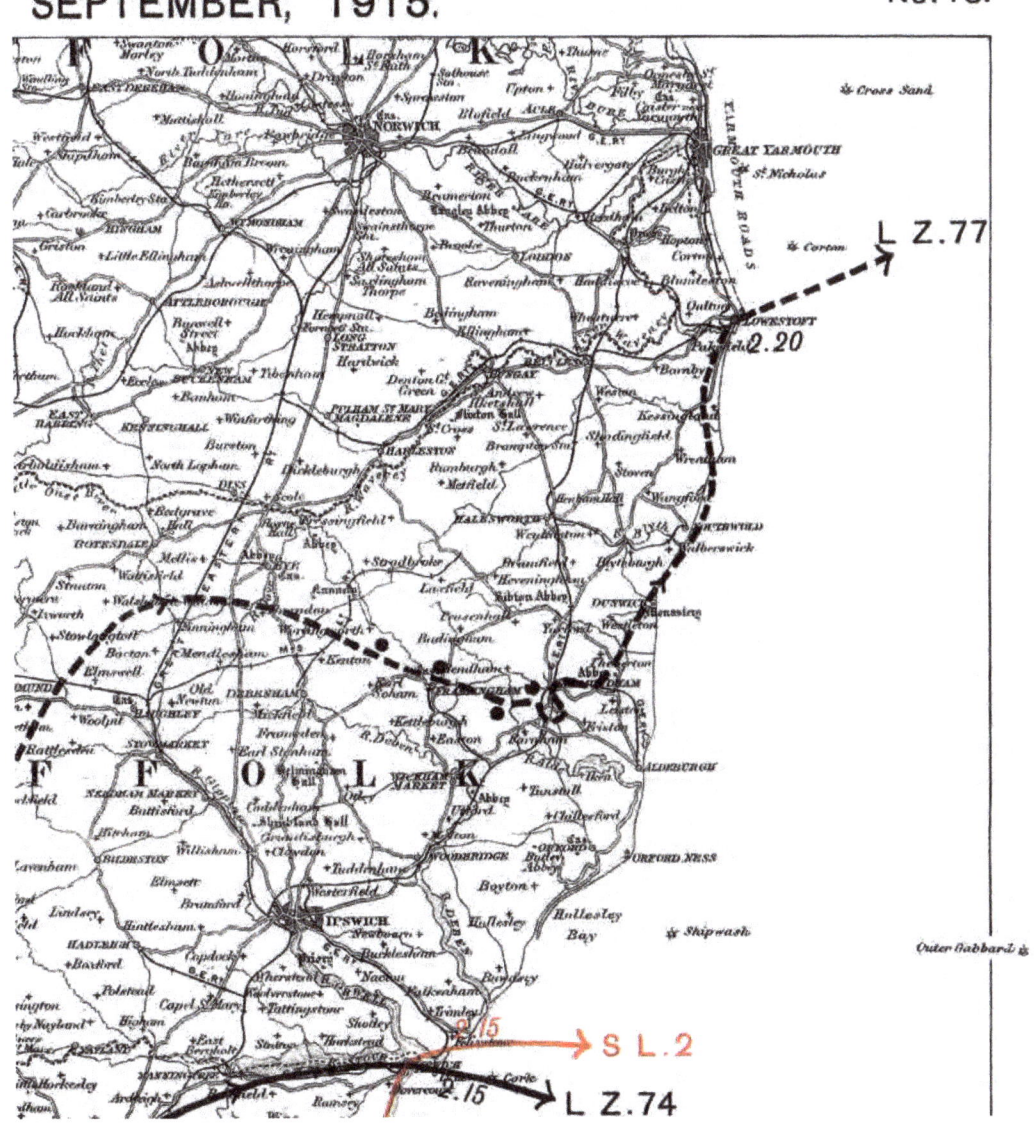

Spread 2

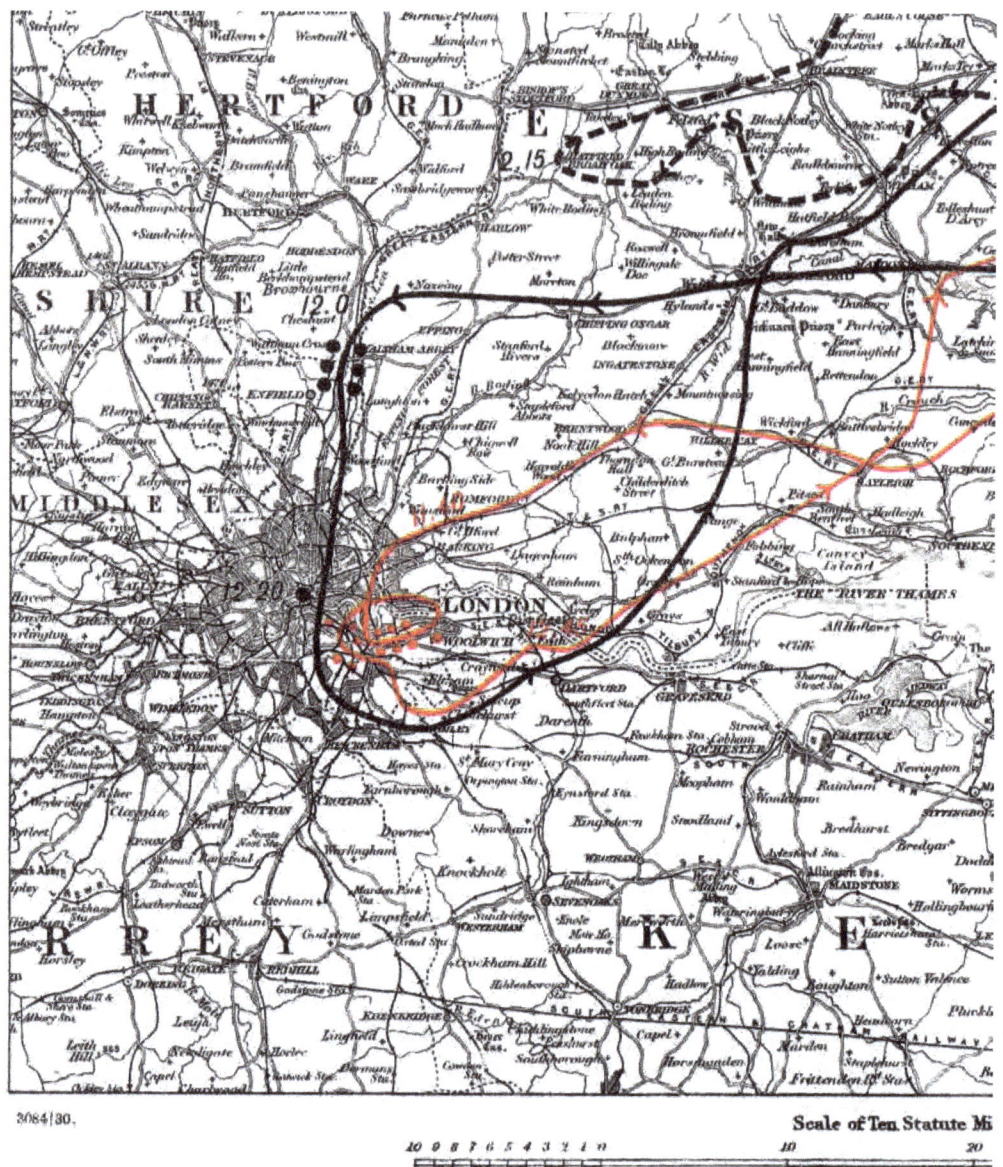

Spread 2

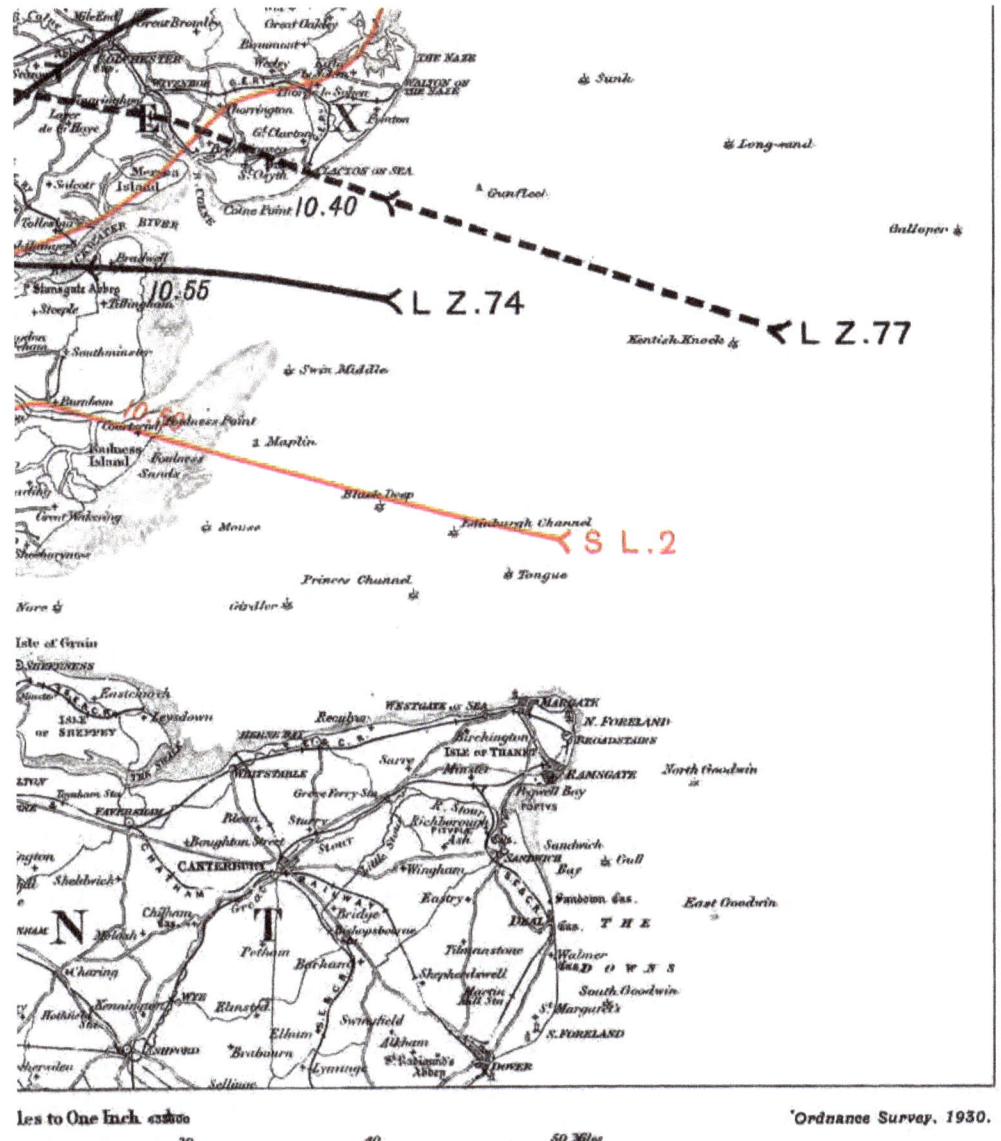

'Ordnance Survey, 1930.

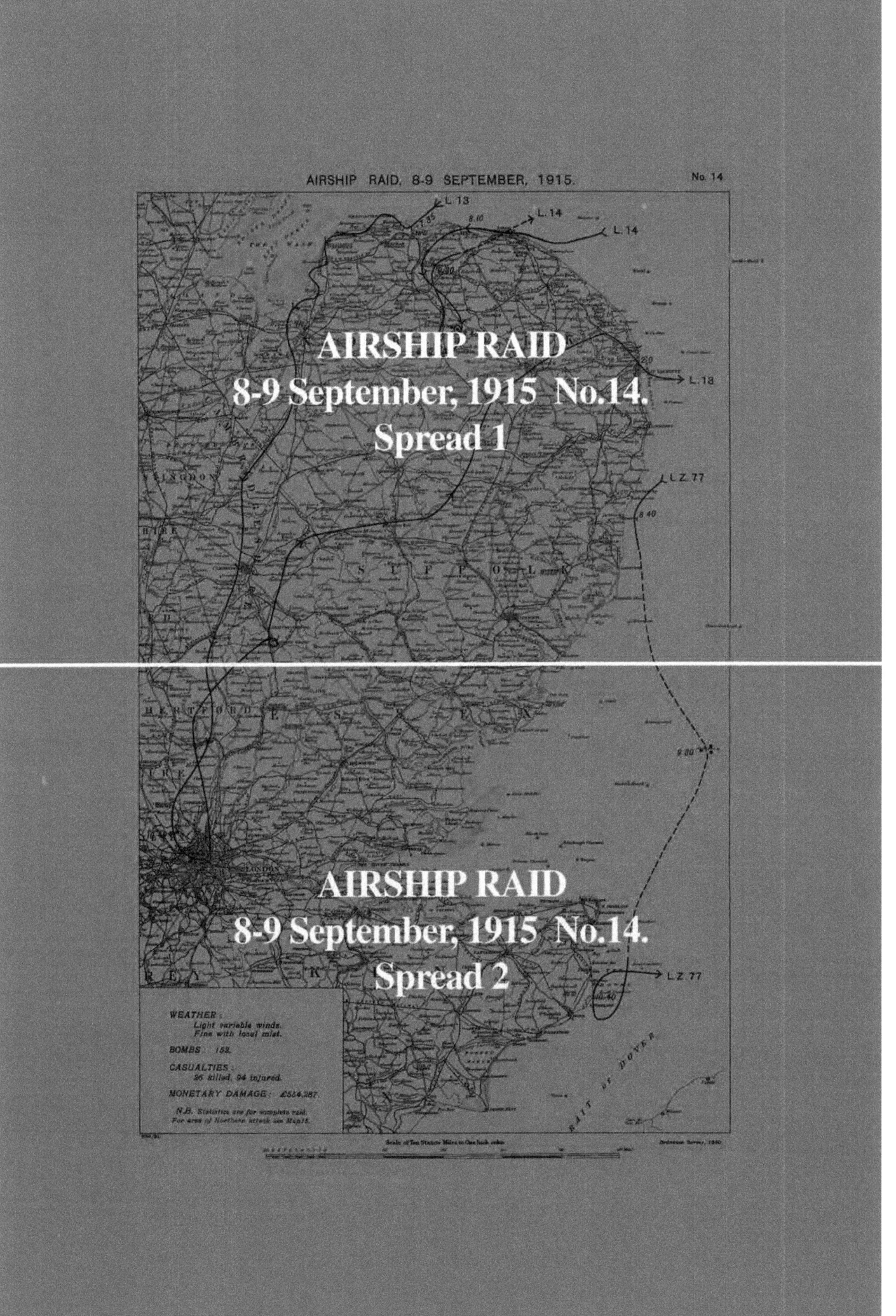

Spread 1

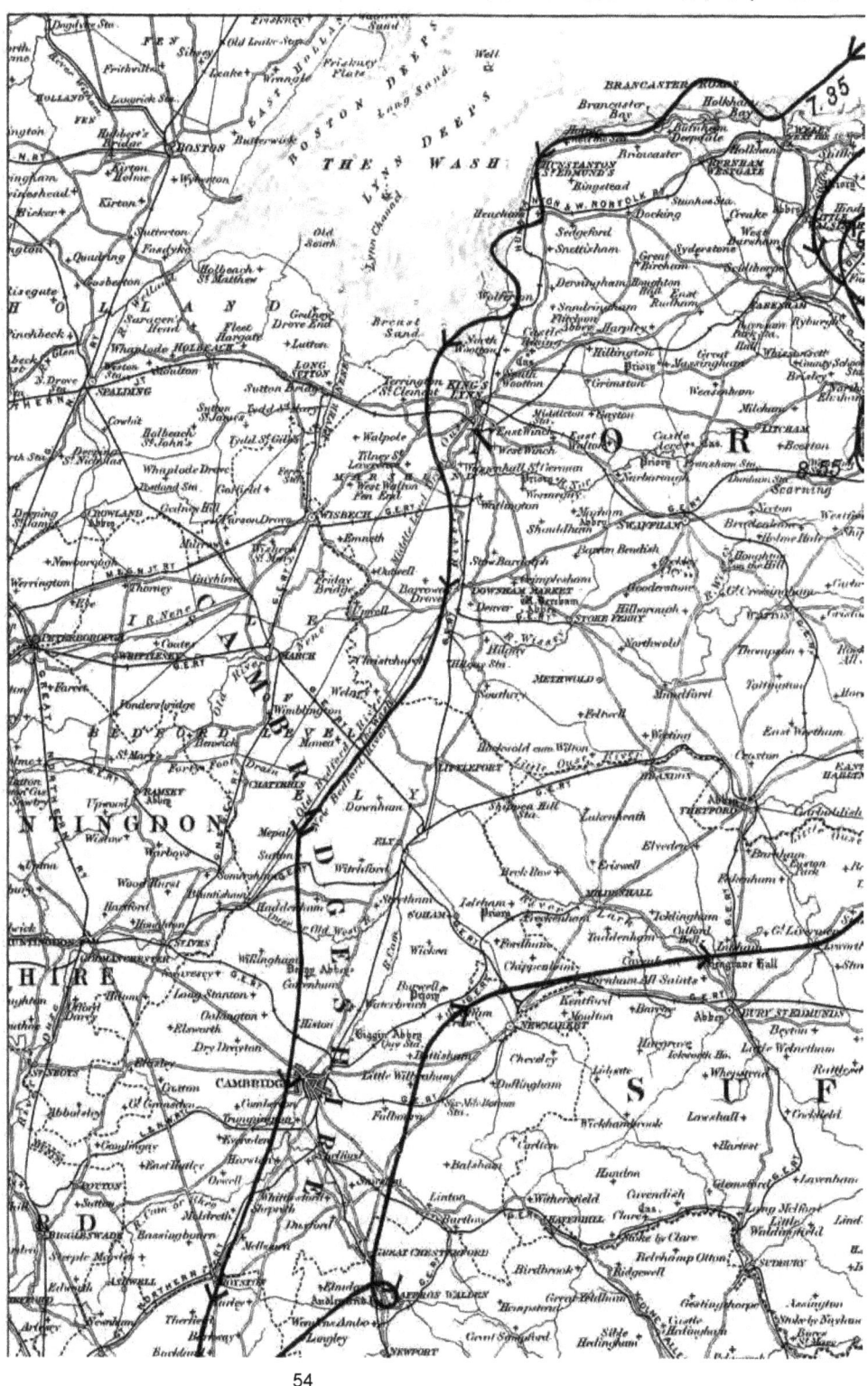

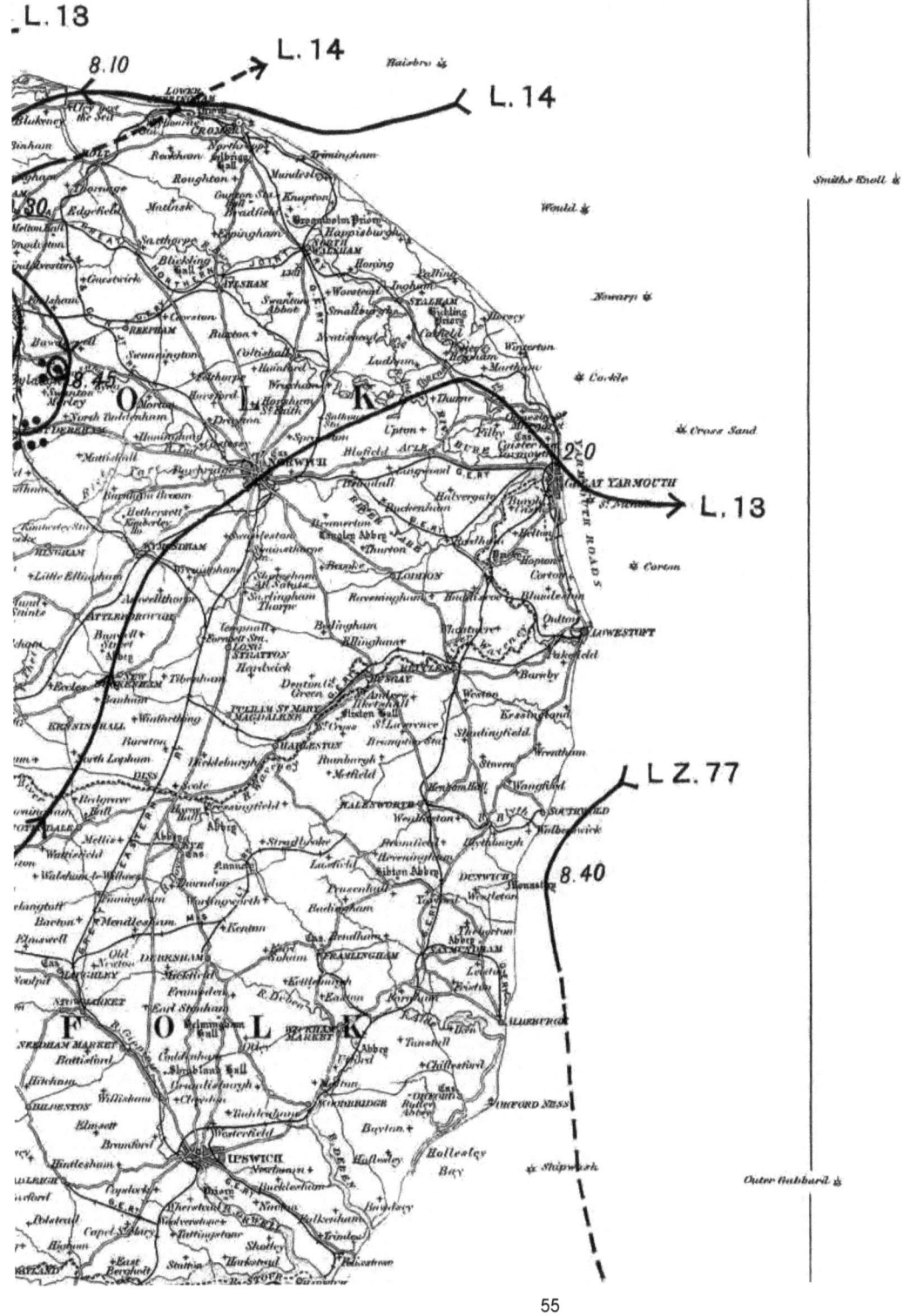

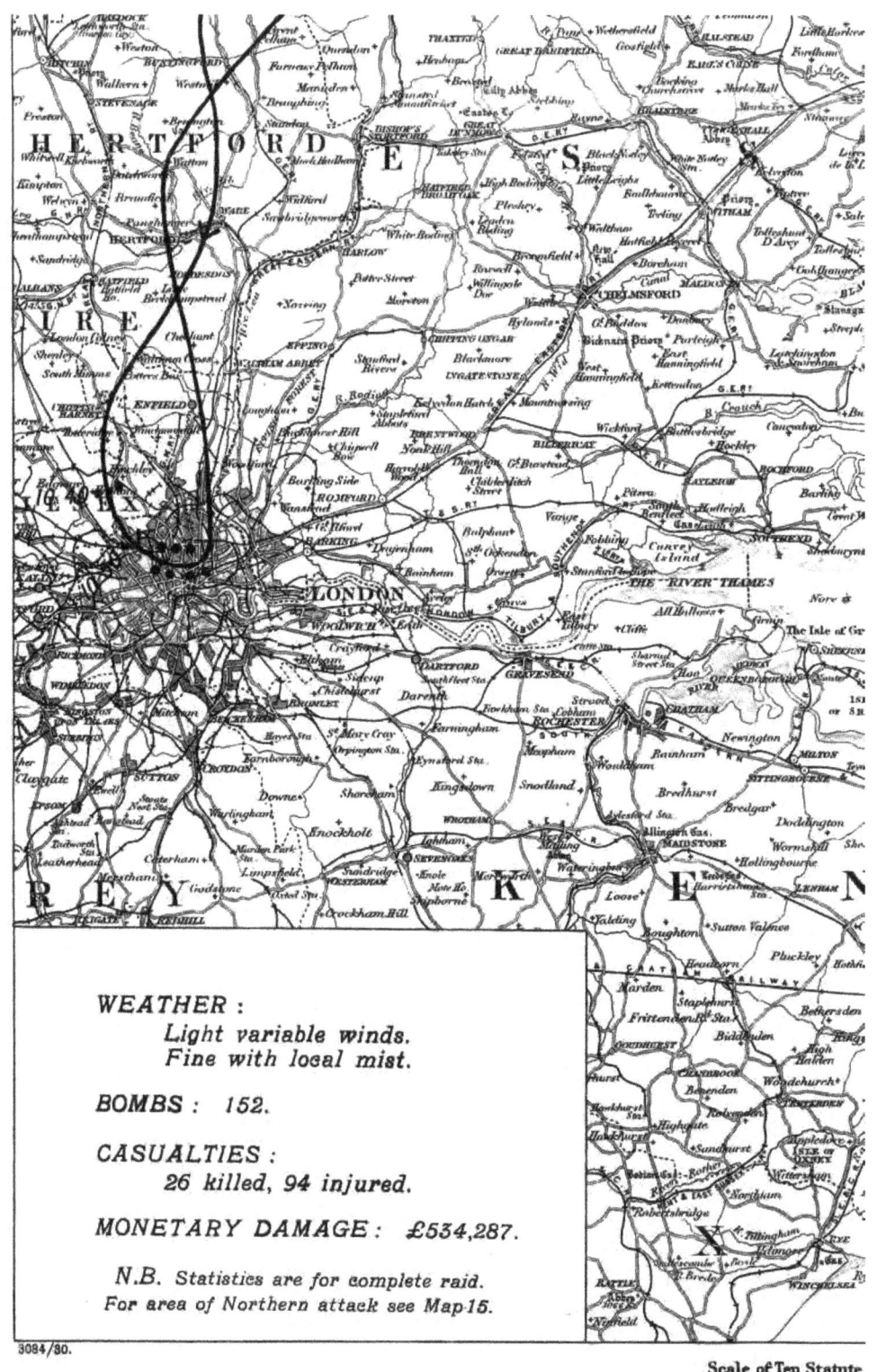

WEATHER:
  Light variable winds.
  Fine with local mist.

BOMBS: 152.

CASUALTIES:
  26 killed, 94 injured.

MONETARY DAMAGE: £534,287.

N.B. Statistics are for complete raid.
For area of Northern attack see Map 15.

Spread 2

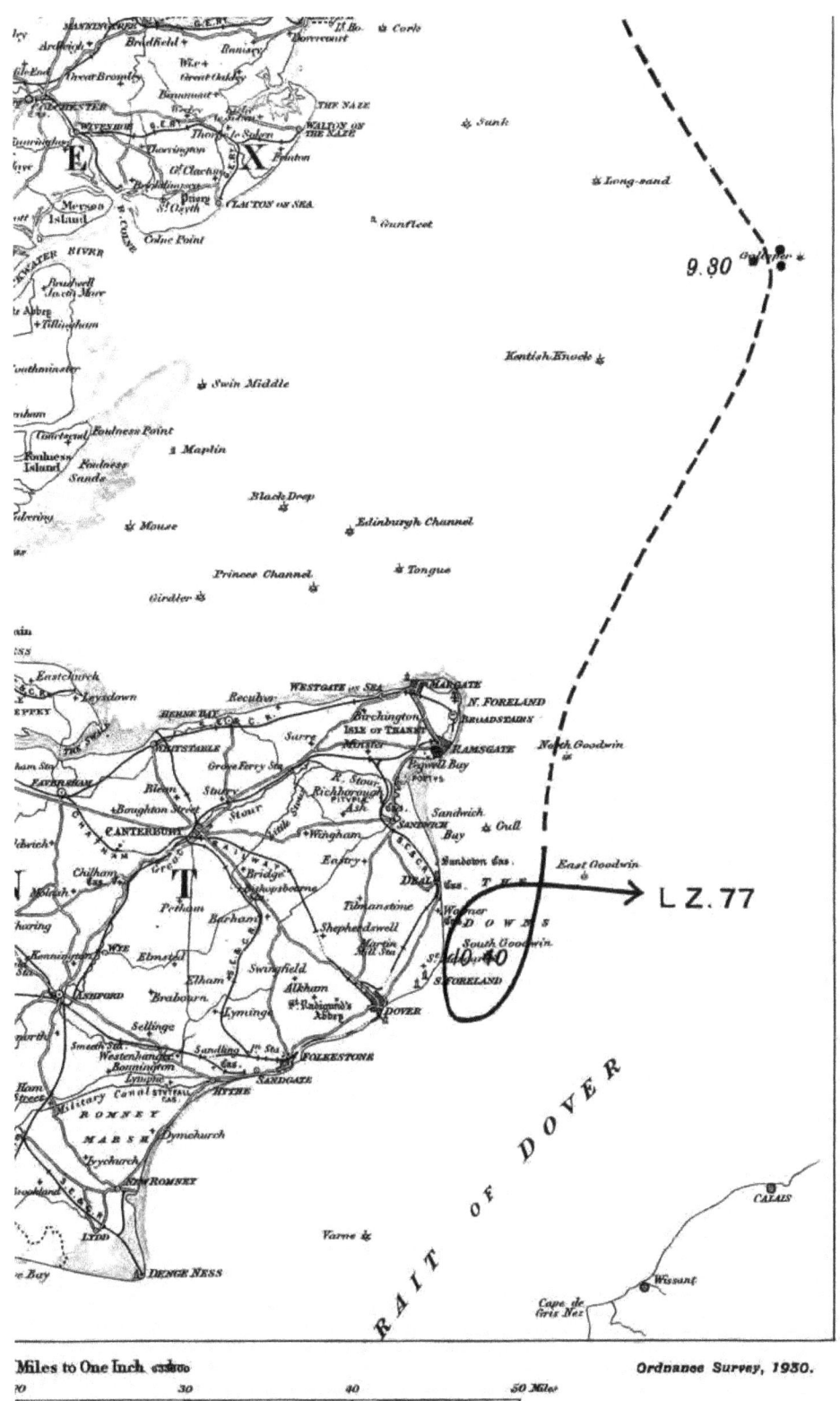

AIRSHIP RAID, 8-9 SEPTEMBER, 1915. No. 15

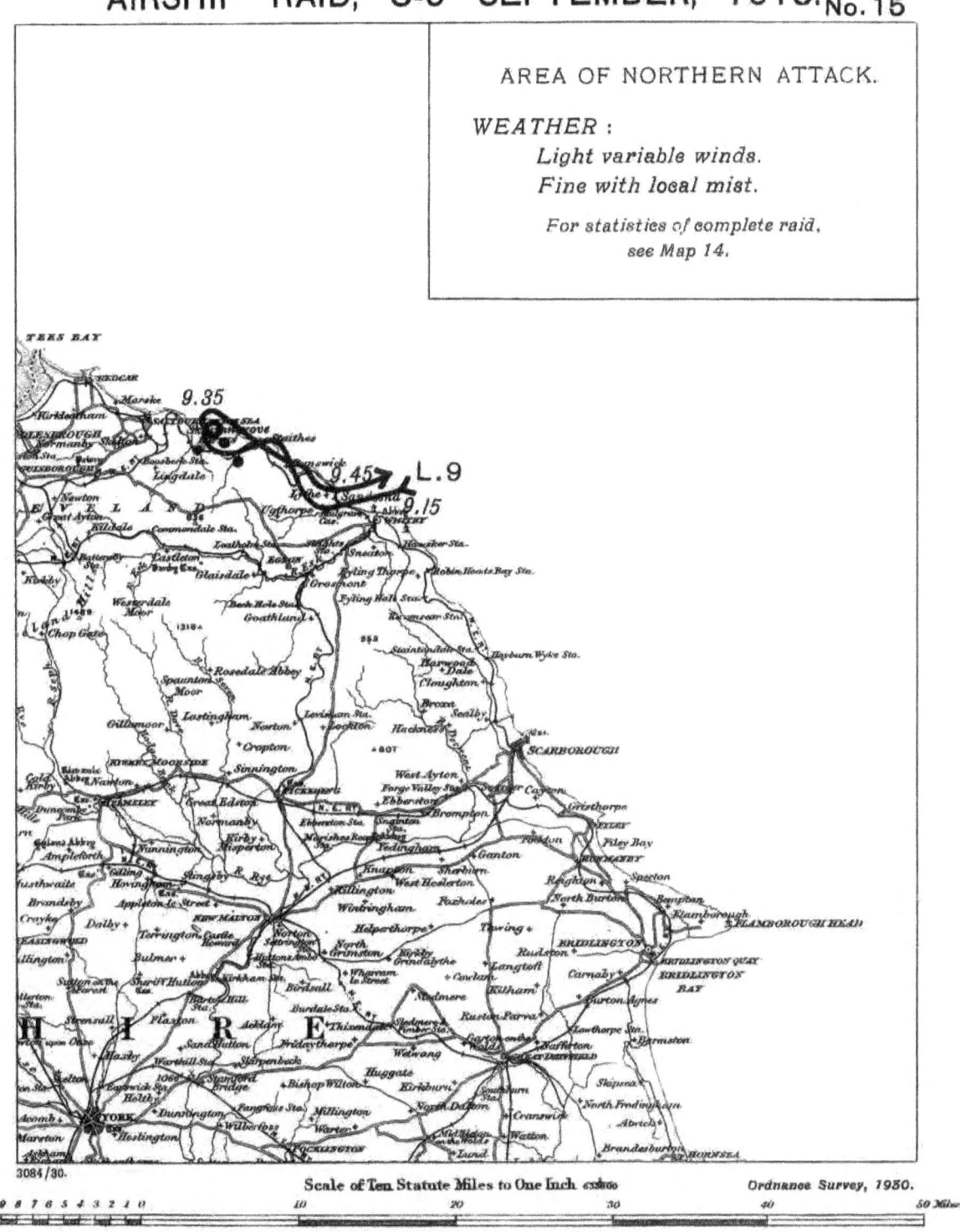

AREA OF NORTHERN ATTACK.

WEATHER:
Light variable winds.
Fine with local mist.

For statistics of complete raid, see Map 14.

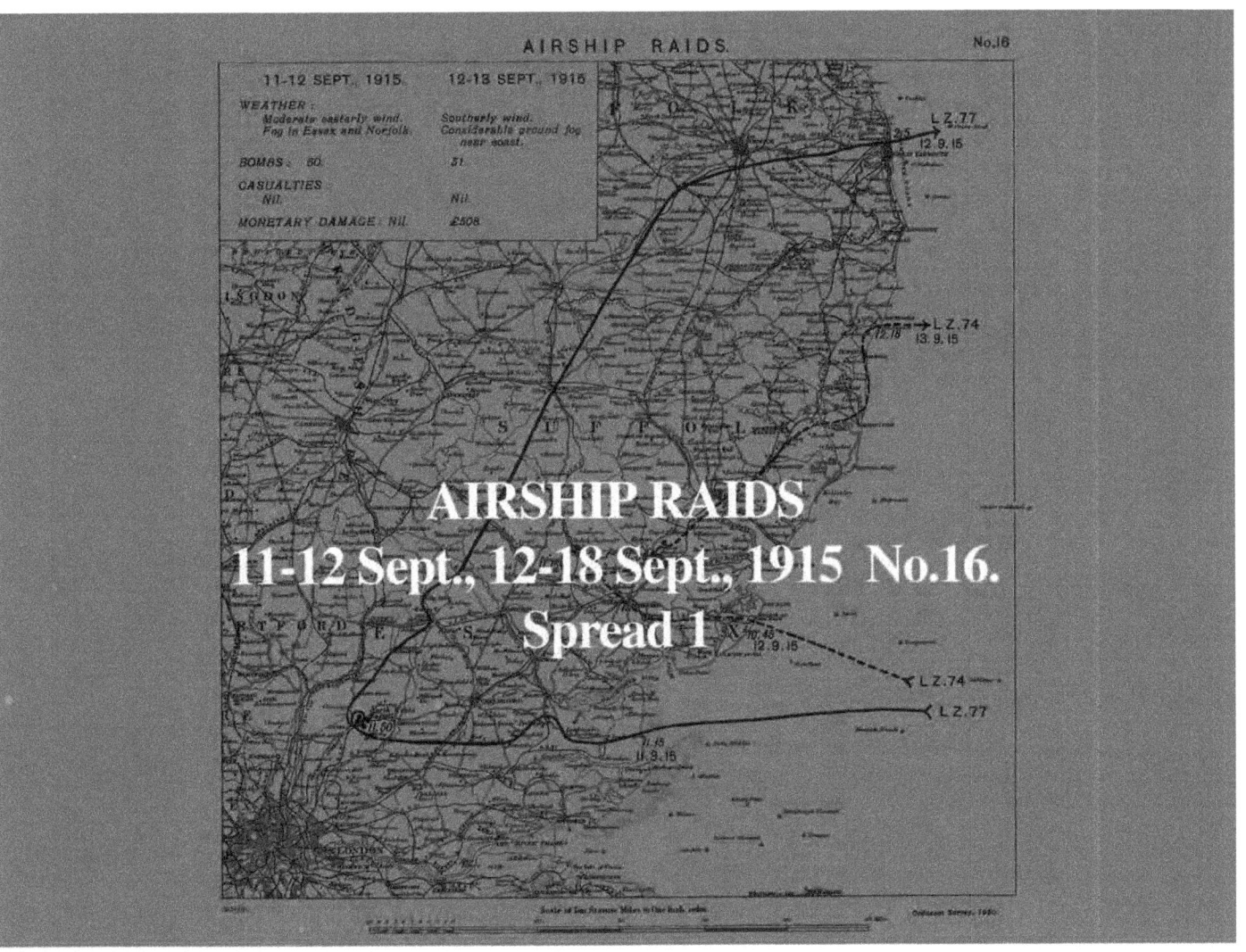

Spread 1

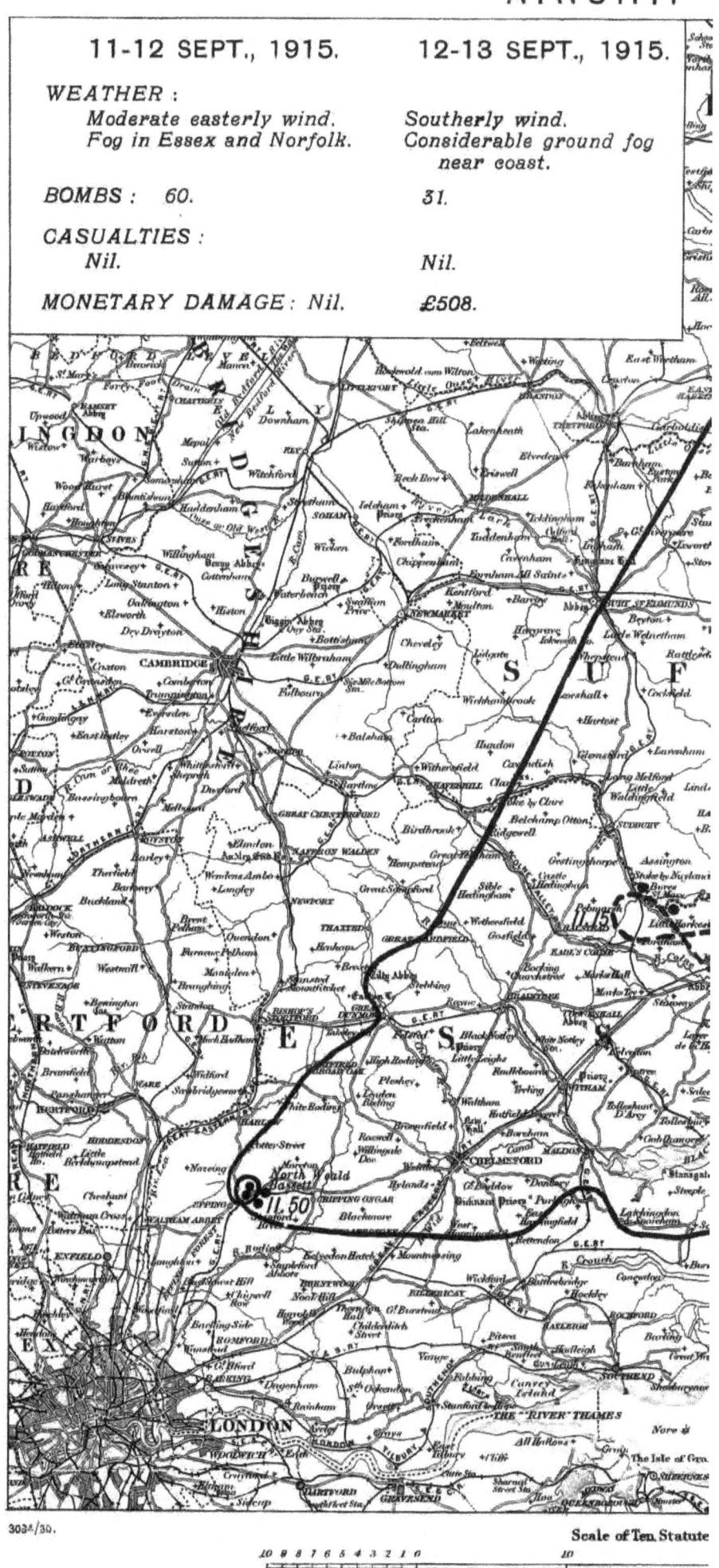

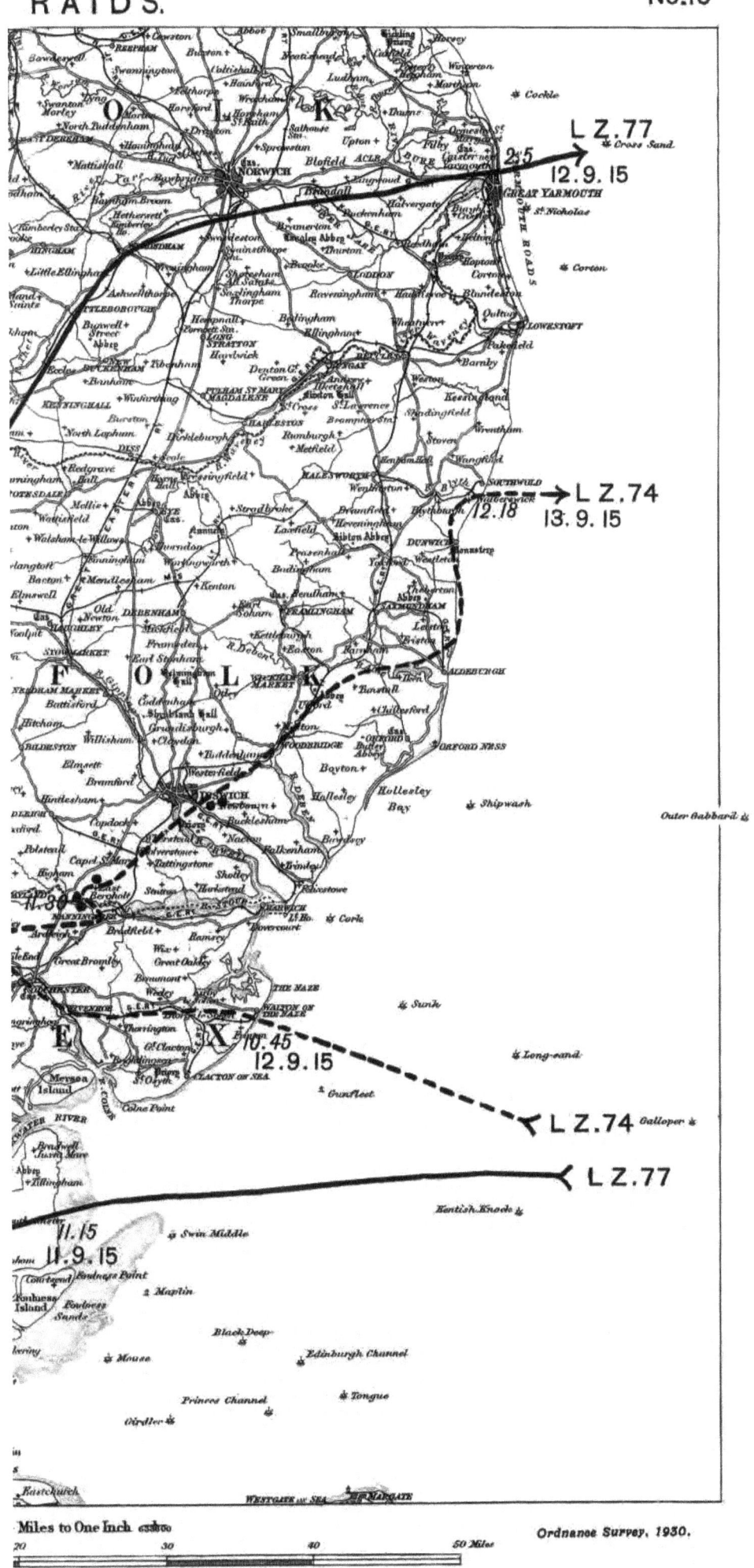

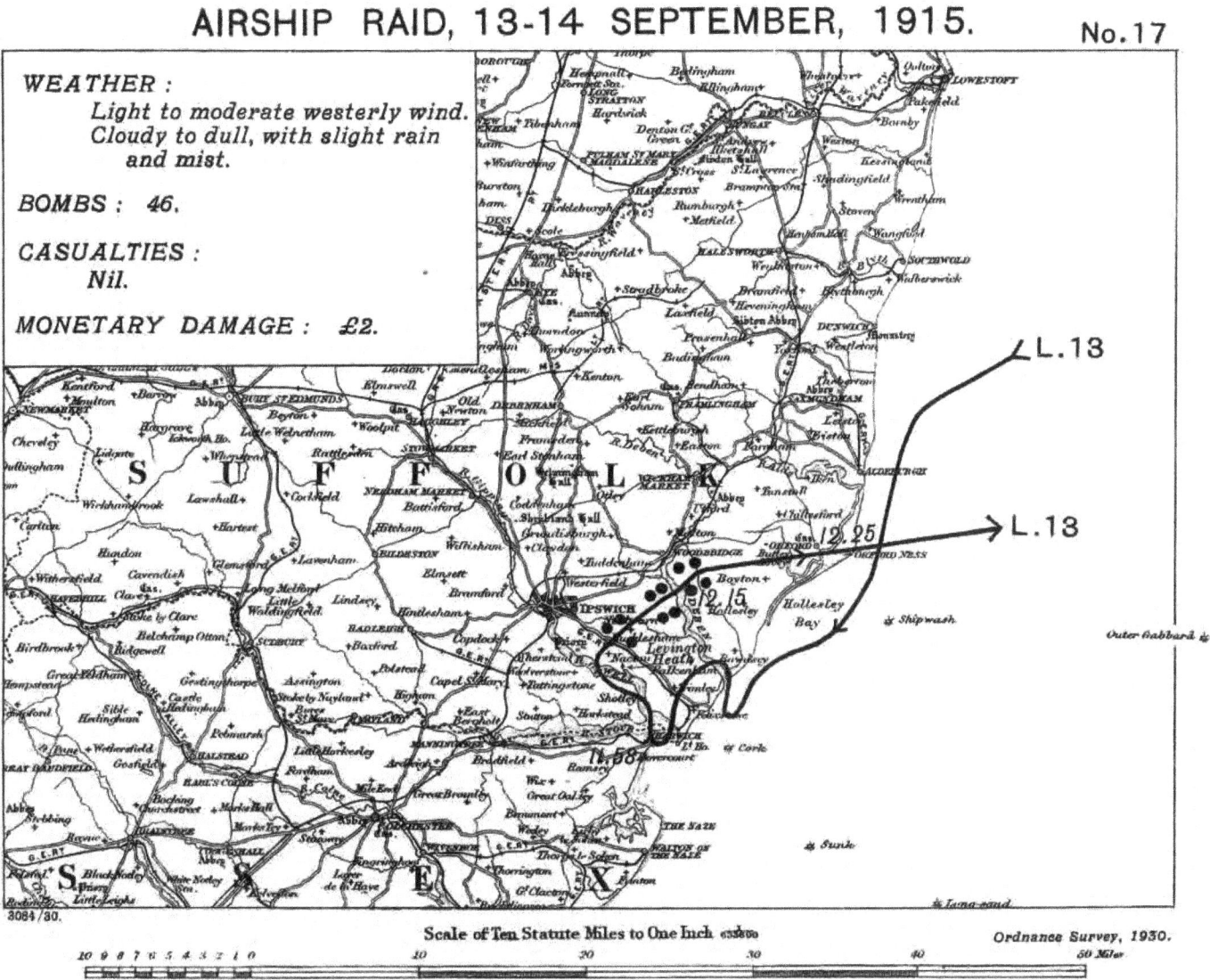

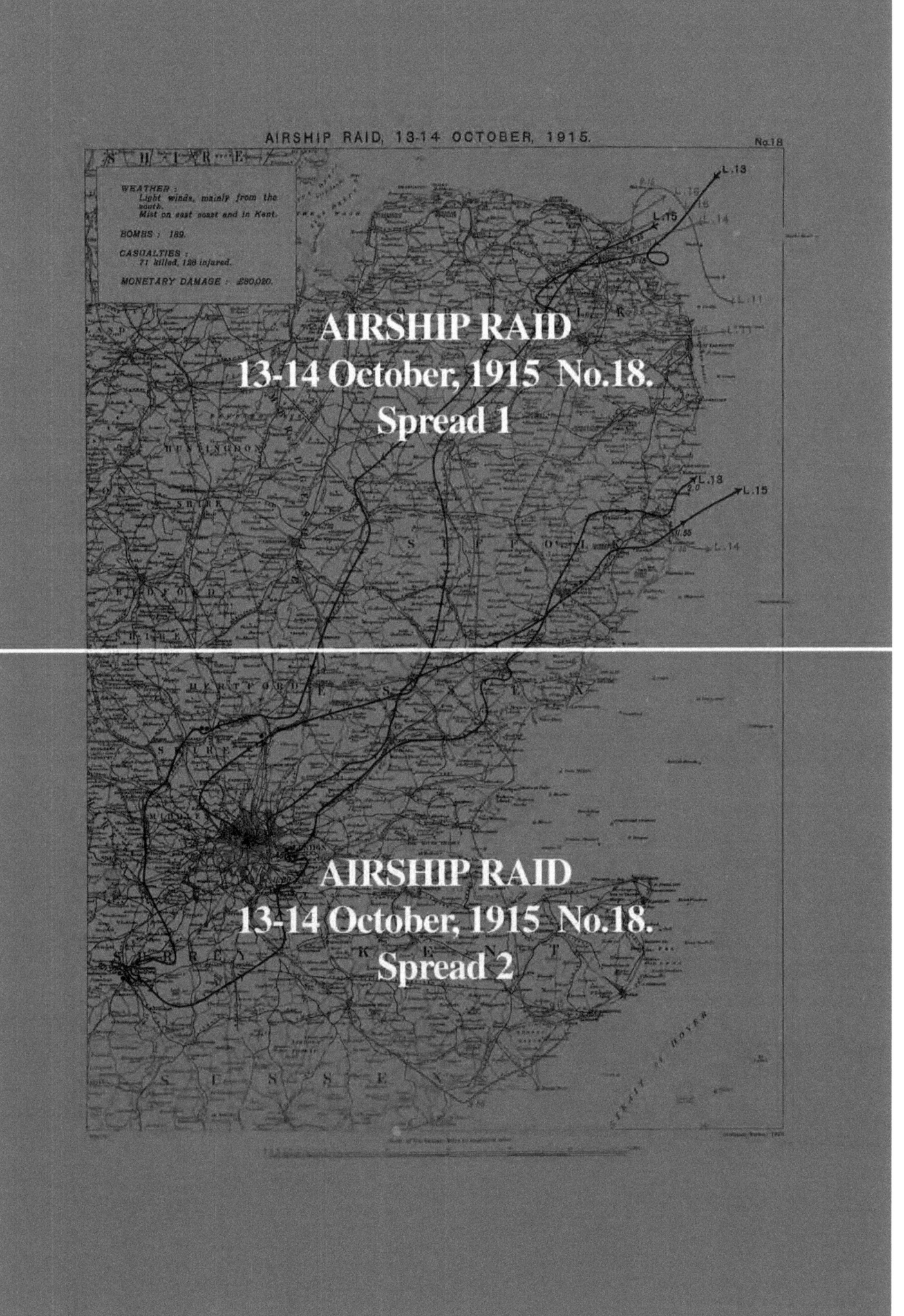

Spread 1

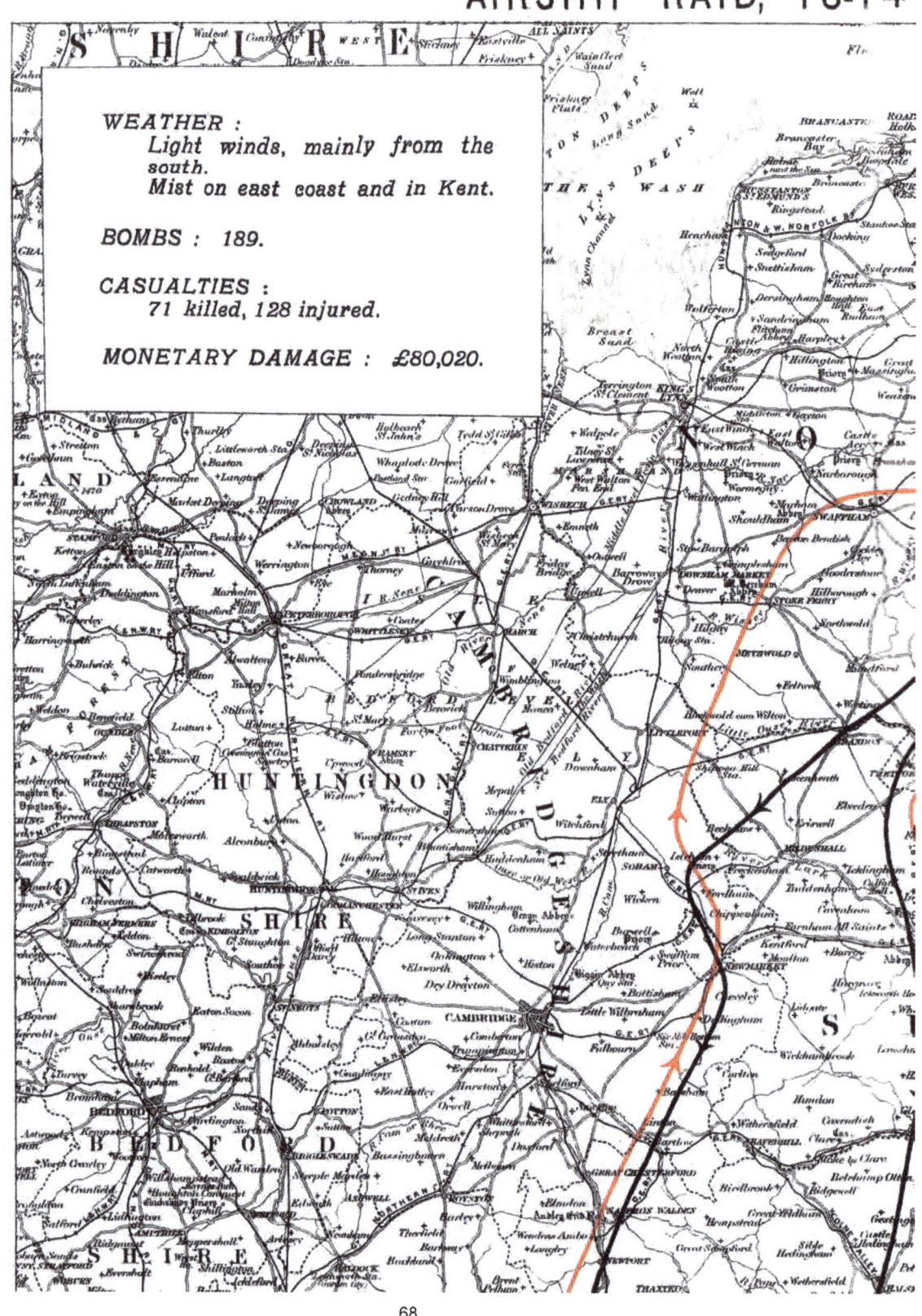

OCTOBER, 1915.

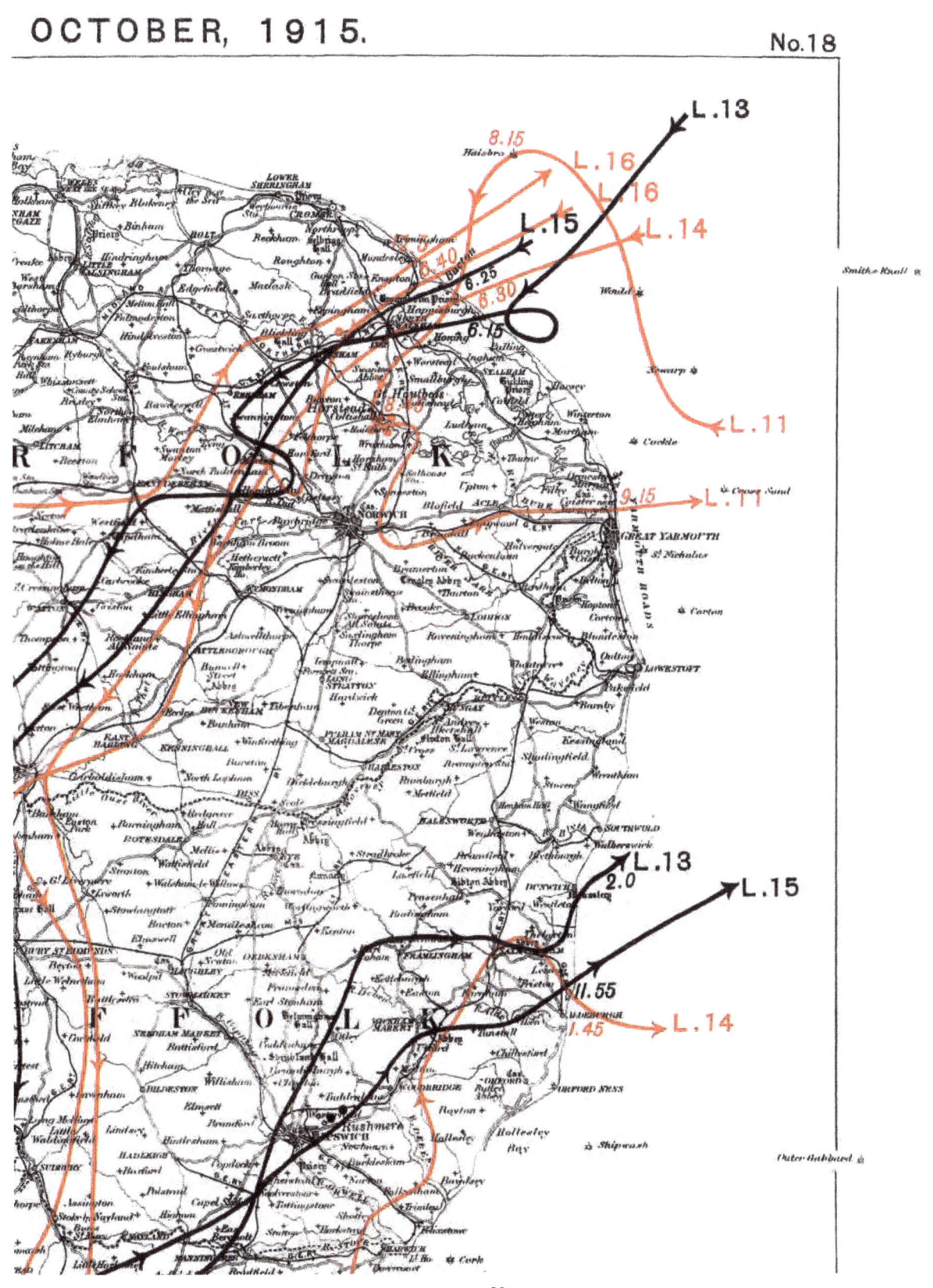

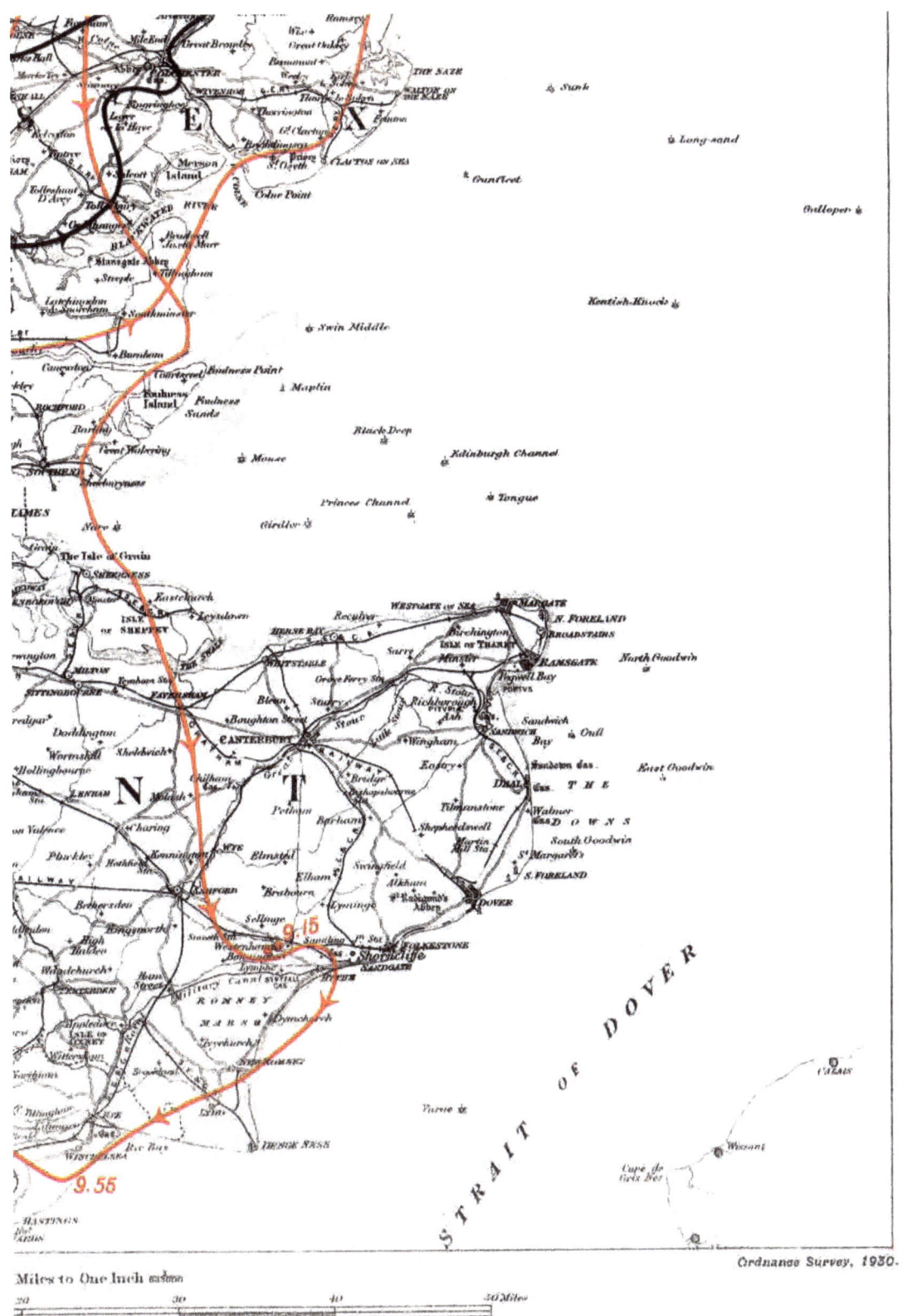

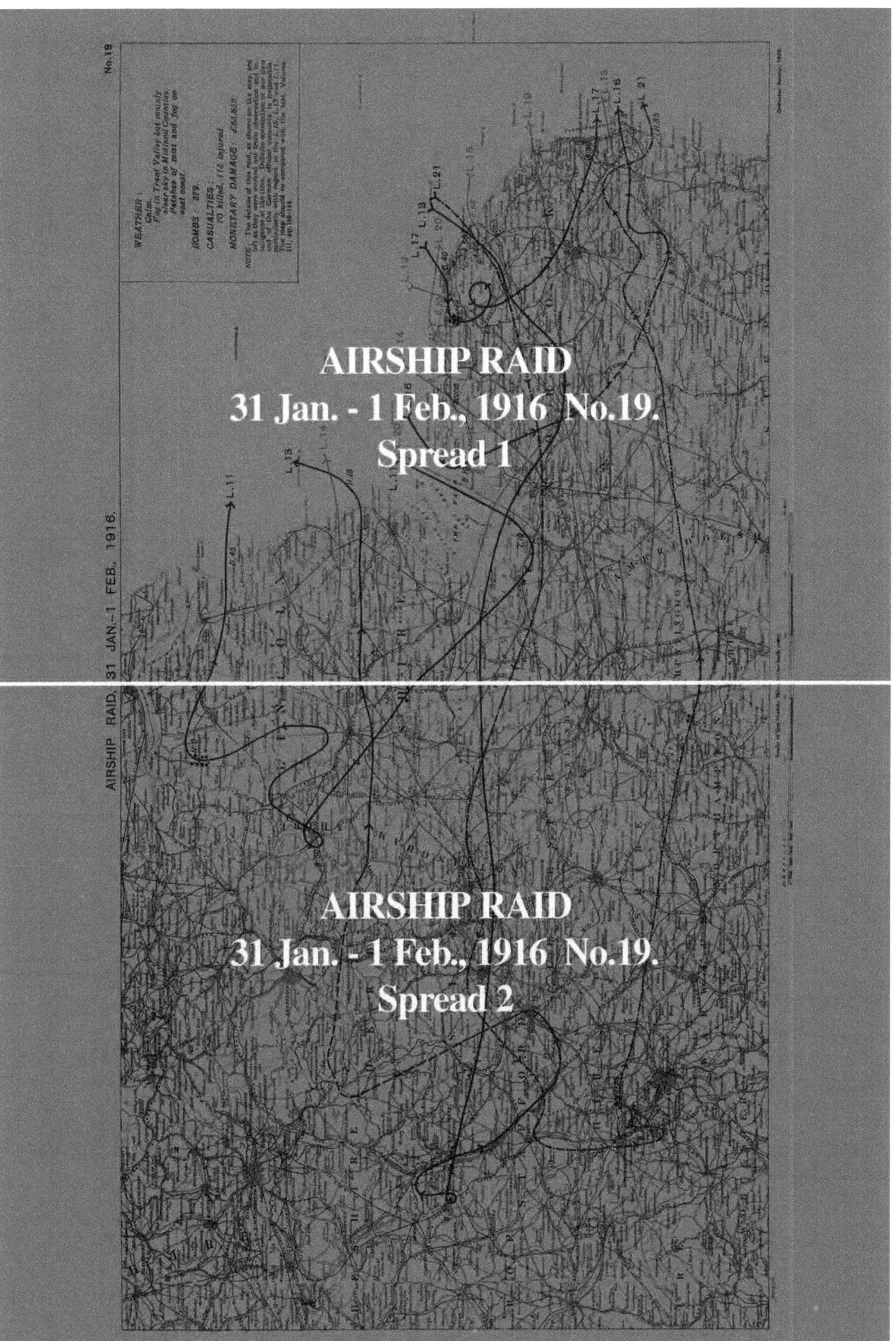

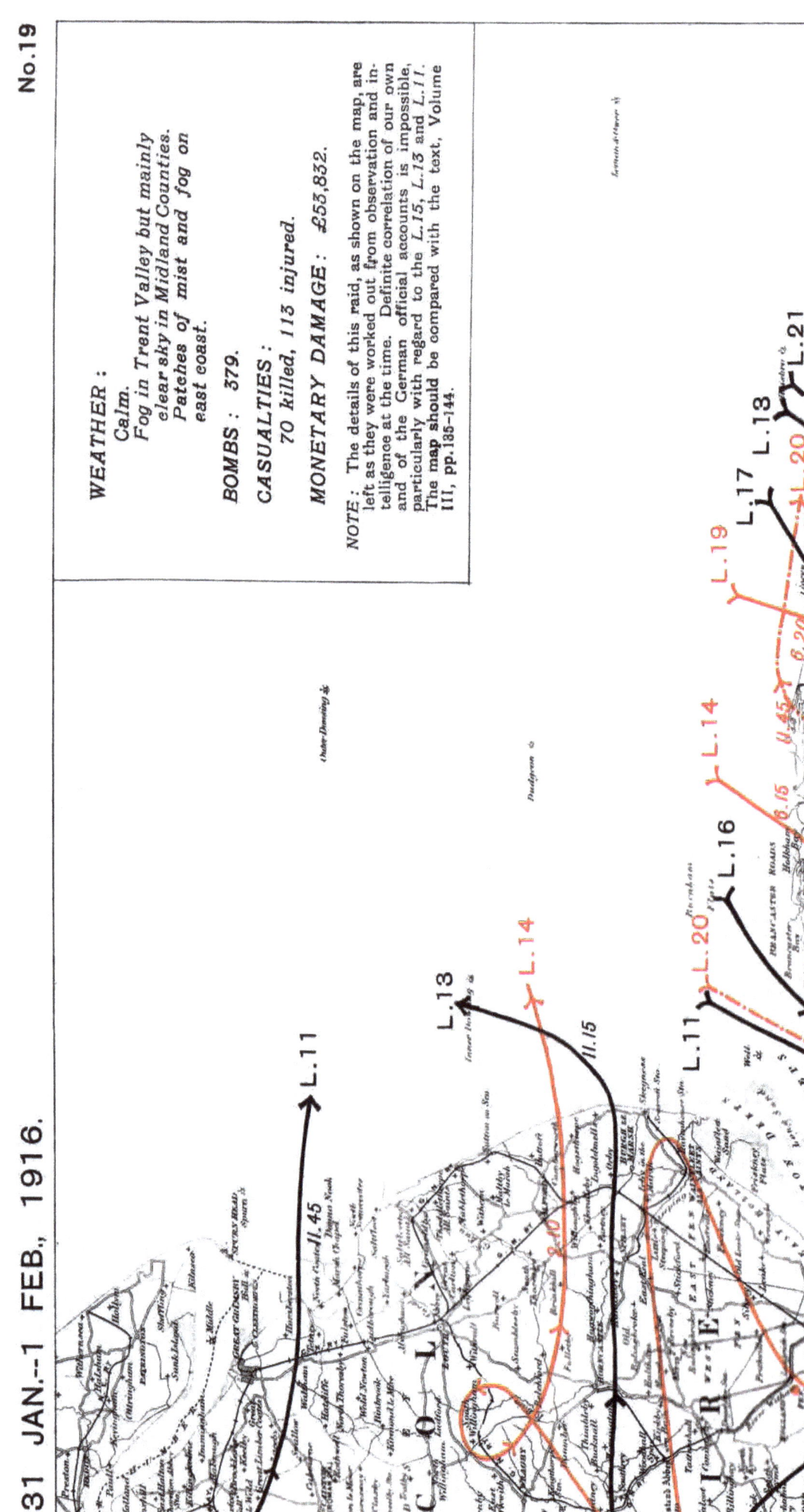

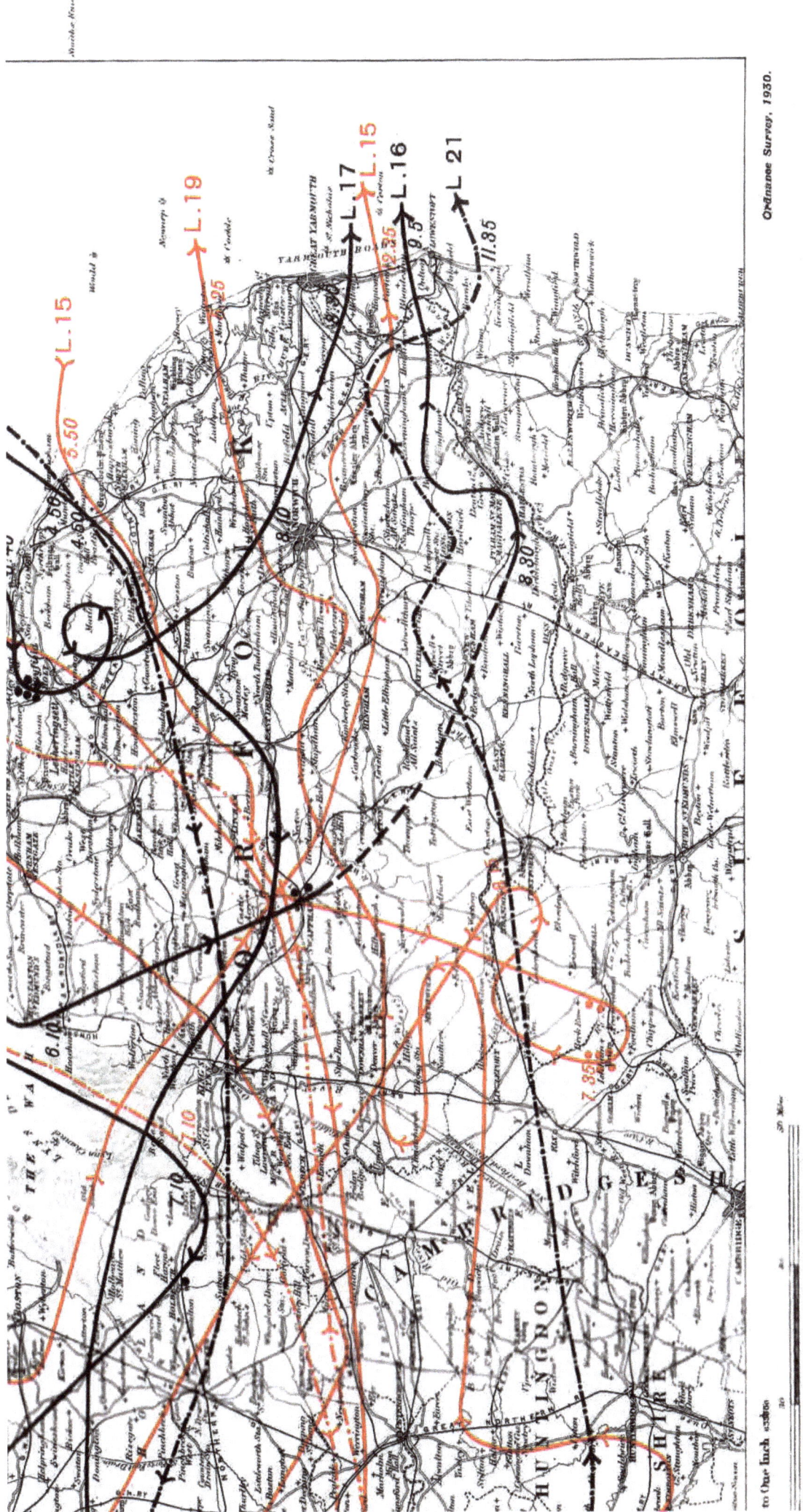

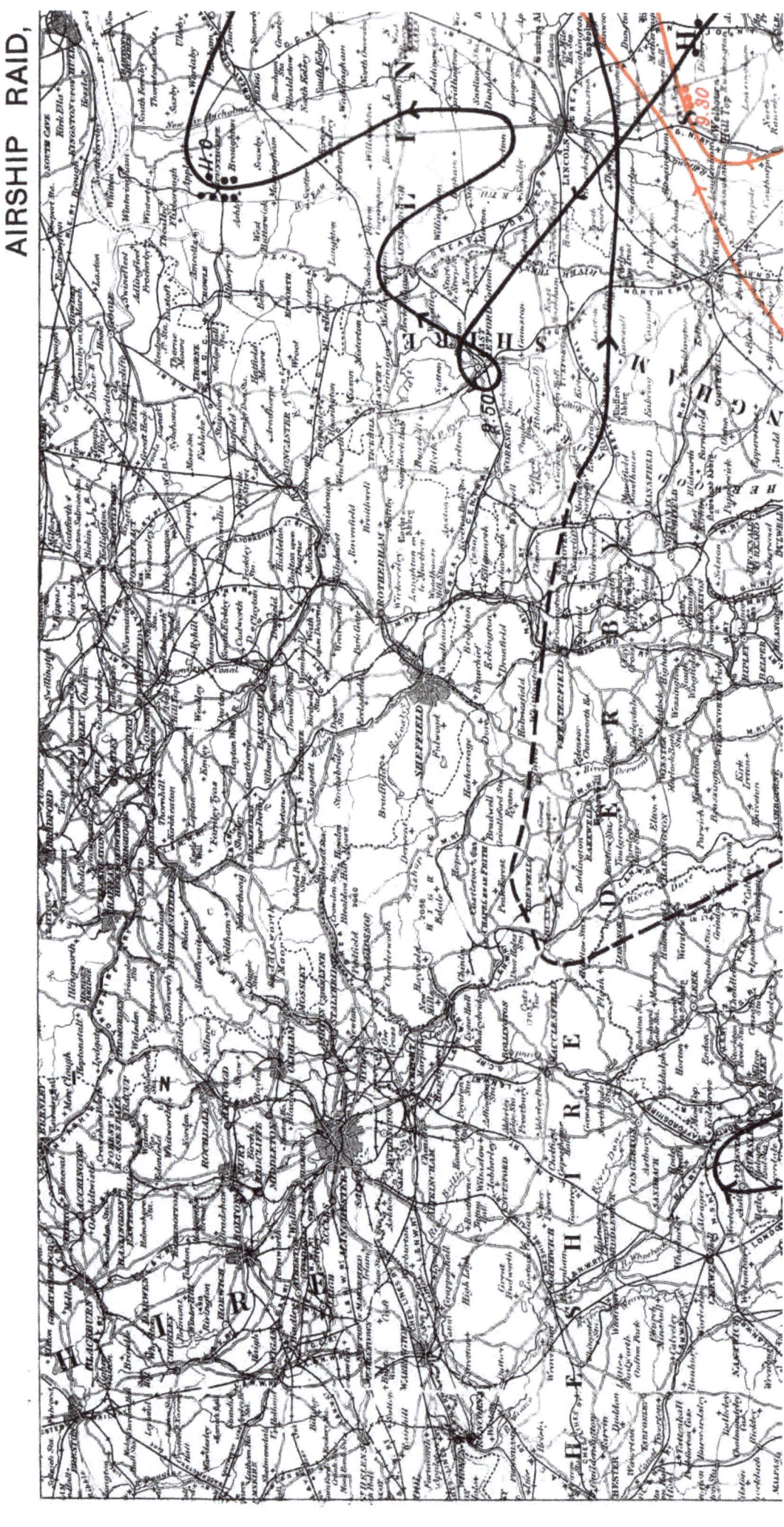

AIRSHIP RAID,

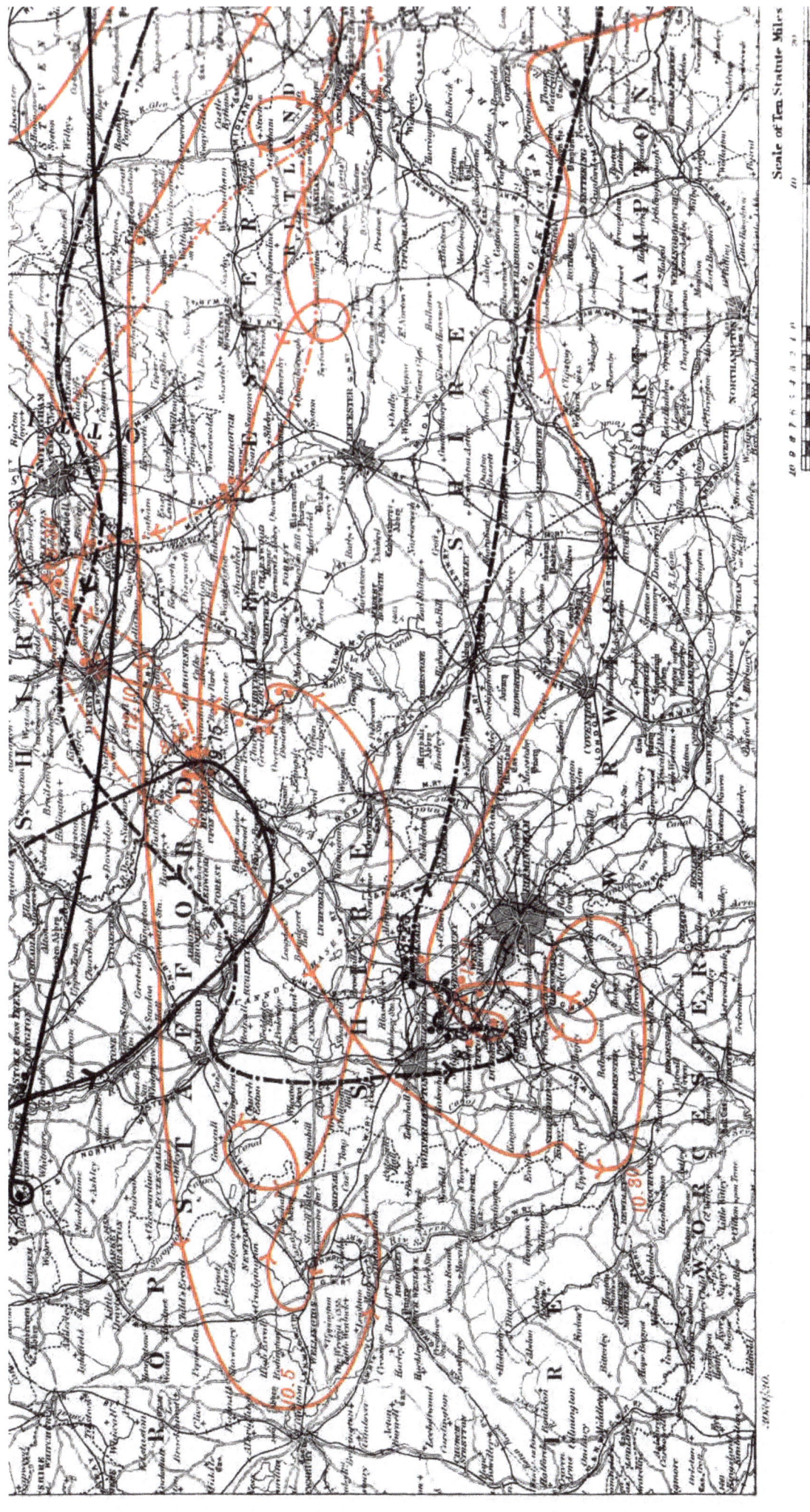

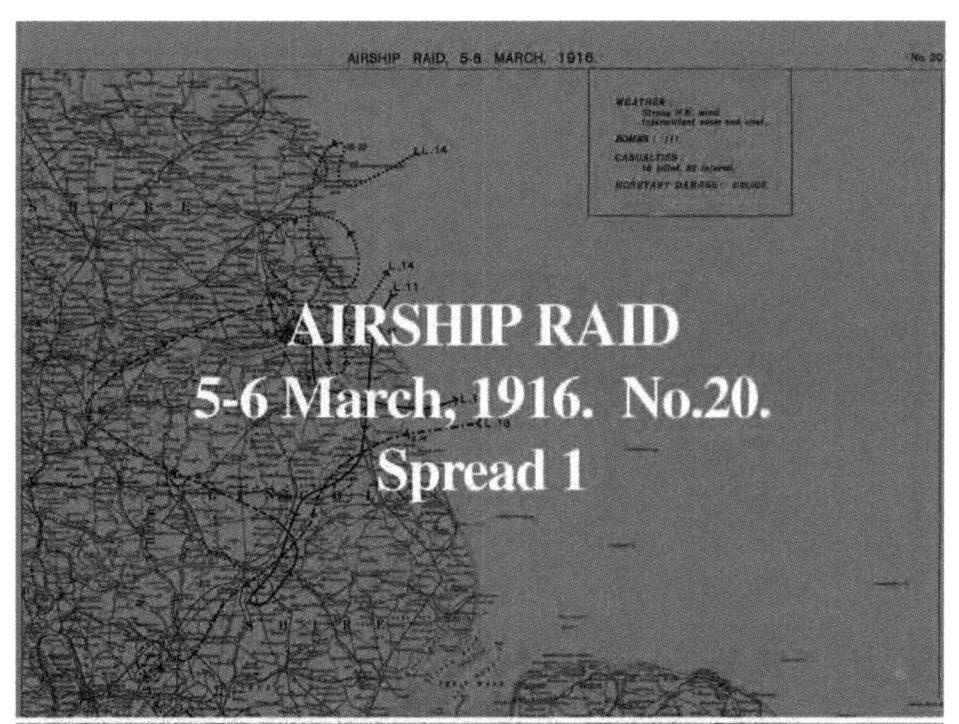

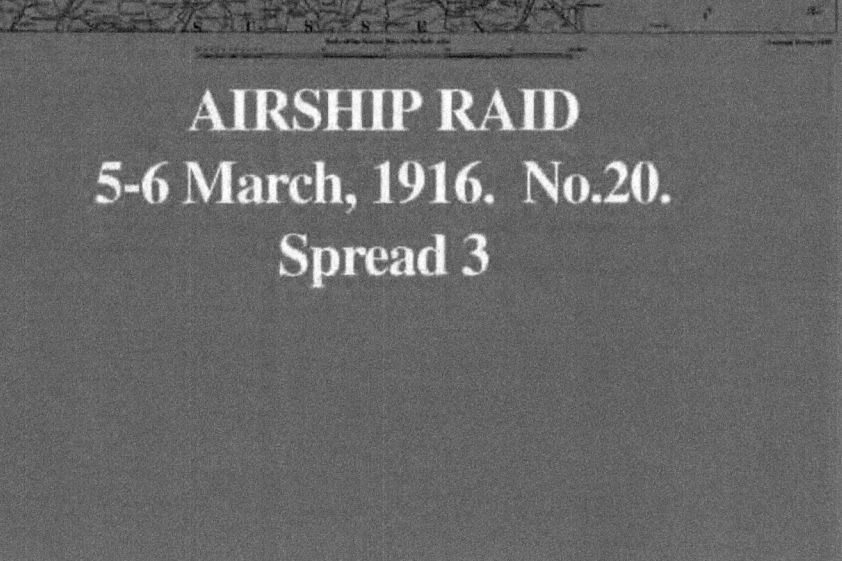

Spread 1

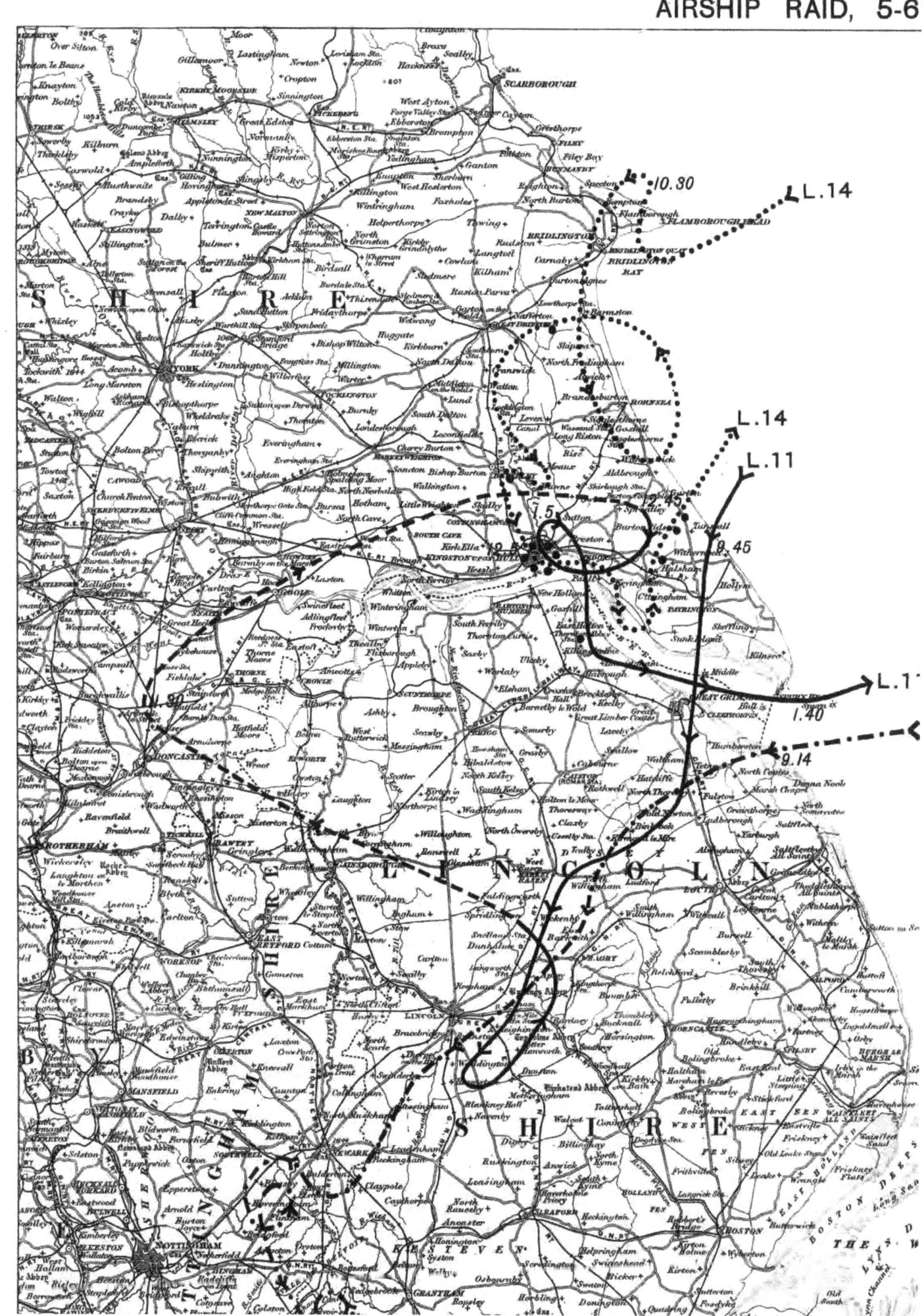

AIRSHIP RAID, 5-6

MARCH, 1916.　　　　　　　　　　　　　　　　　　No. 20

> **WEATHER:**
>   Strong N.E. wind.
>   Intermittent snow and sleet.
>
> **BOMBS:** 111.
>
> **CASUALTIES:**
>   18 killed, 52 injured.
>
> **MONETARY DAMAGE:** £25,005.

L.13

Spread 2

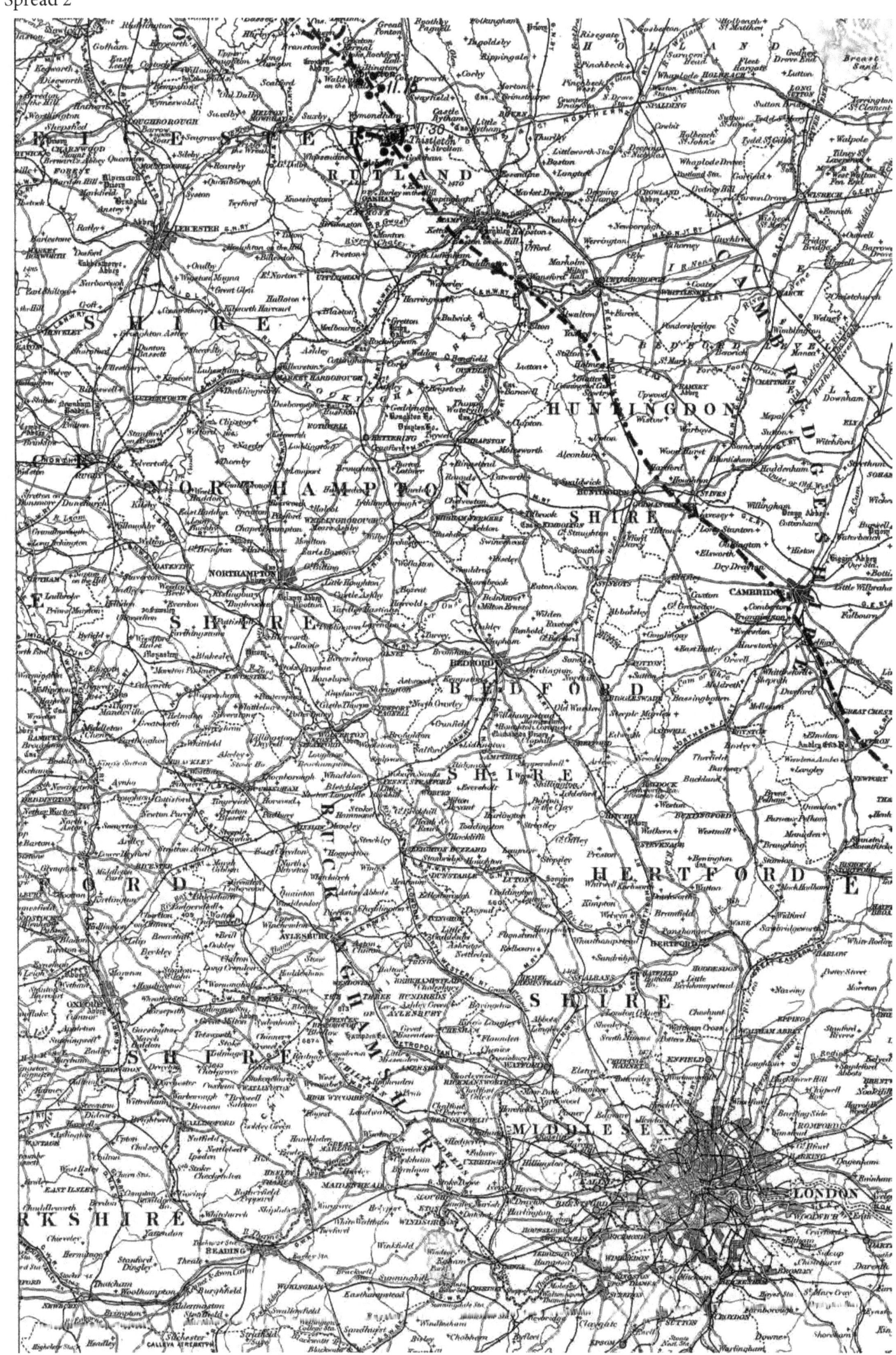

Spread 2

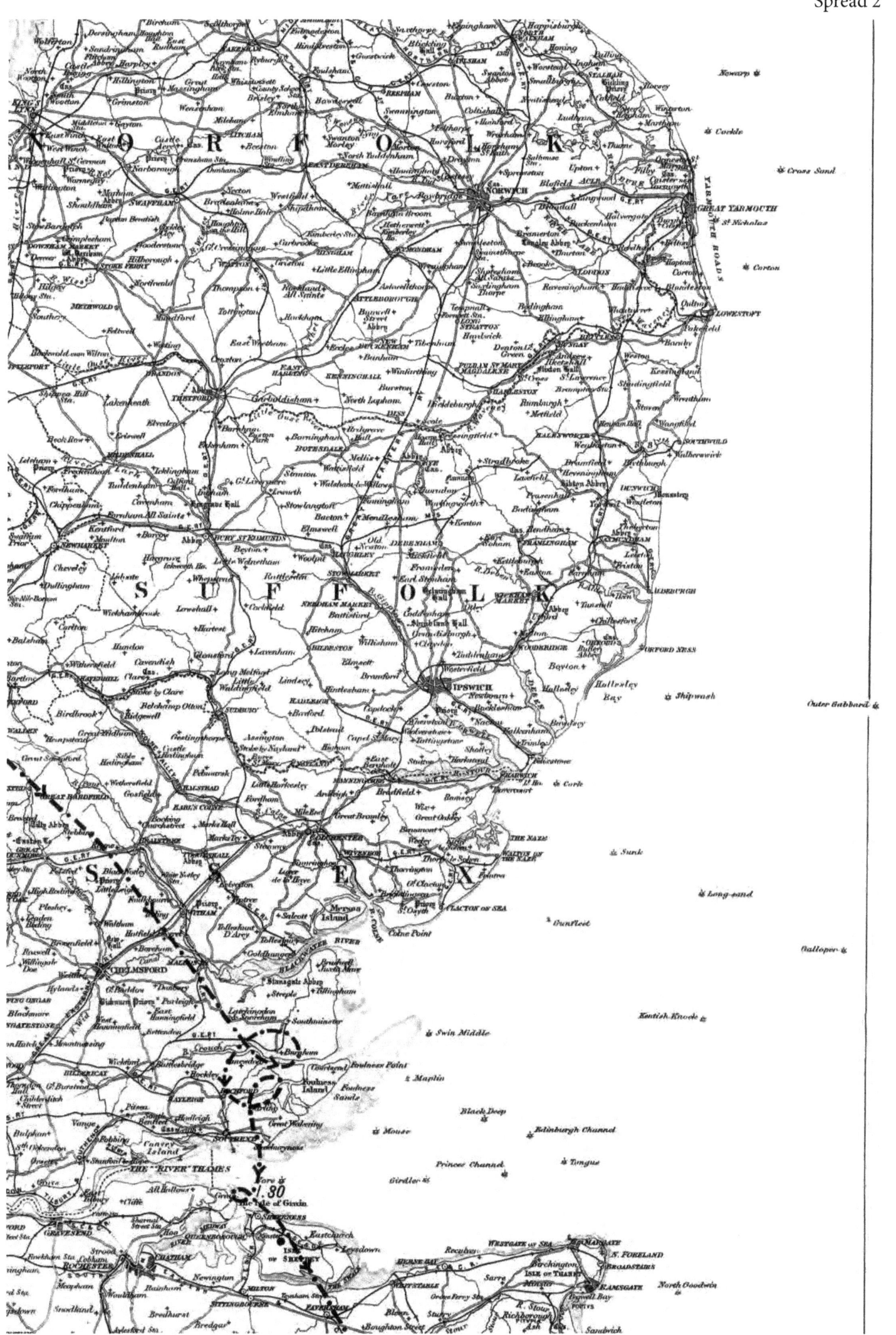

Spread 3

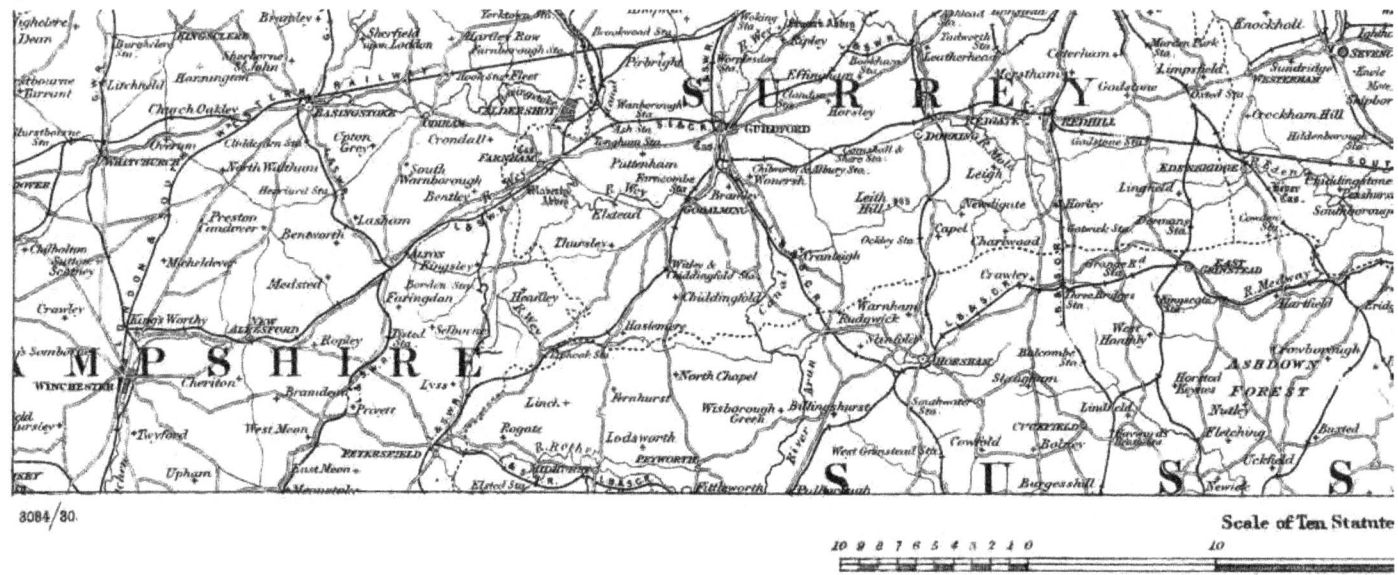

Spread 3

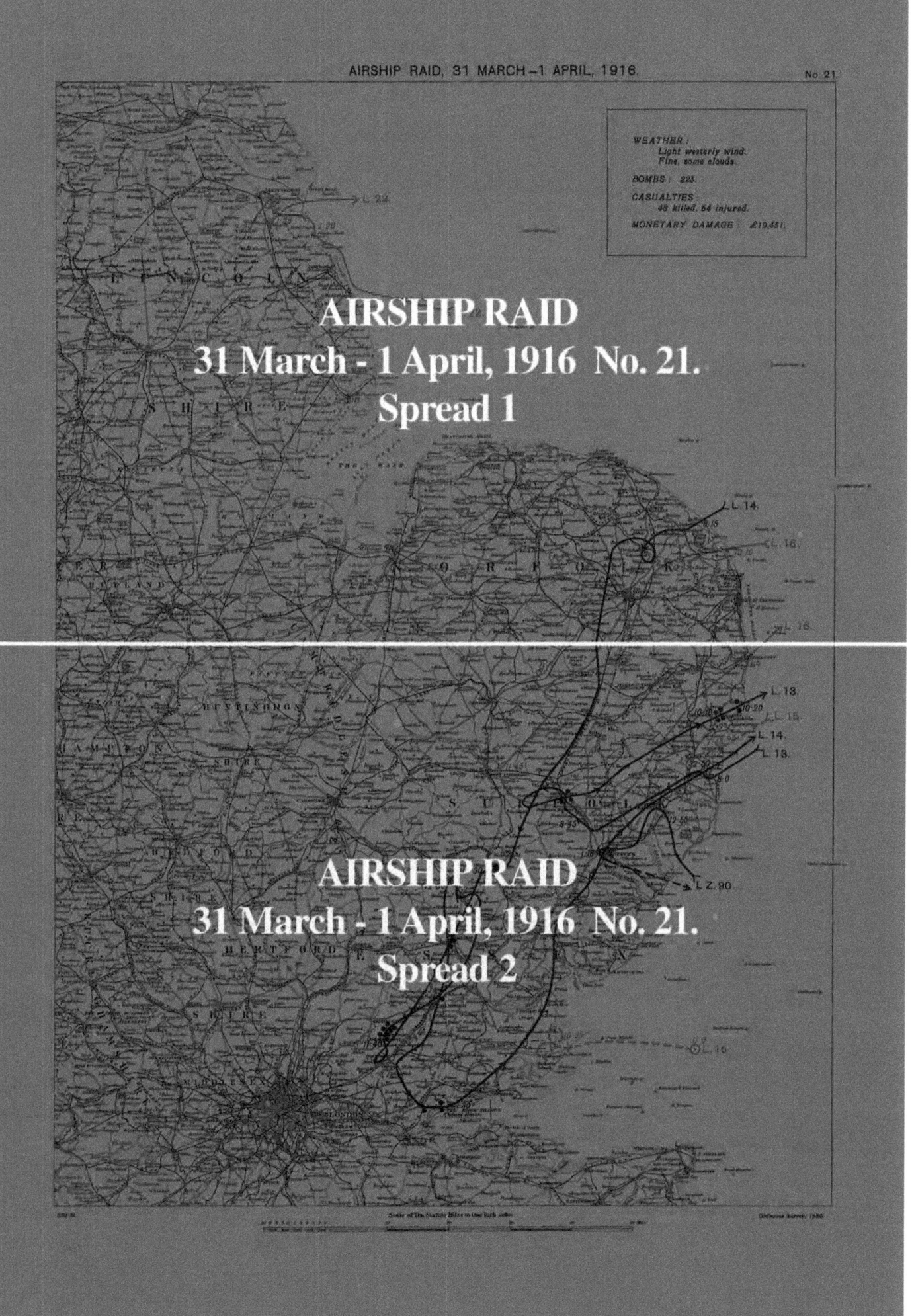

Spread 1

AIRSHIP RAID,

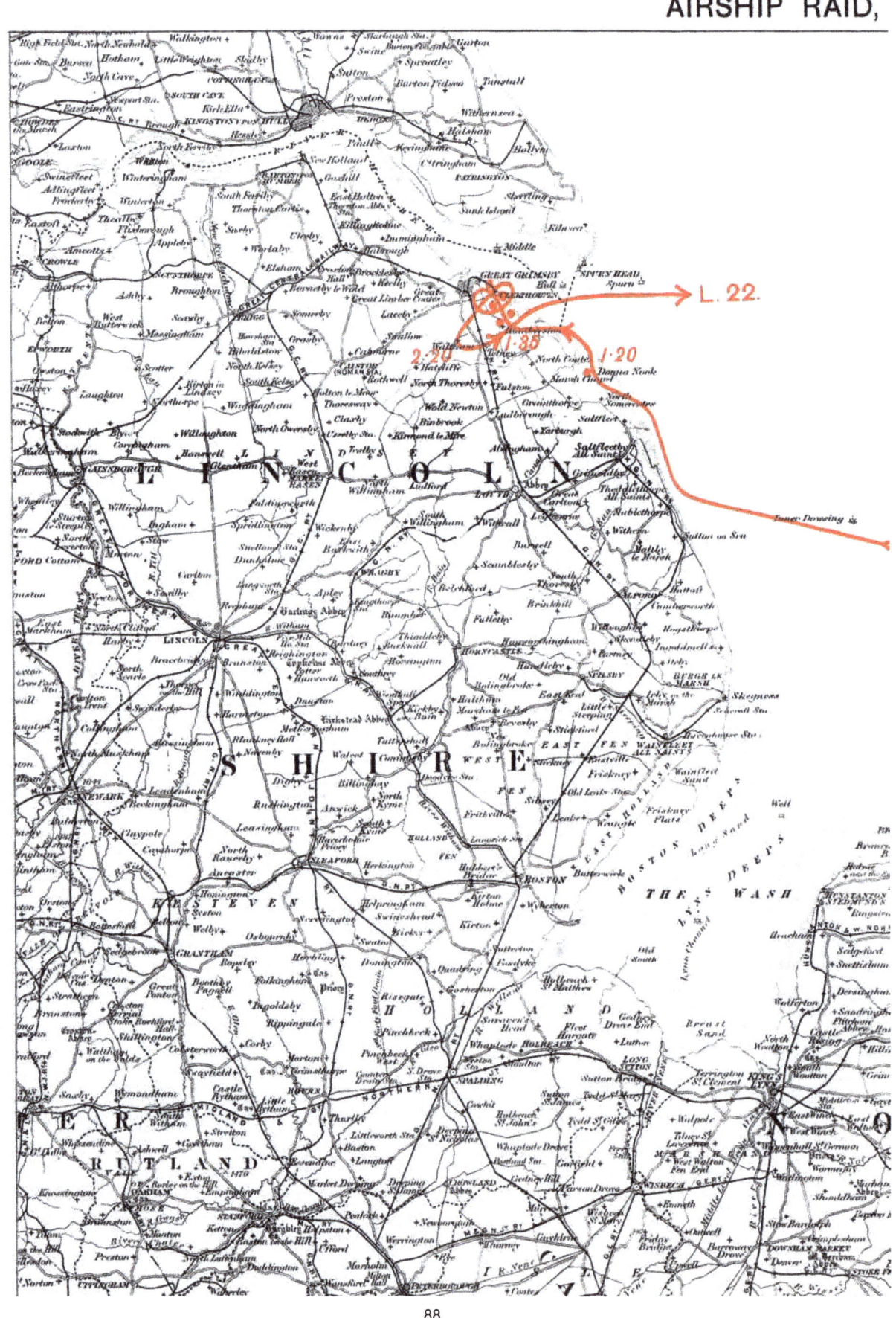

31 MARCH – 1 APRIL, 1916.

No. 21.

```
WEATHER:
    Light westerly wind.
    Fine, some clouds.

BOMBS: 223.

CASUALTIES:
    48 killed, 64 injured.

MONETARY DAMAGE: £19,431.
```

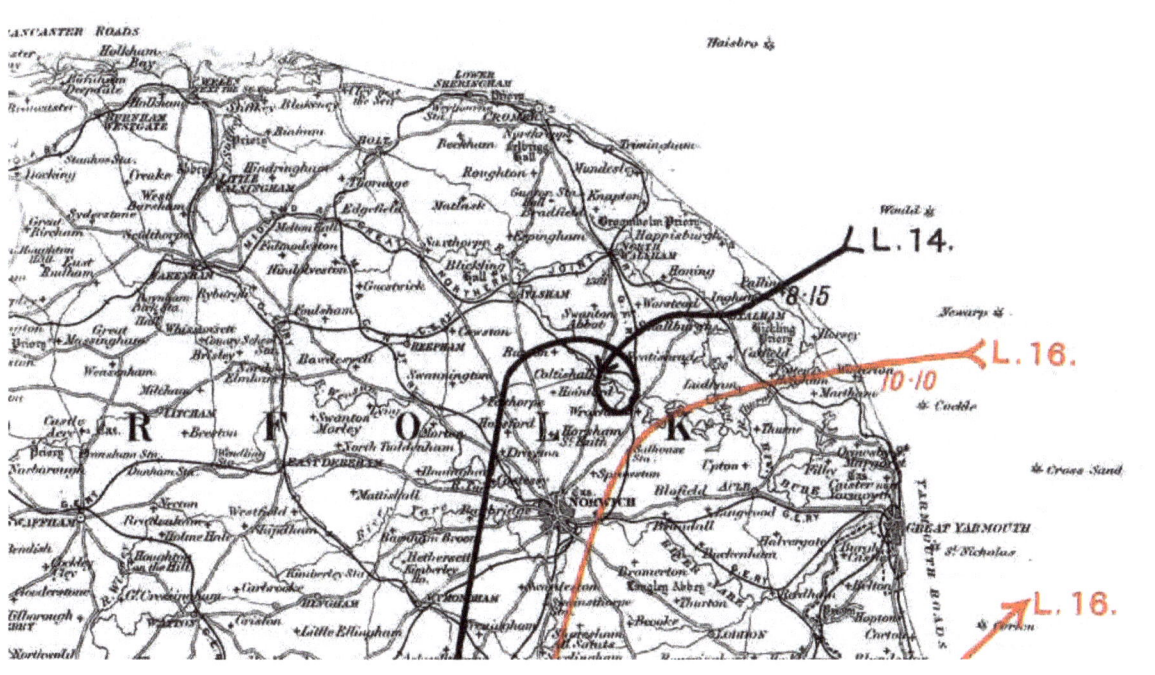

Spread 2

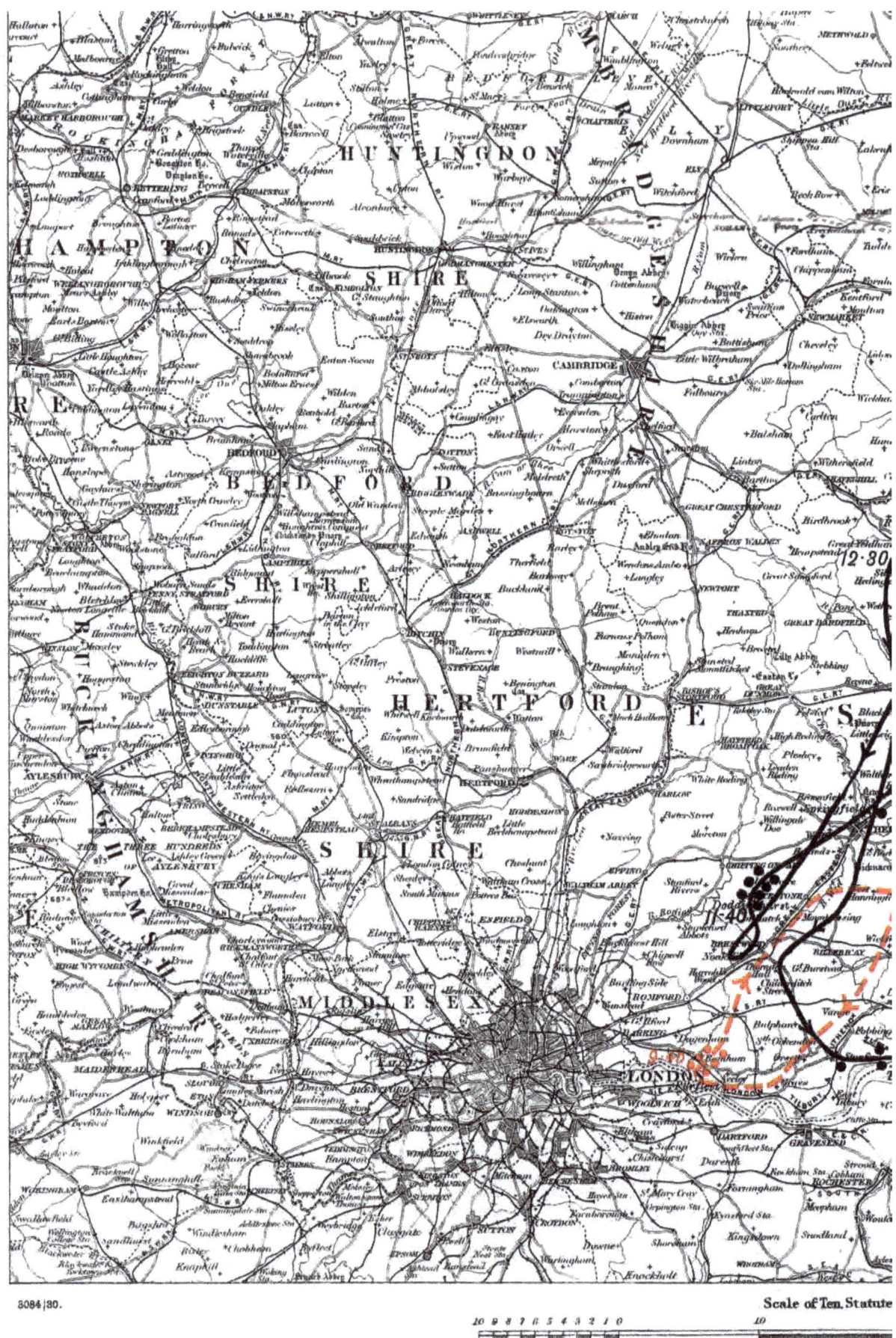

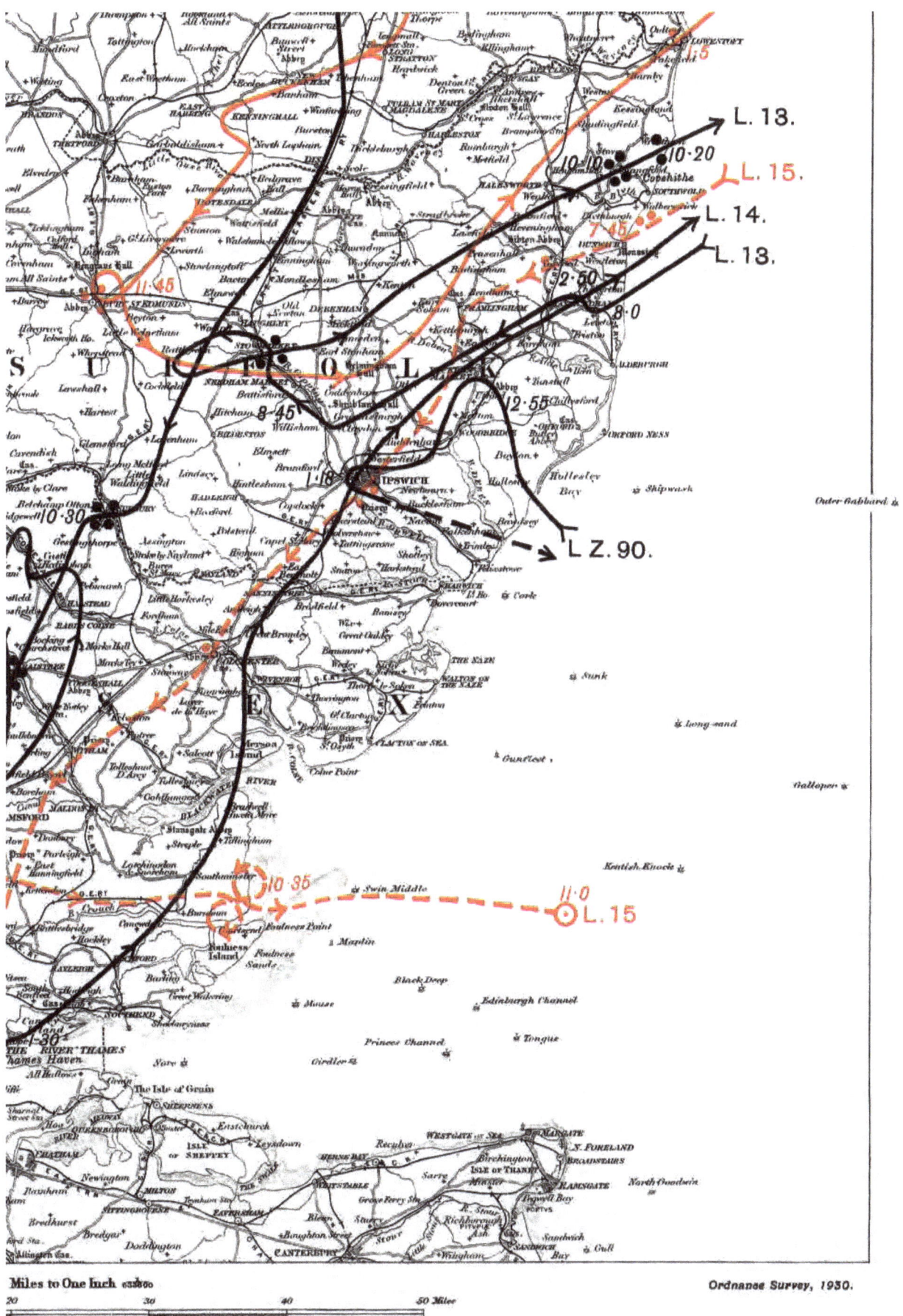

Spread 2

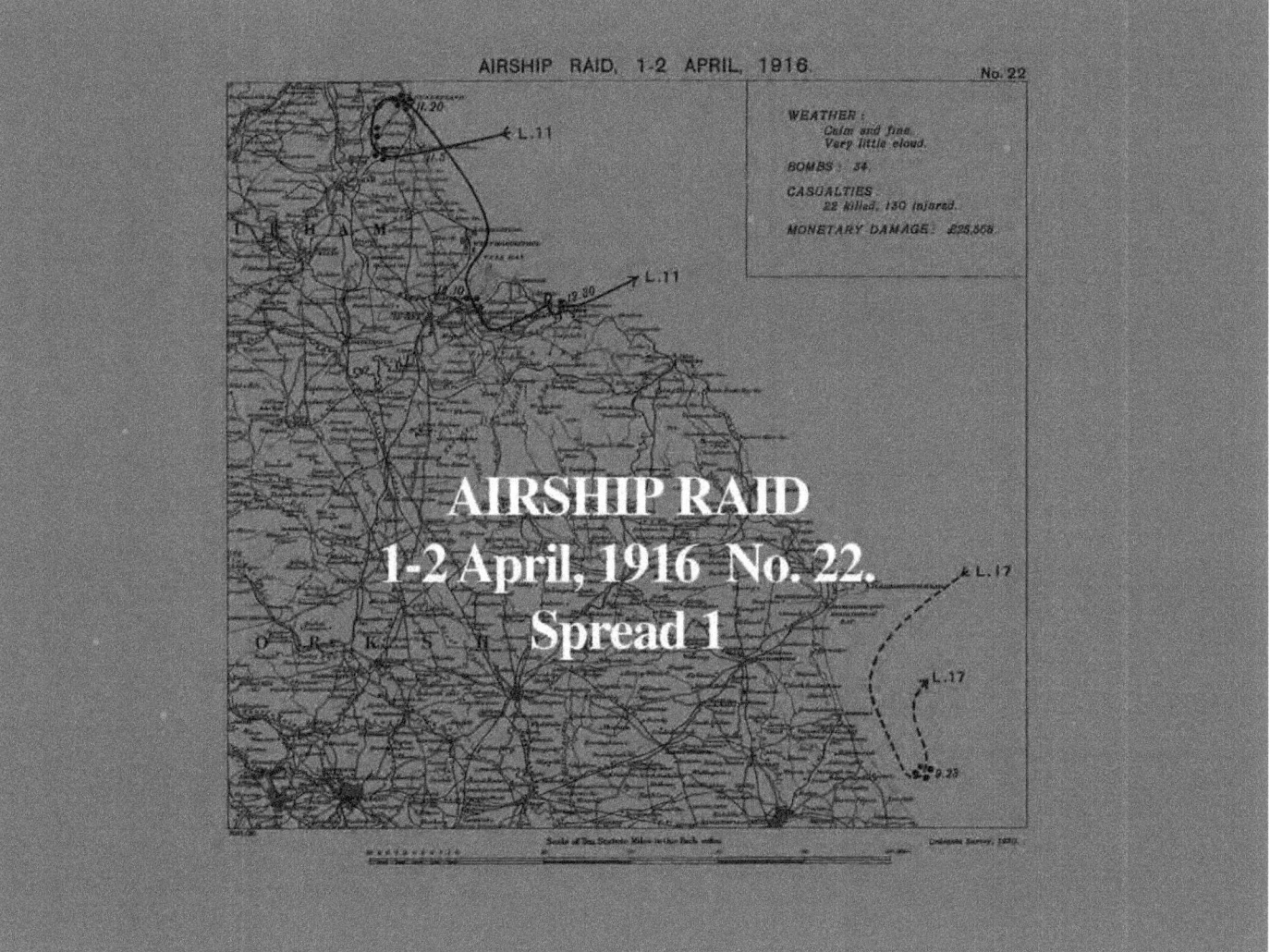

Spread 1

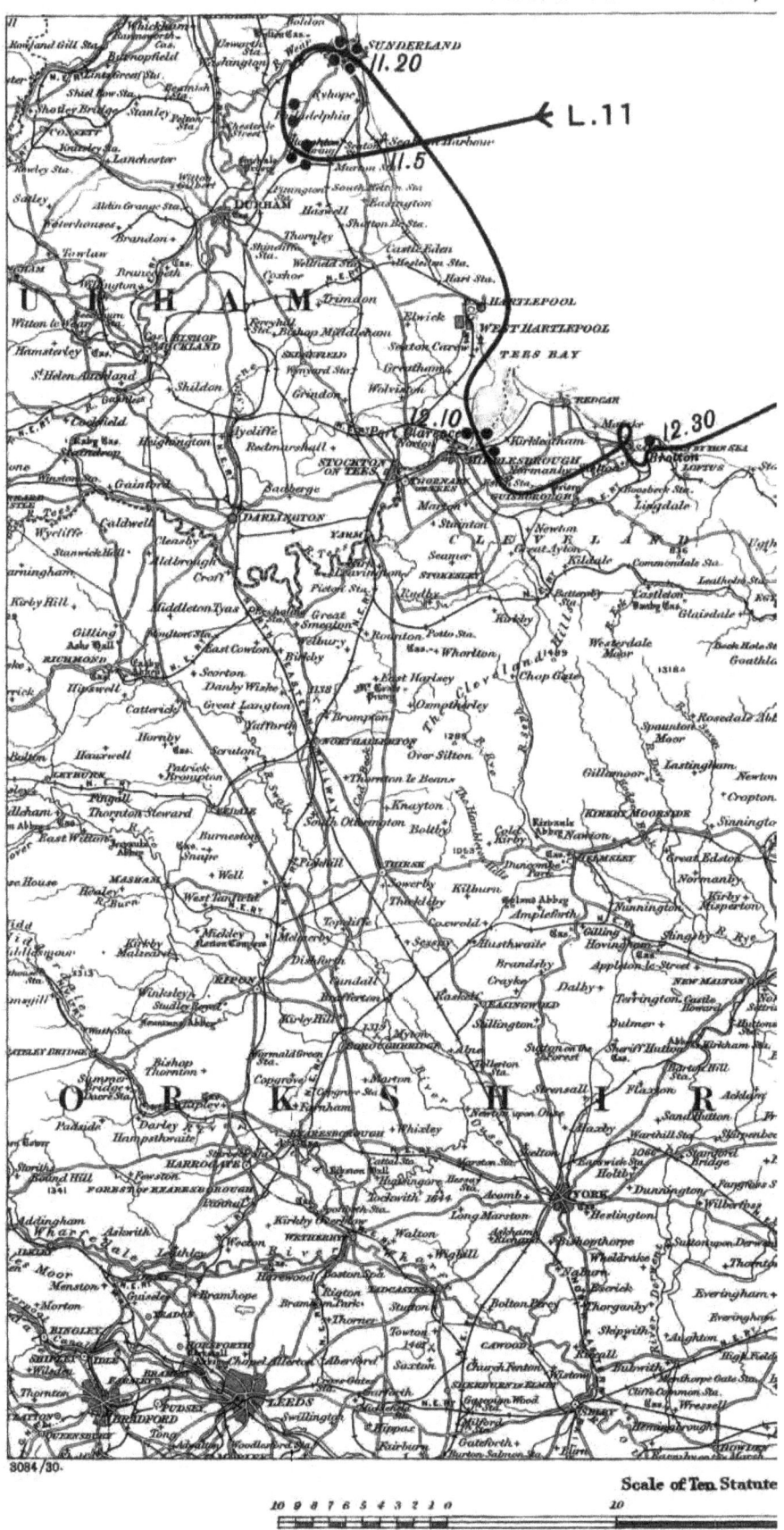

1-2 APRIL, 1916.

No. 22

WEATHER:
  Calm and fine.
  Very little cloud.

BOMBS: 34.

CASUALTIES:
  22 killed, 130 injured.

MONETARY DAMAGE: £25,568.

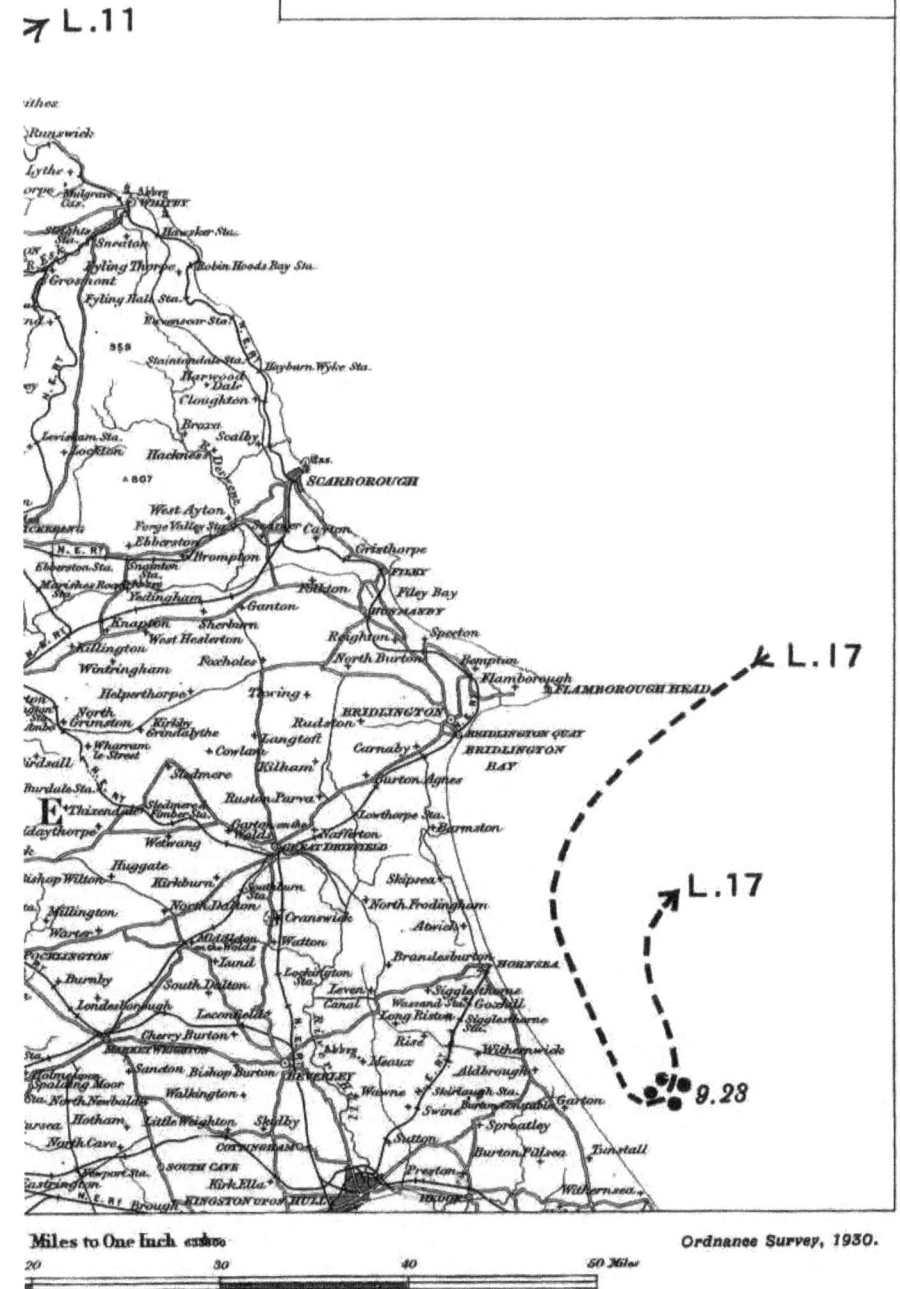

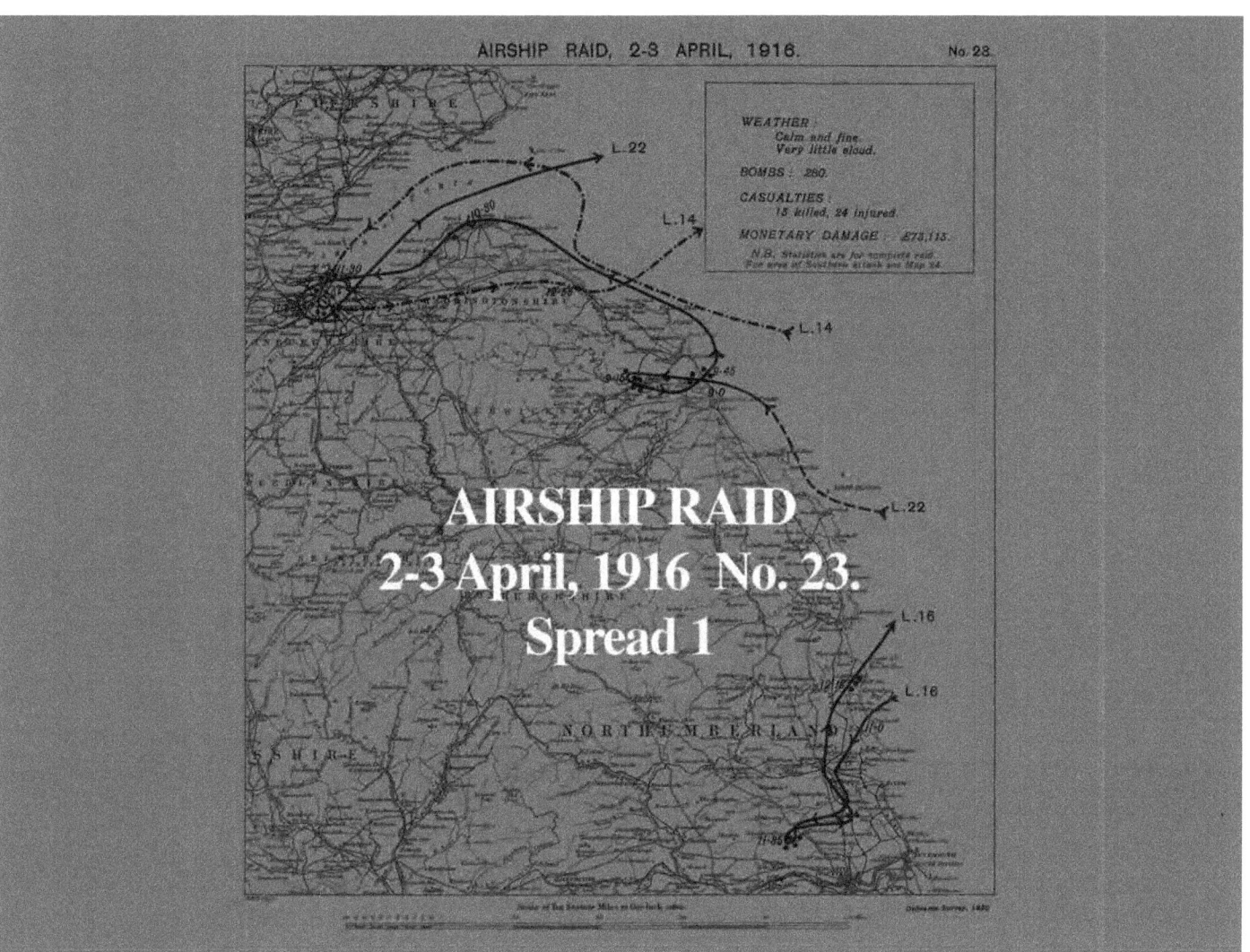

Spread 1

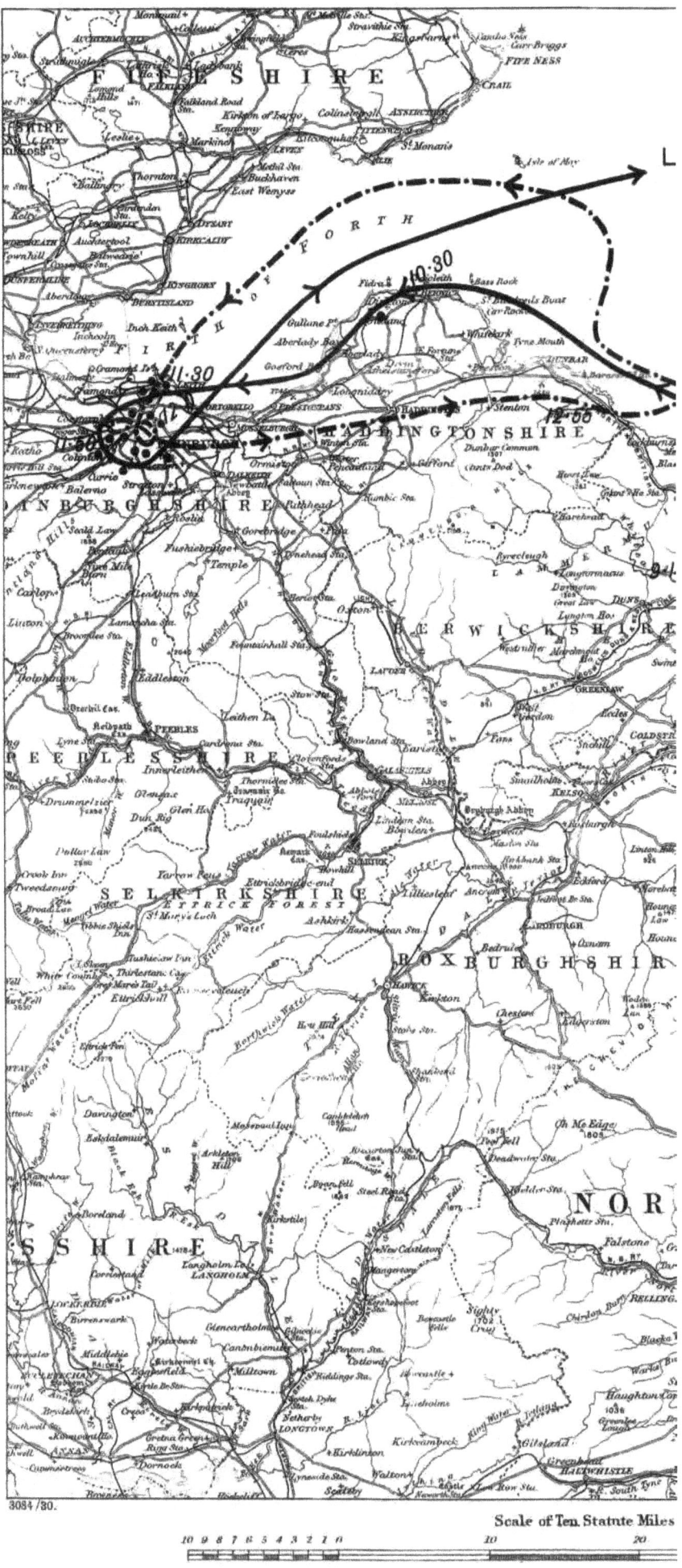

2-3 APRIL, 1916. No. 23.

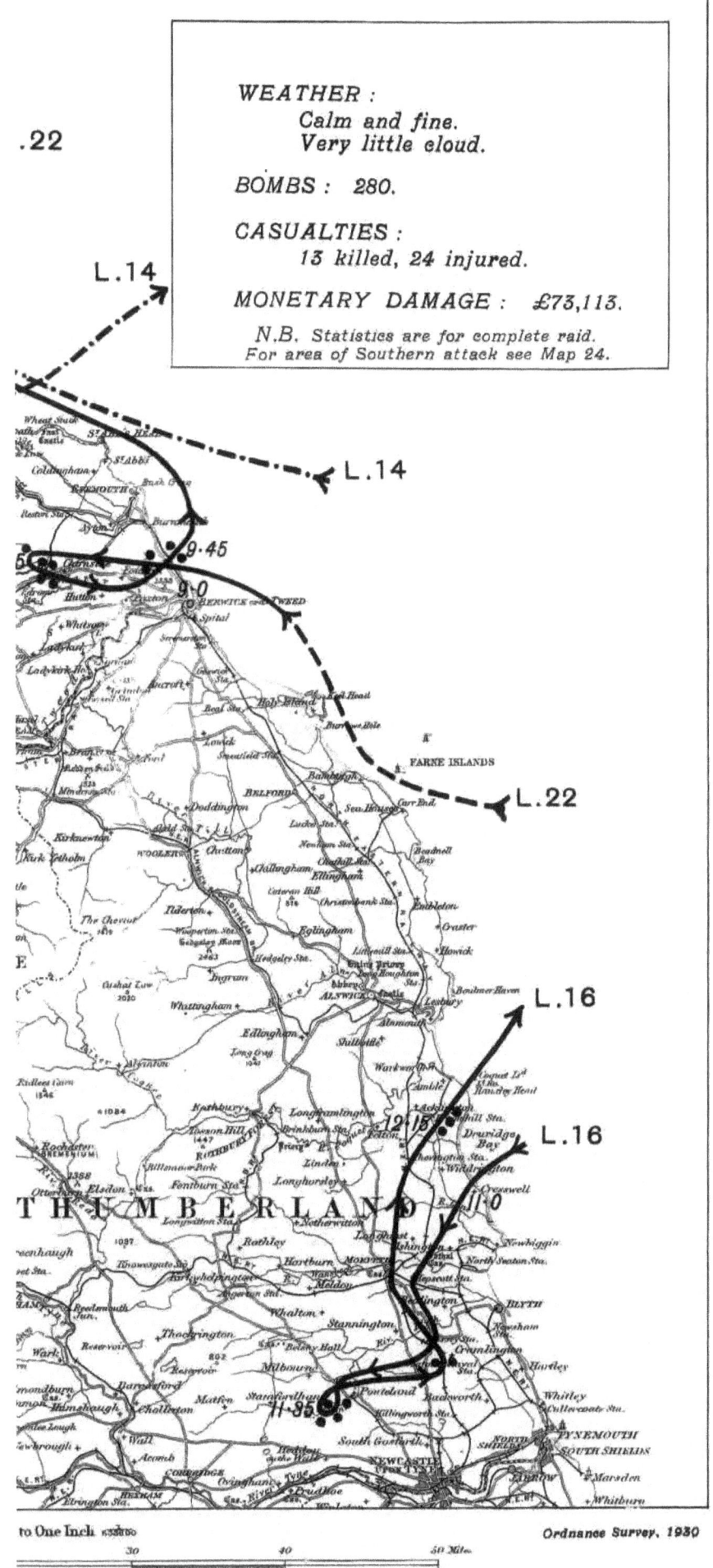

WEATHER:
  Calm and fine.
  Very little cloud.

BOMBS: 280.

CASUALTIES:
  13 killed, 24 injured.

MONETARY DAMAGE: £73,113.

N.B. Statistics are for complete raid. For area of Southern attack see Map 24.

AIRSHIP RAID, 3-4 APRIL, 1916. No.25

WEATHER: Calm and fine at first, then mist and rising northerly wind on east coast.

BOMBS: 13.

CASUALTIES: Nil.

MONETARY DAMAGE: Nil.

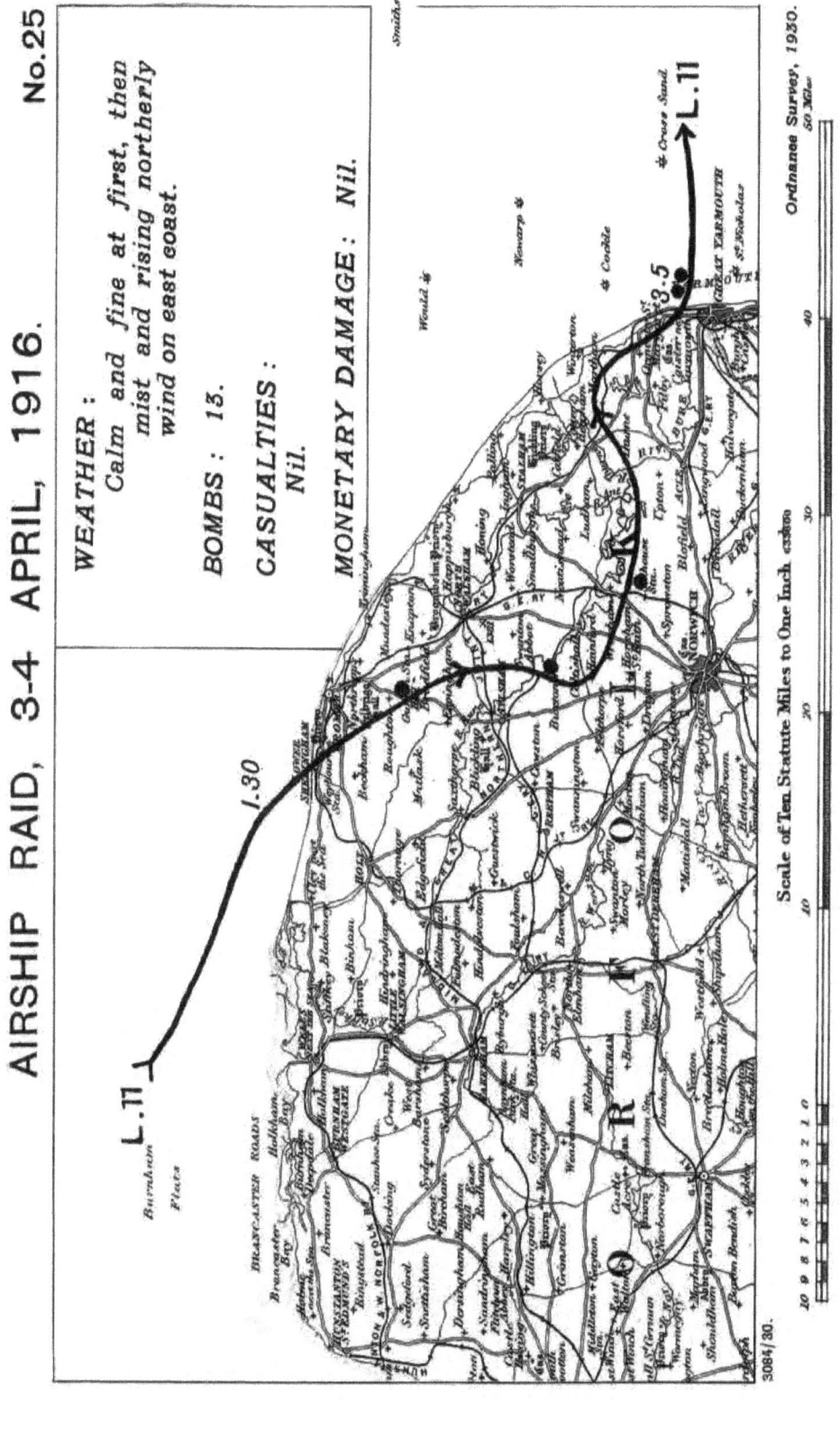

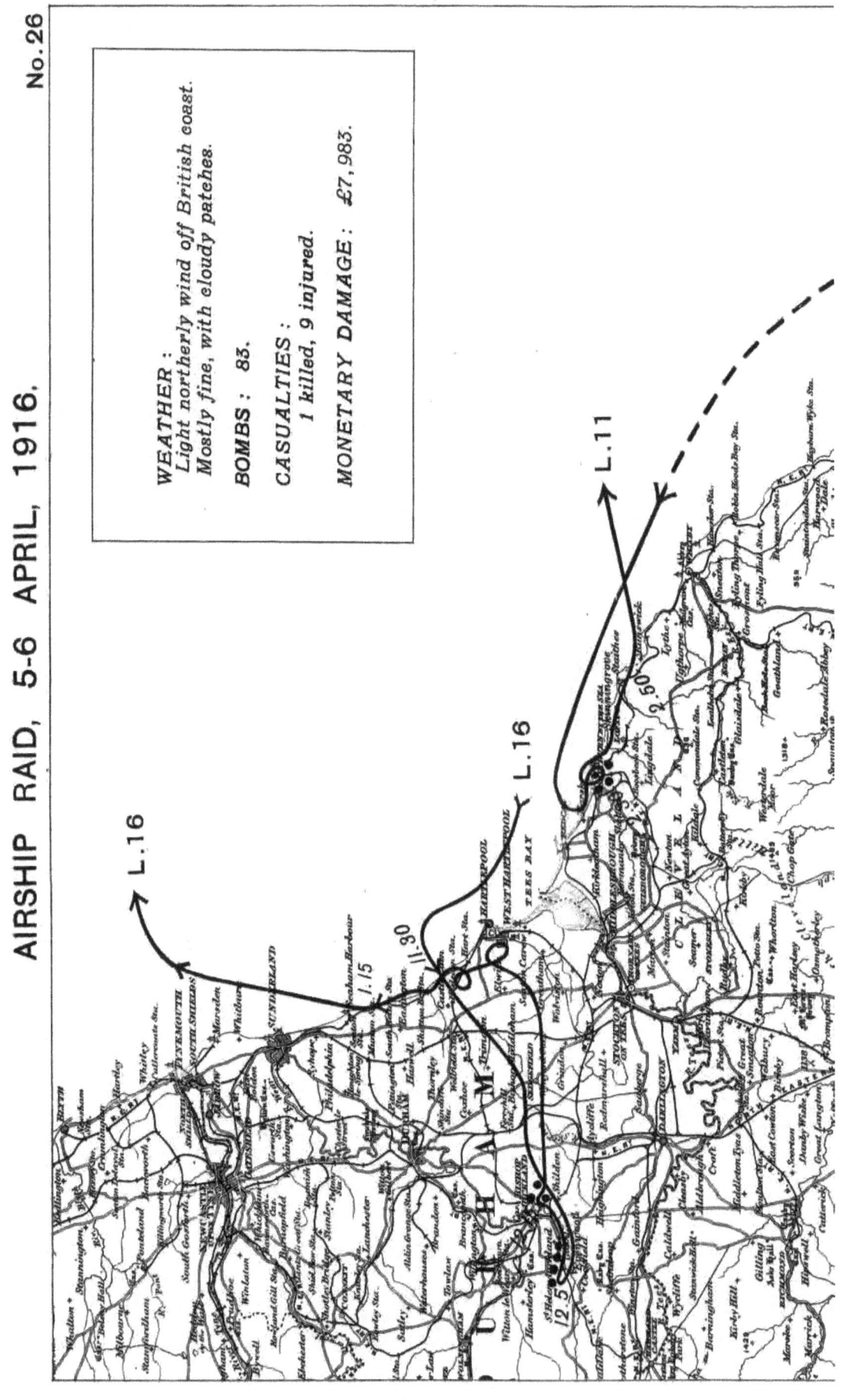

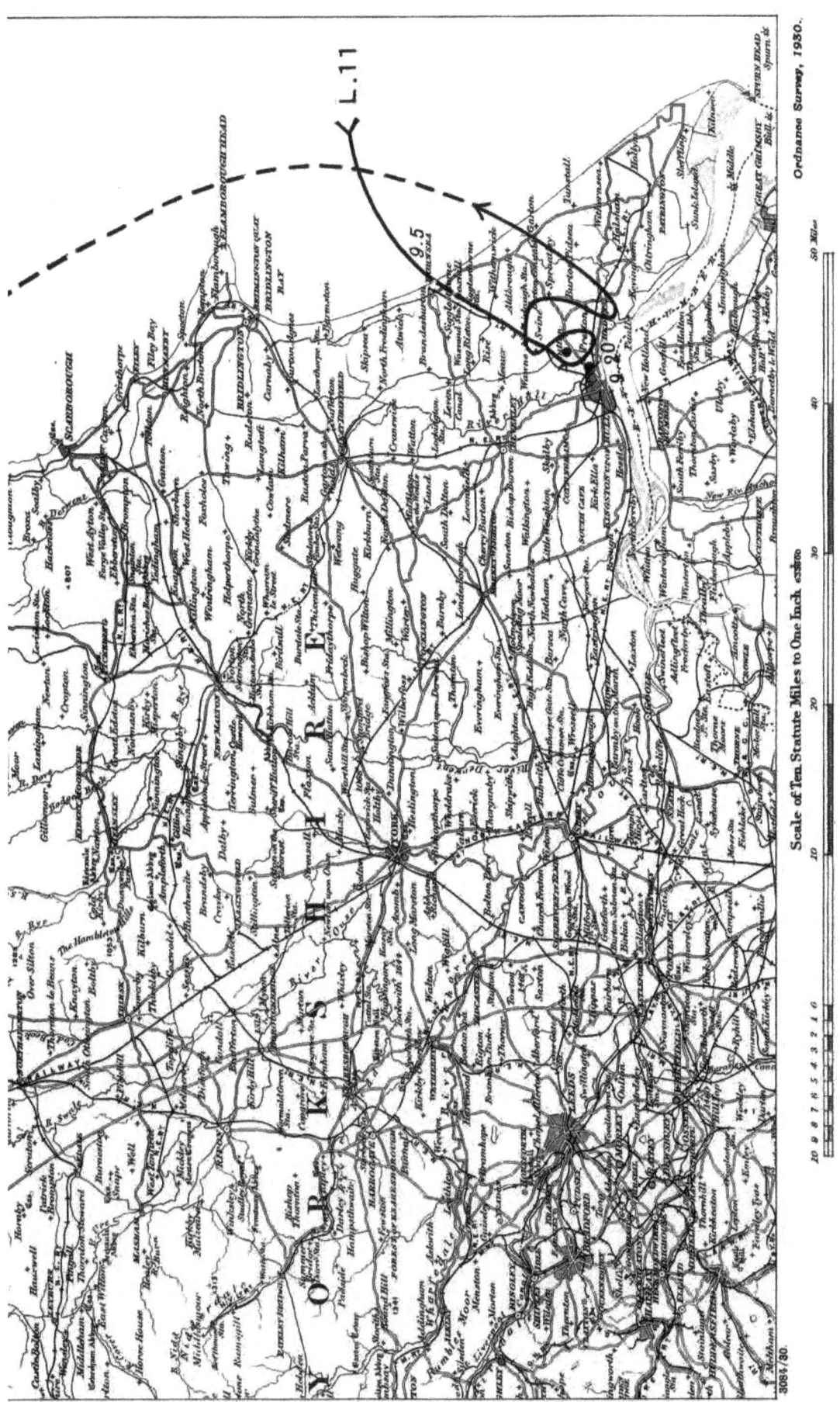

Ordnance Survey, 1930.

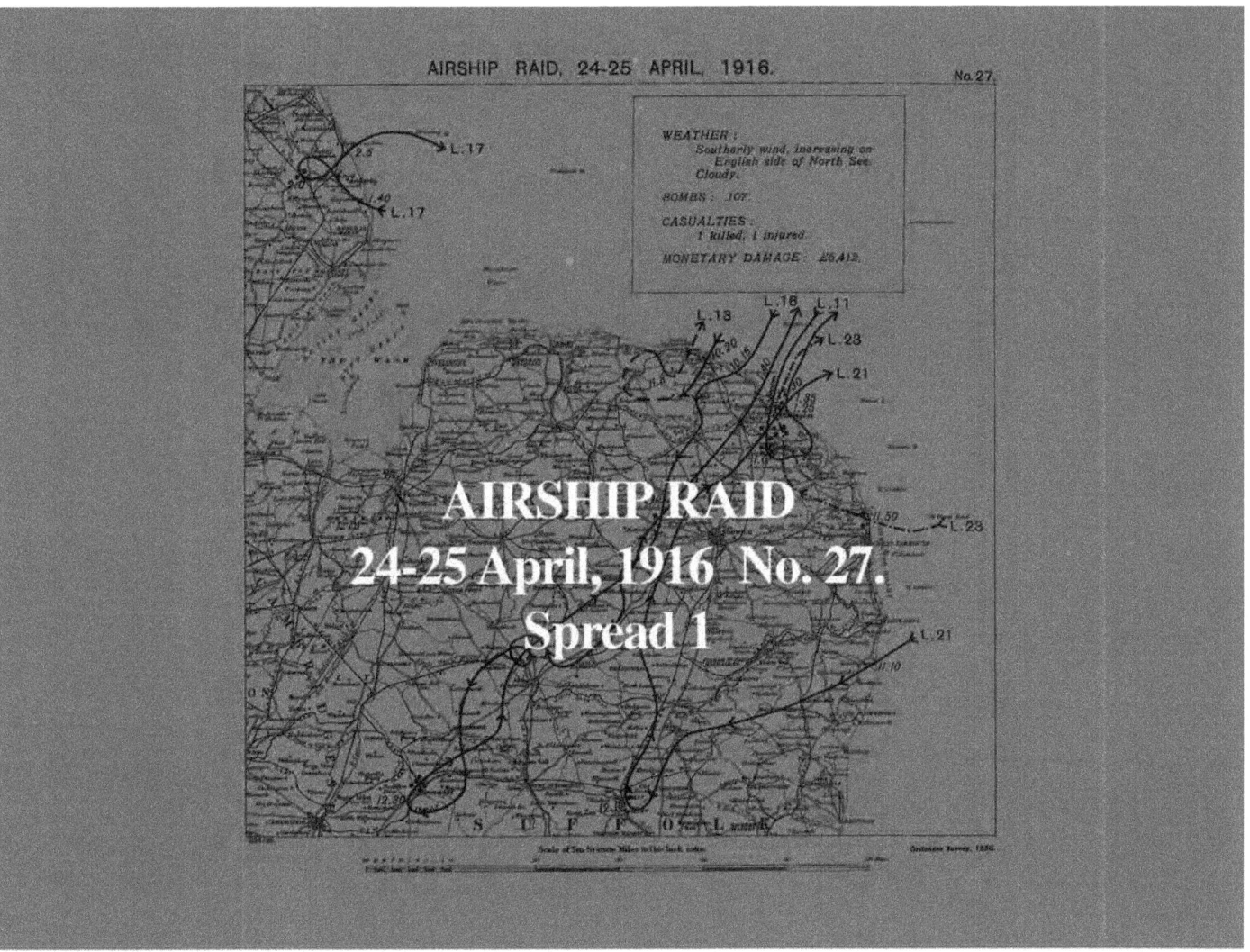

Spread 1

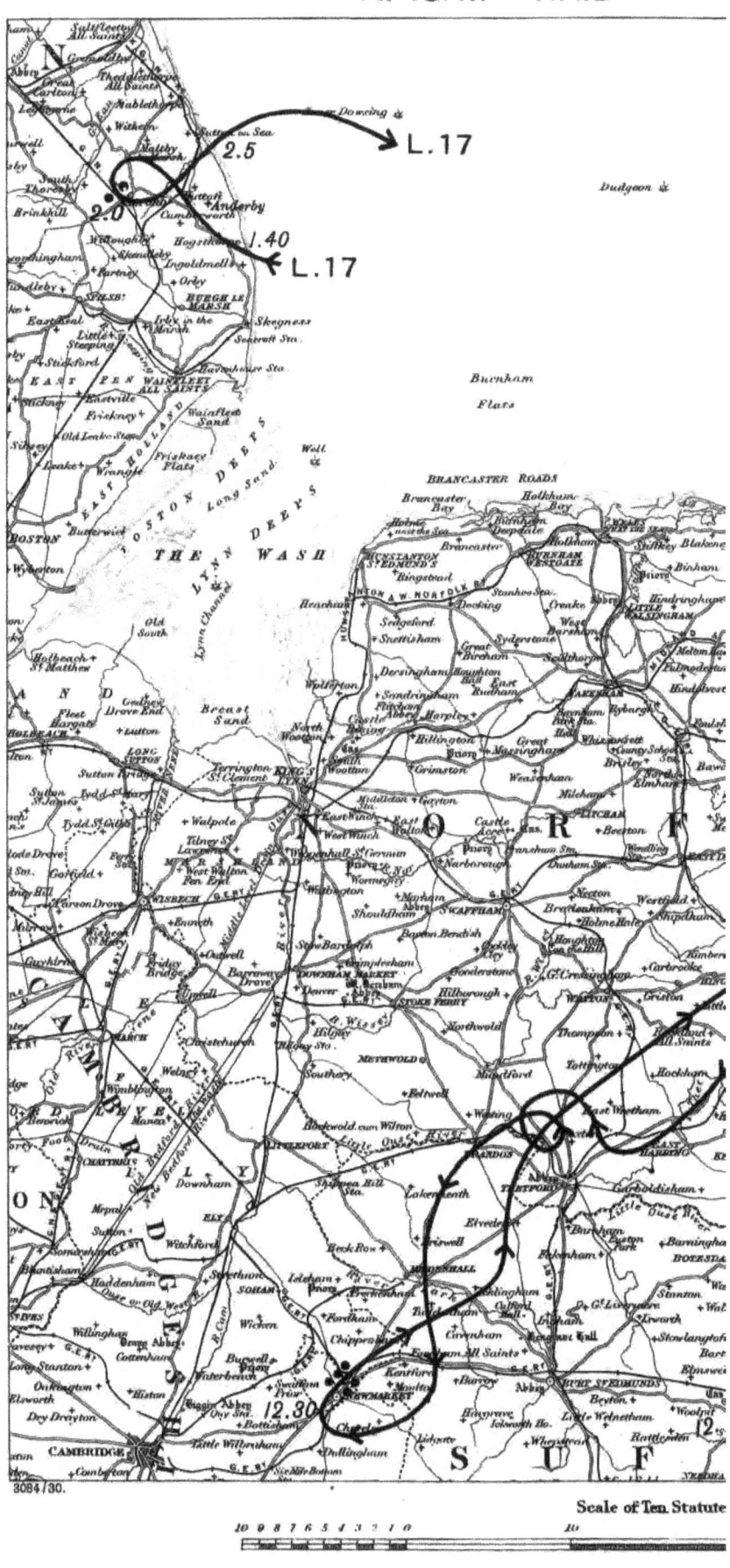

24-25 APRIL, 1916.

No. 27.

WEATHER:
　　Southerly wind, increasing on English side of North Sea. Cloudy.

BOMBS: 107.

CASUALTIES:
　　1 killed, 1 injured.

MONETARY DAMAGE: £6,412.

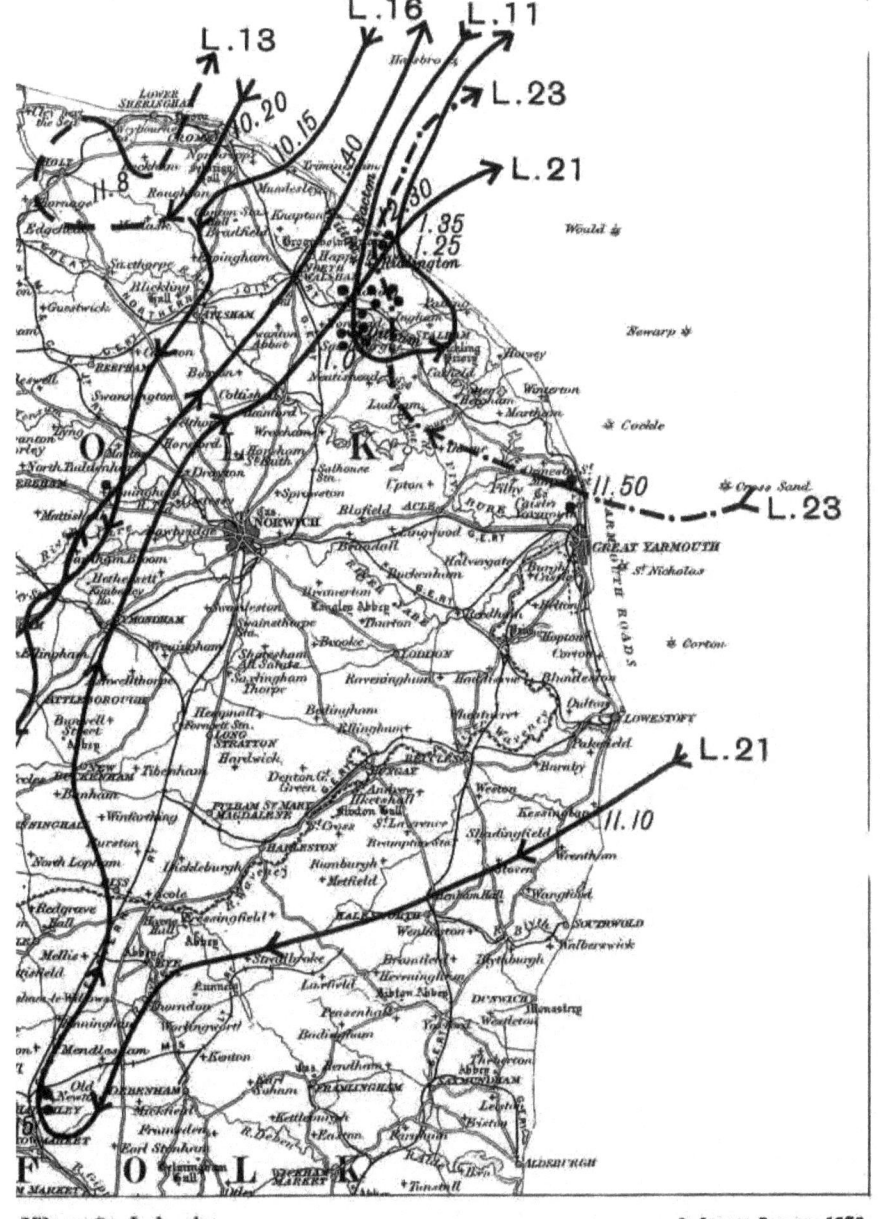

Miles to One Inch

Ordnance Survey, 1930.

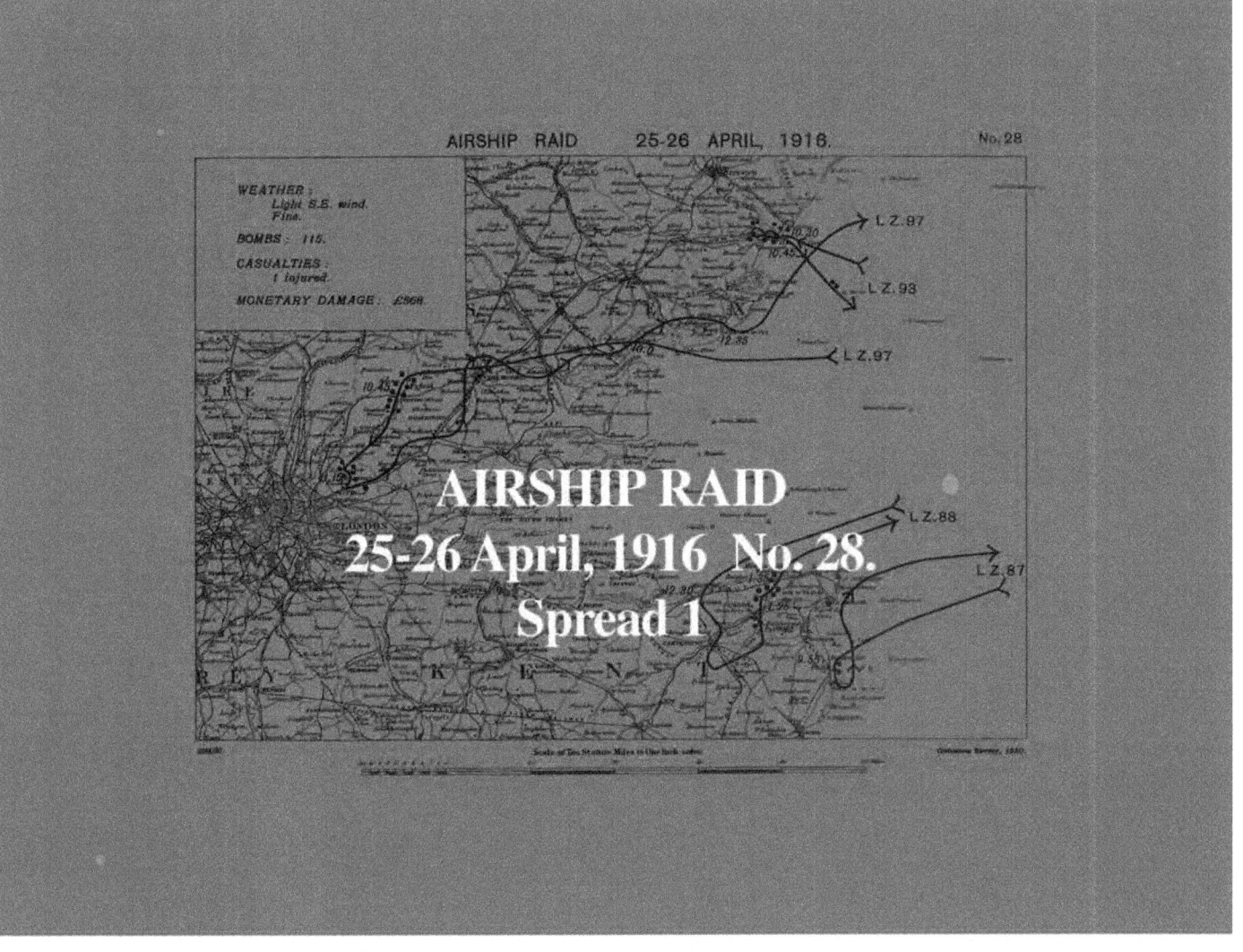

Spread 1

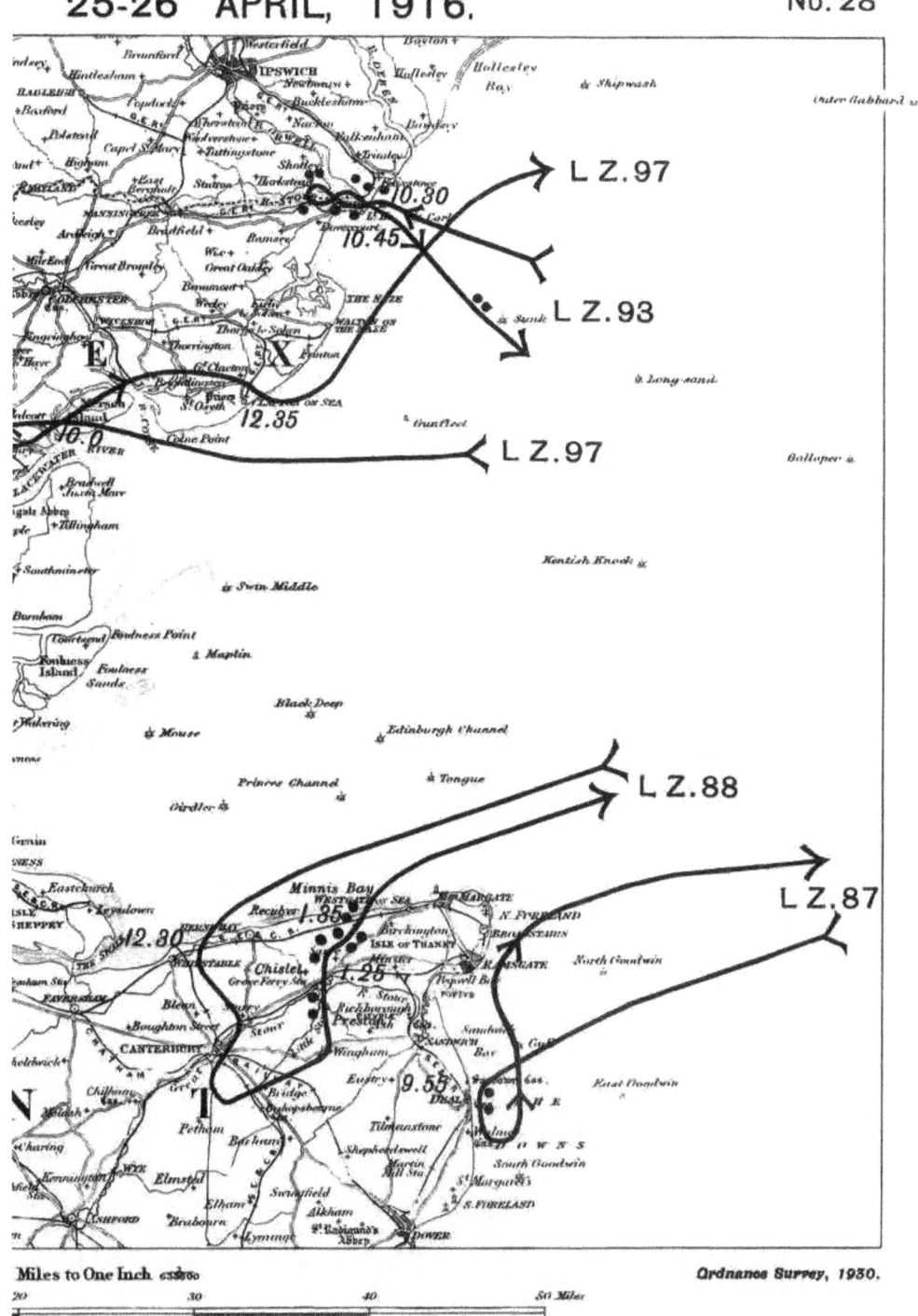

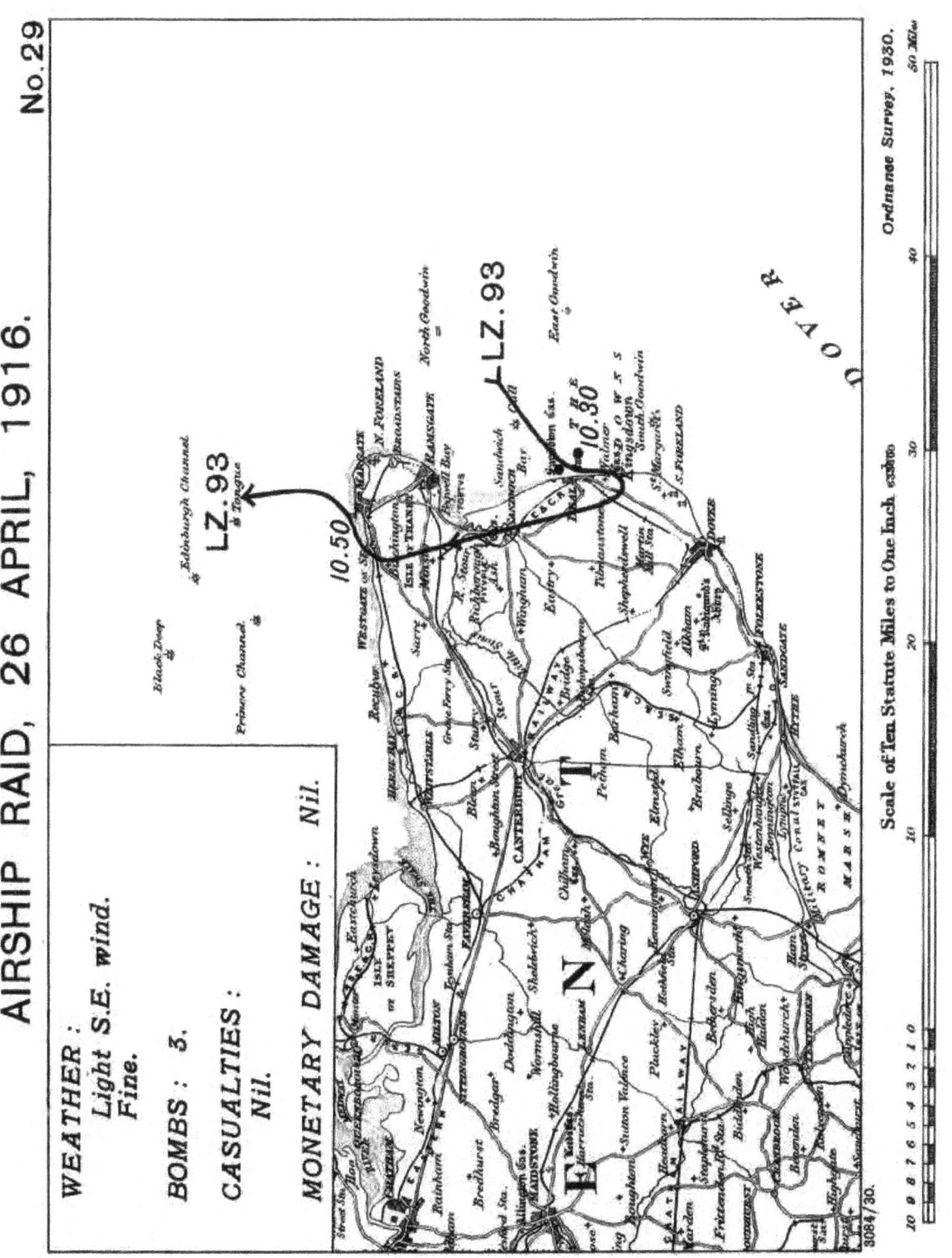

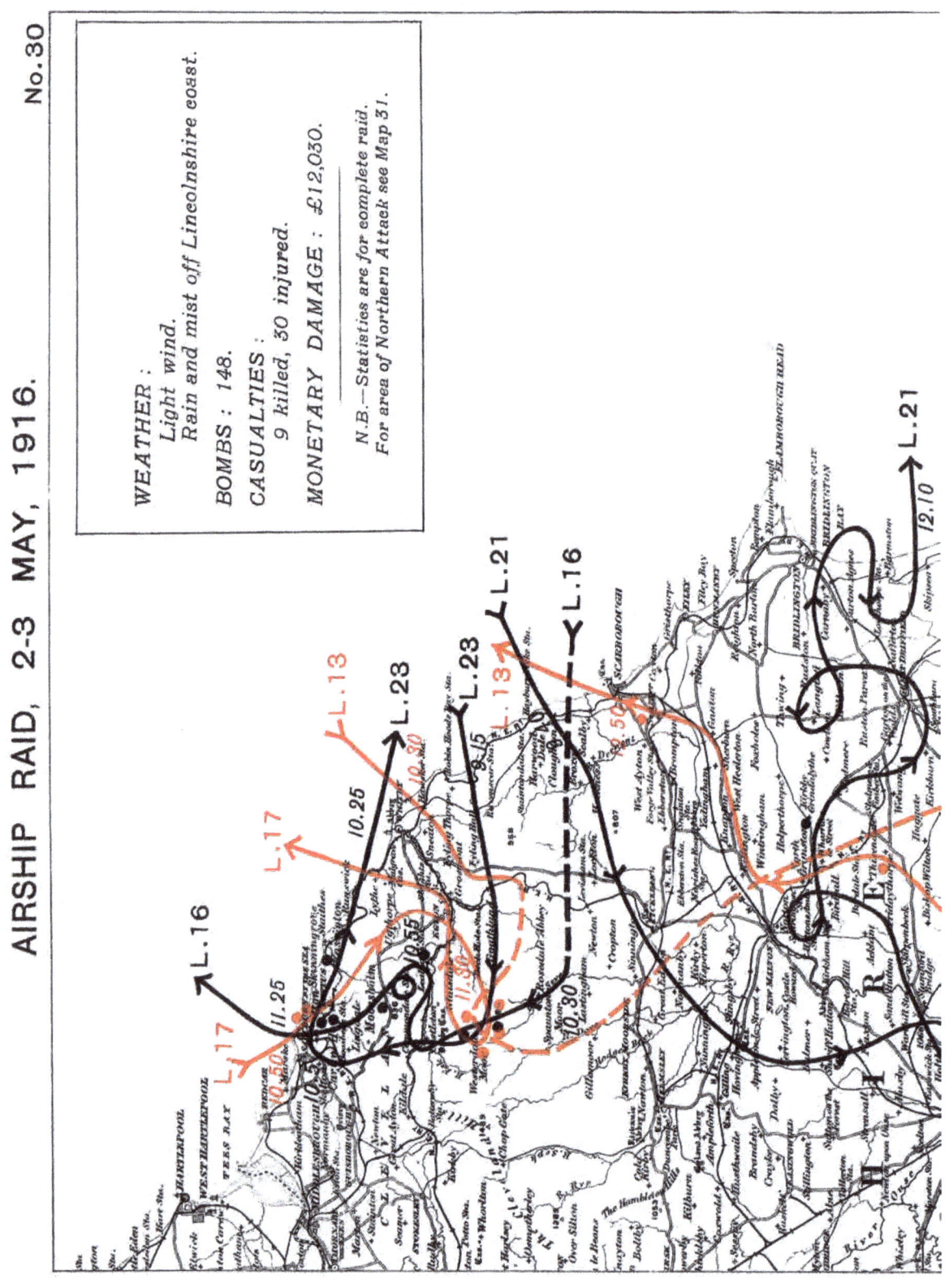

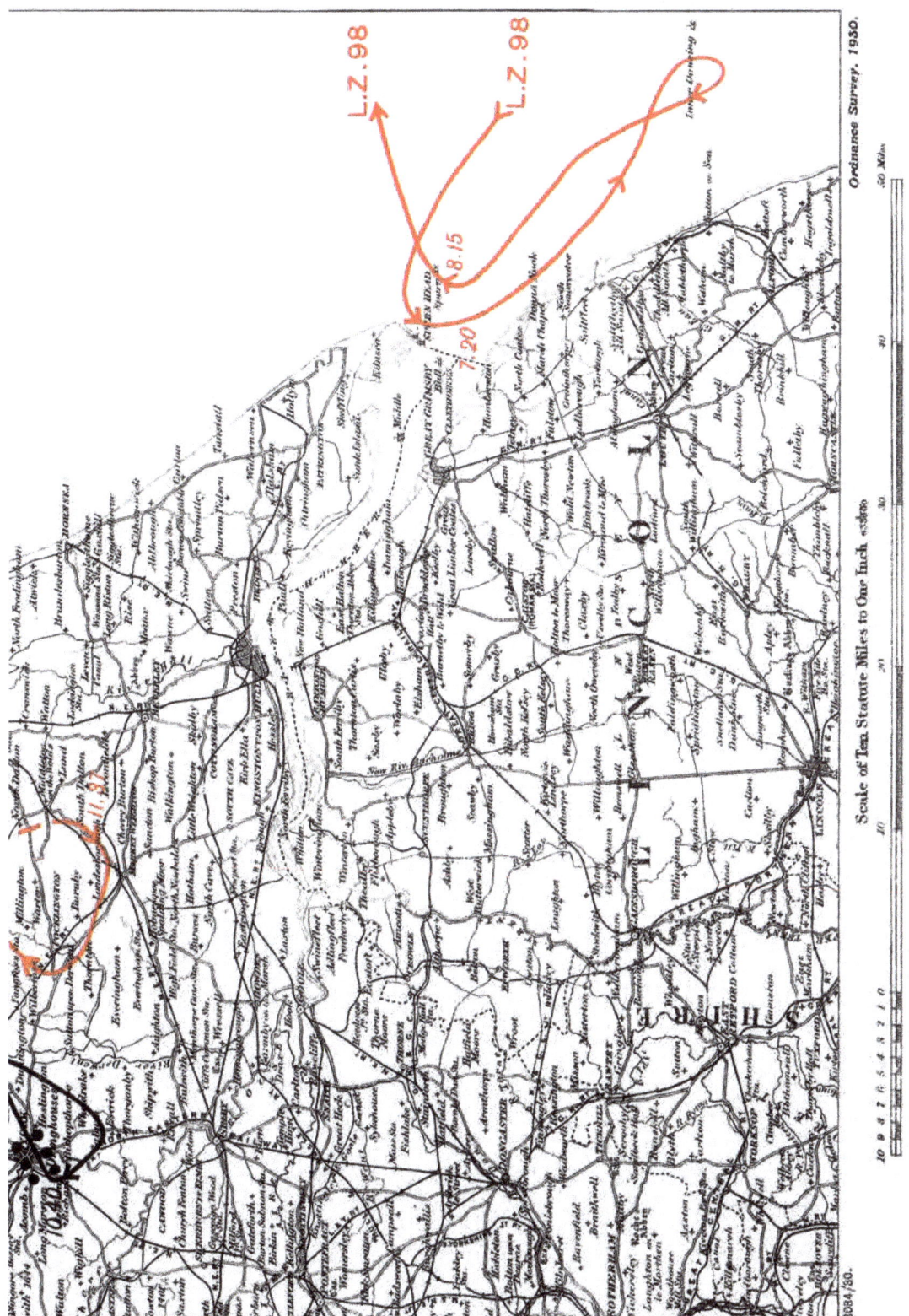

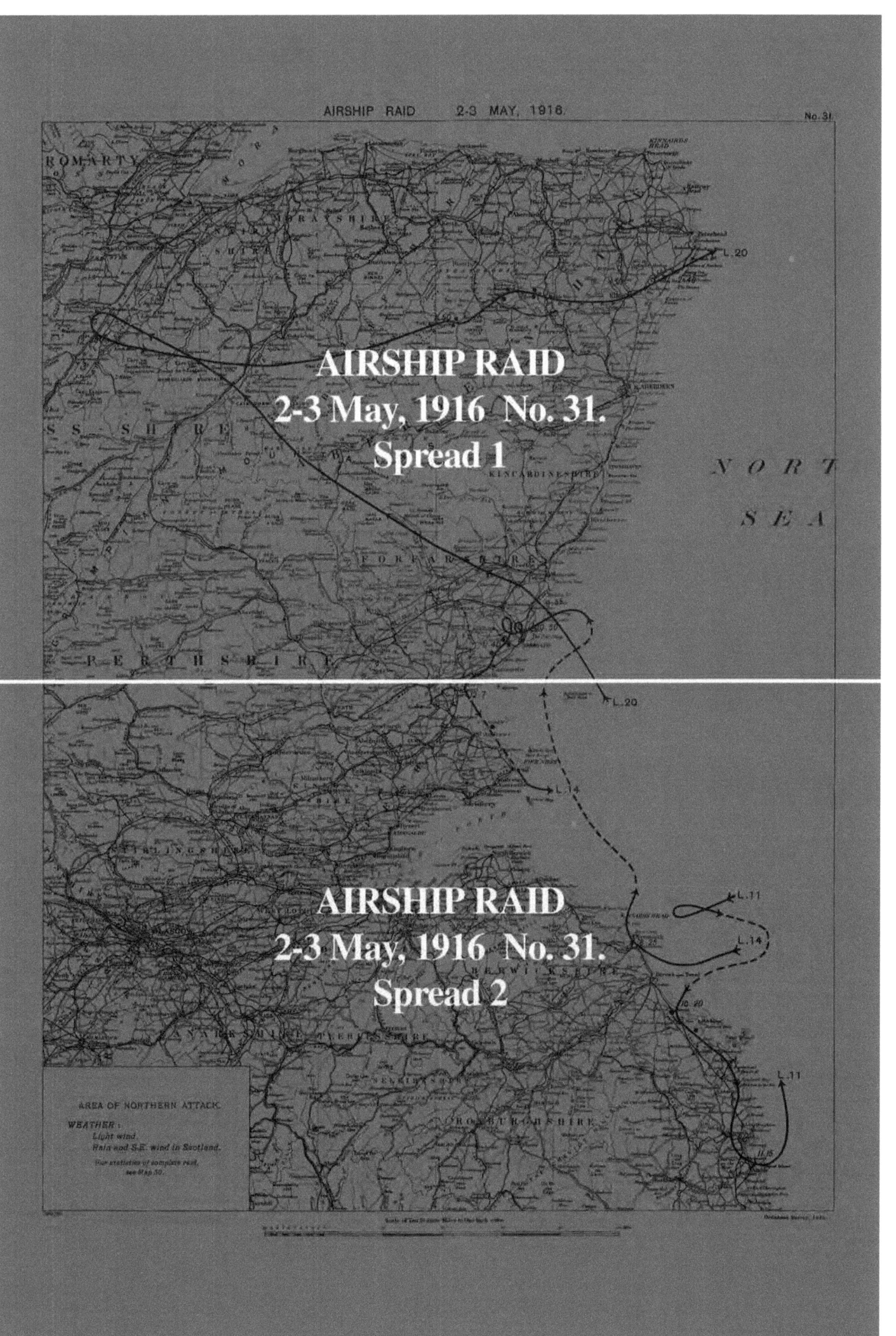

Spread 1

AIRSHIP RAID

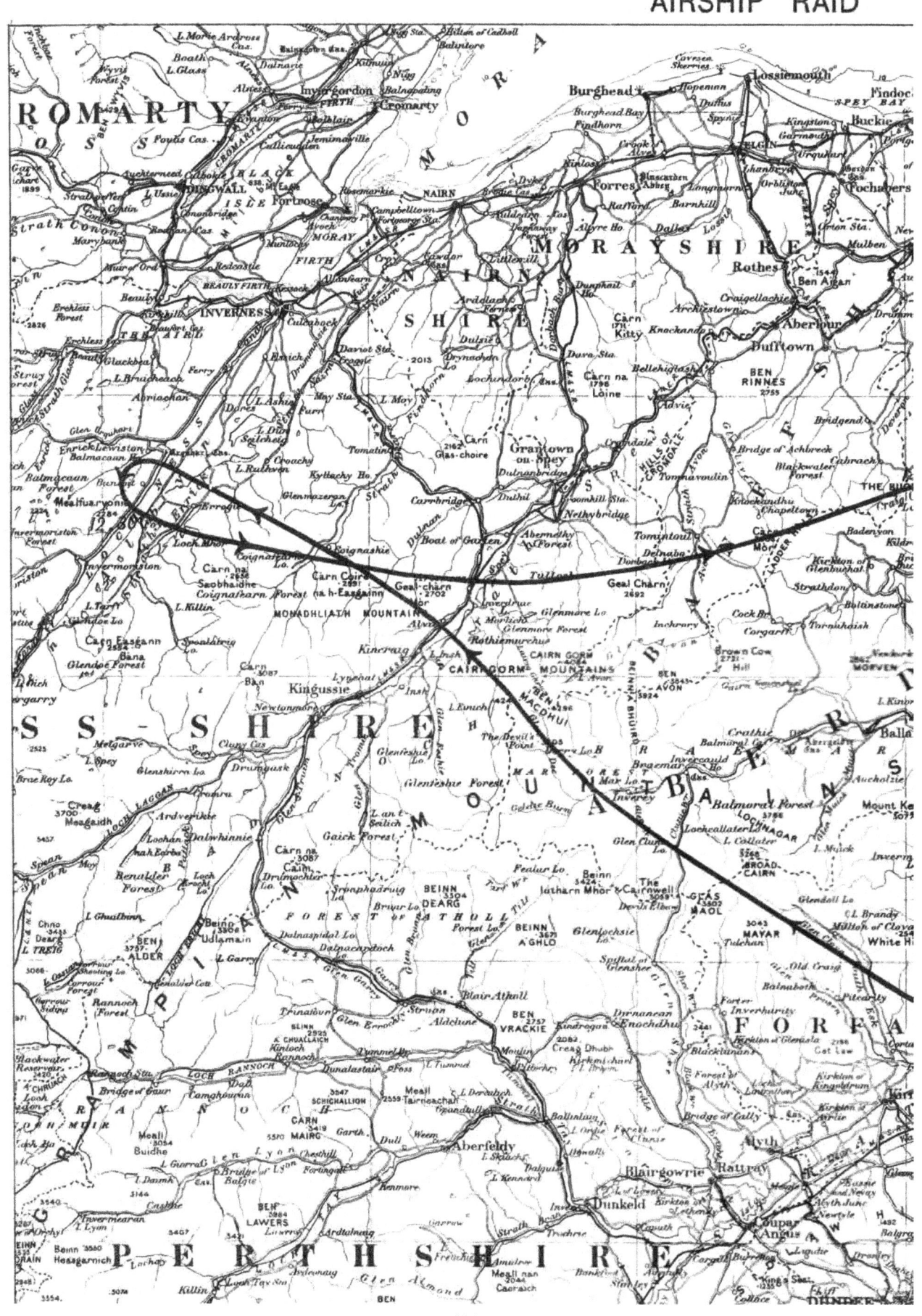

2-3 MAY, 1916.   No. 31.

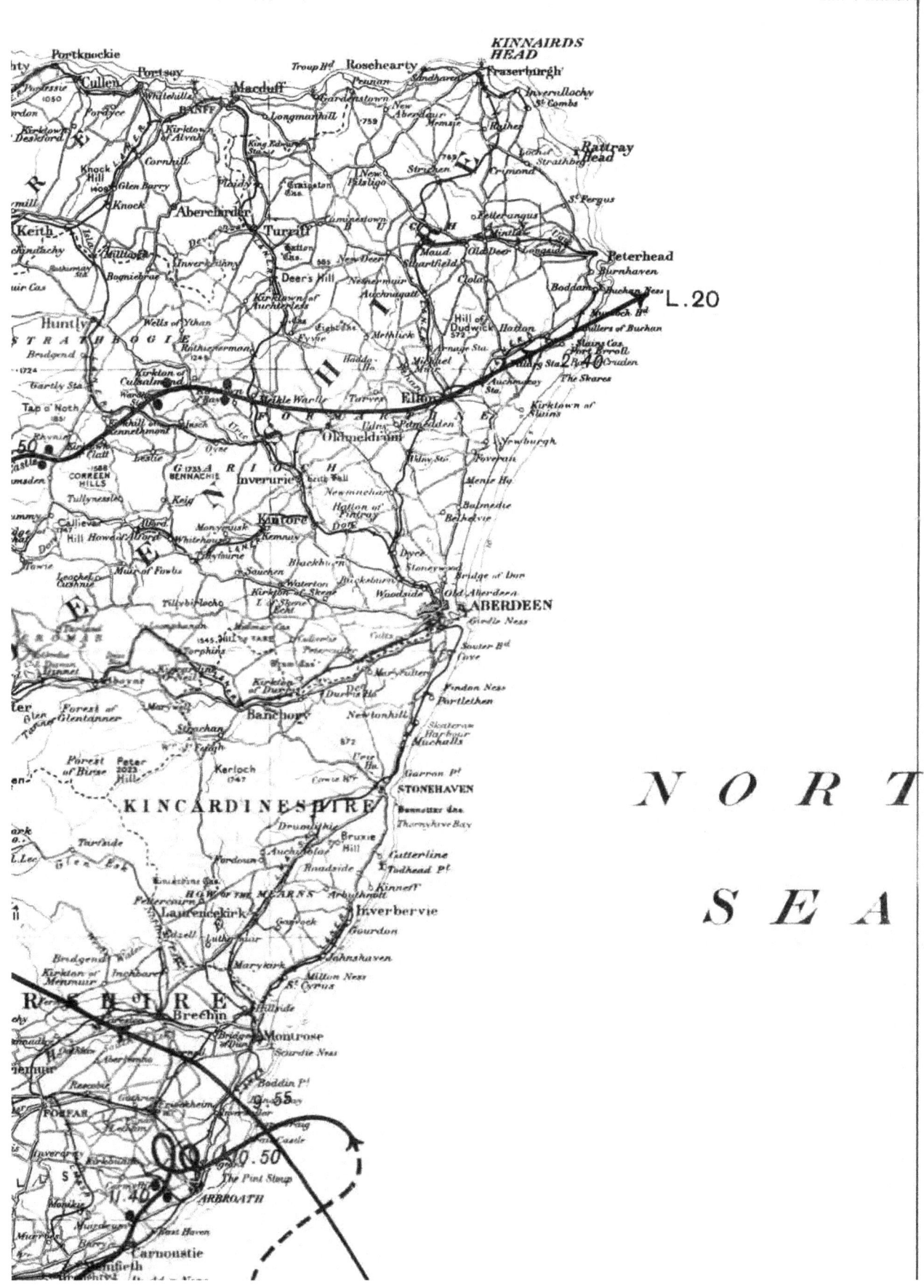

AREA OF NORTHERN ATTACK.

WEATHER:
  Light wind.
  Rain and S.E. wind in Scotland.

For statistics of complete raid,
see Map 30.

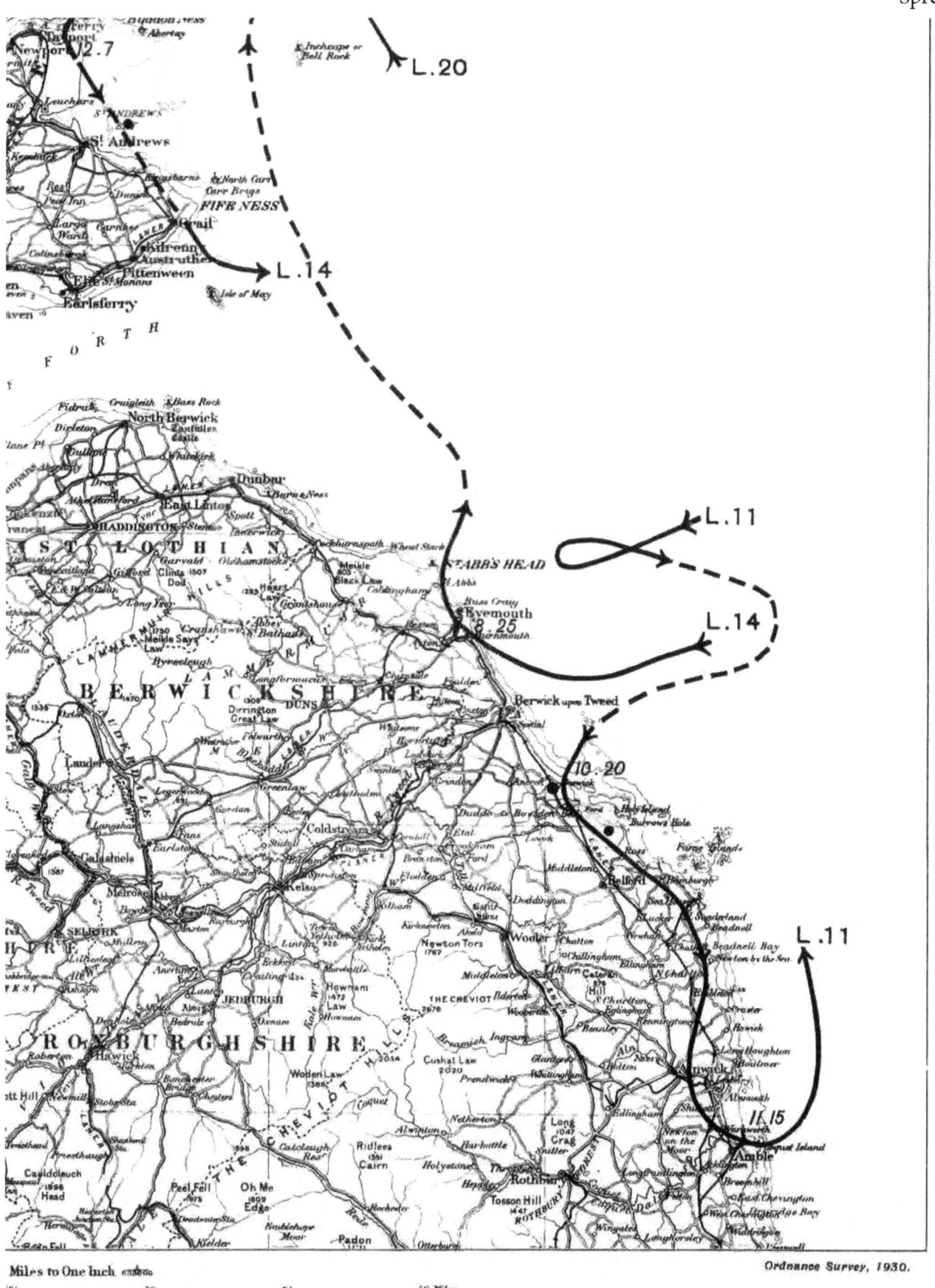

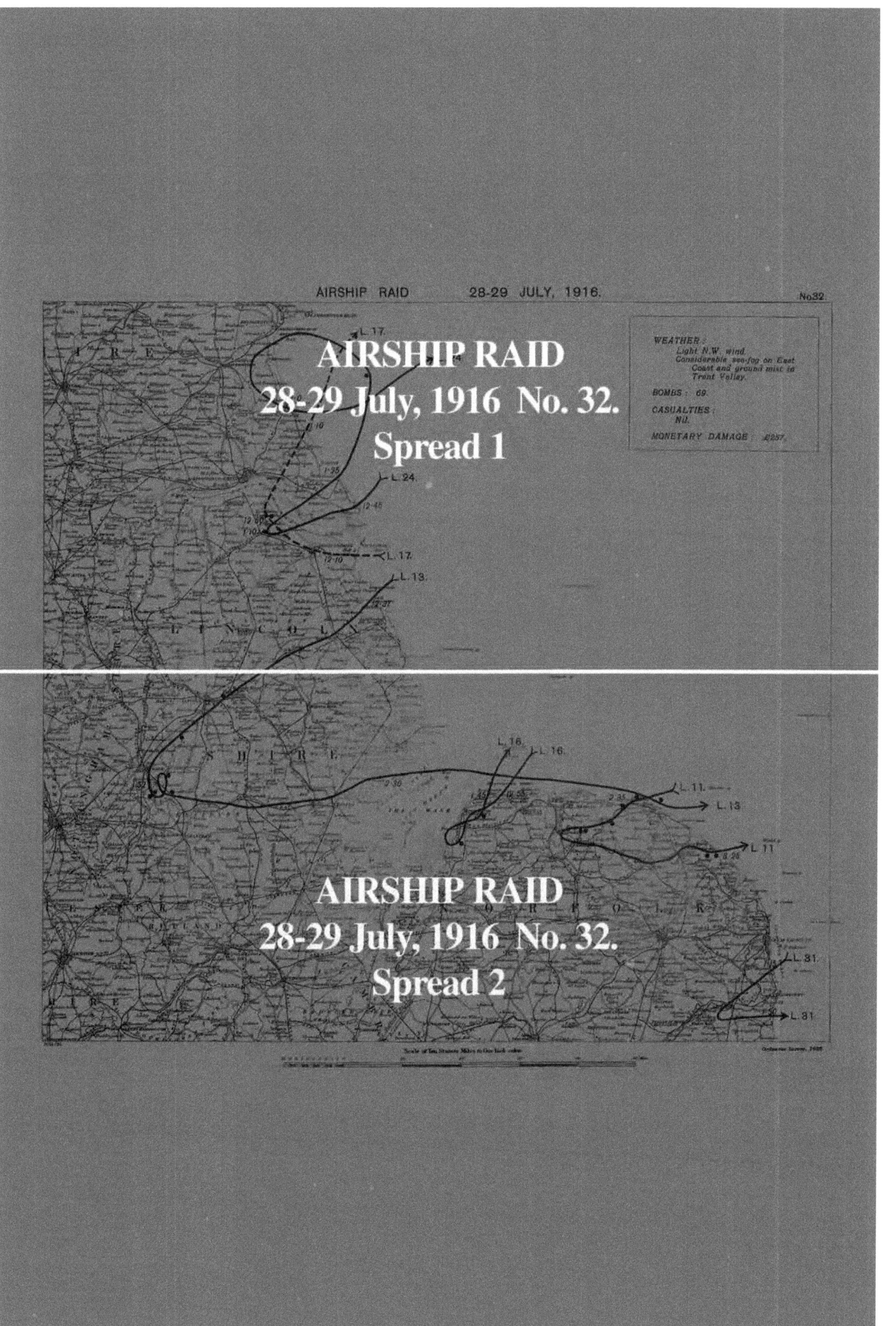

Spread 1

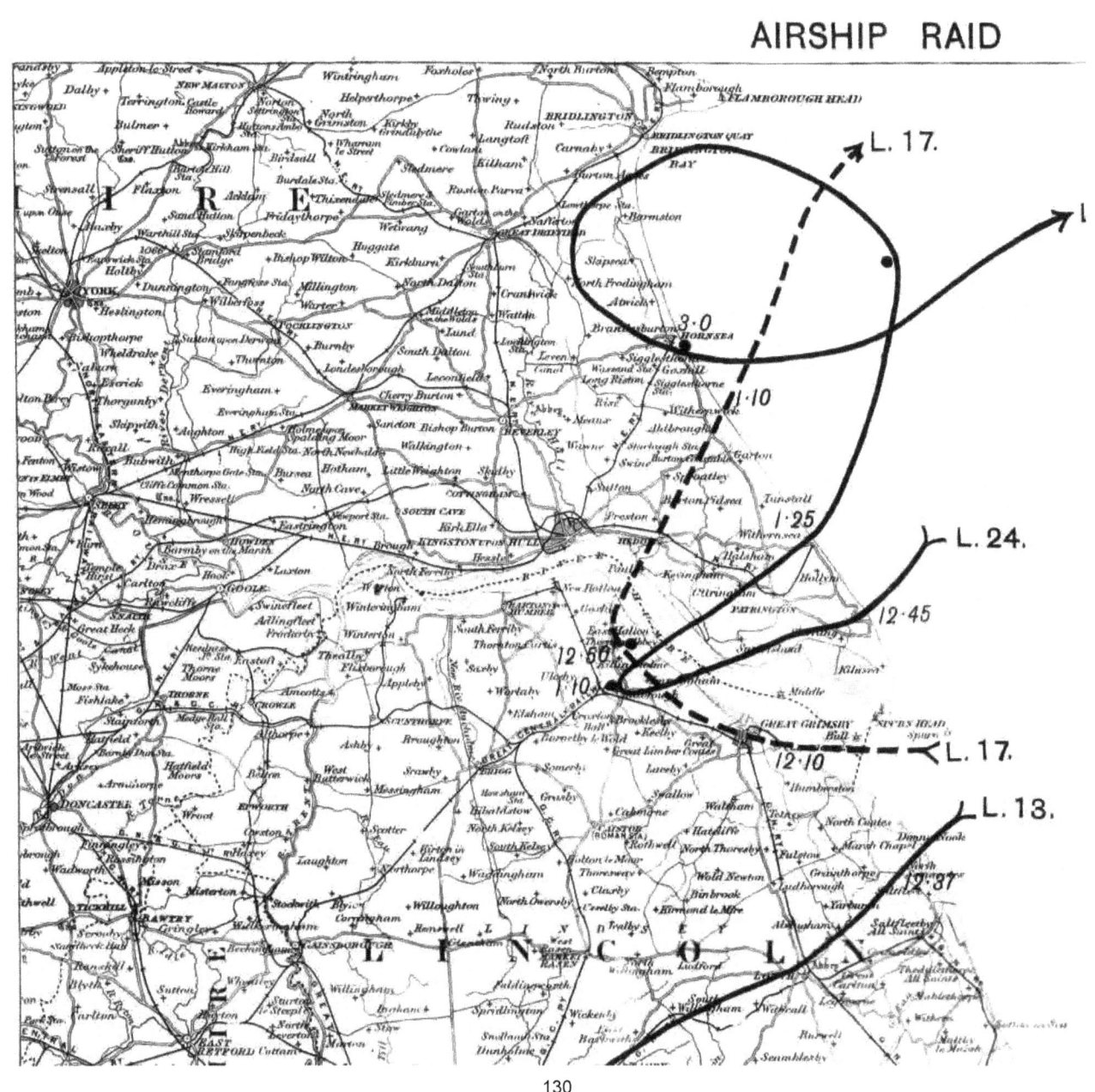

AIRSHIP RAID

28-29 JULY, 1916.   No. 32.

_. 24.

> WEATHER :
>   Light N.W. wind.
>   Considerable sea-fog on East Coast and ground mist in Trent Valley.
>
> BOMBS : 69.
>
> CASUALTIES :
>   Nil.
>
> MONETARY DAMAGE : £257.

Outer Dowsing

Inner Dowsing

Spread 2

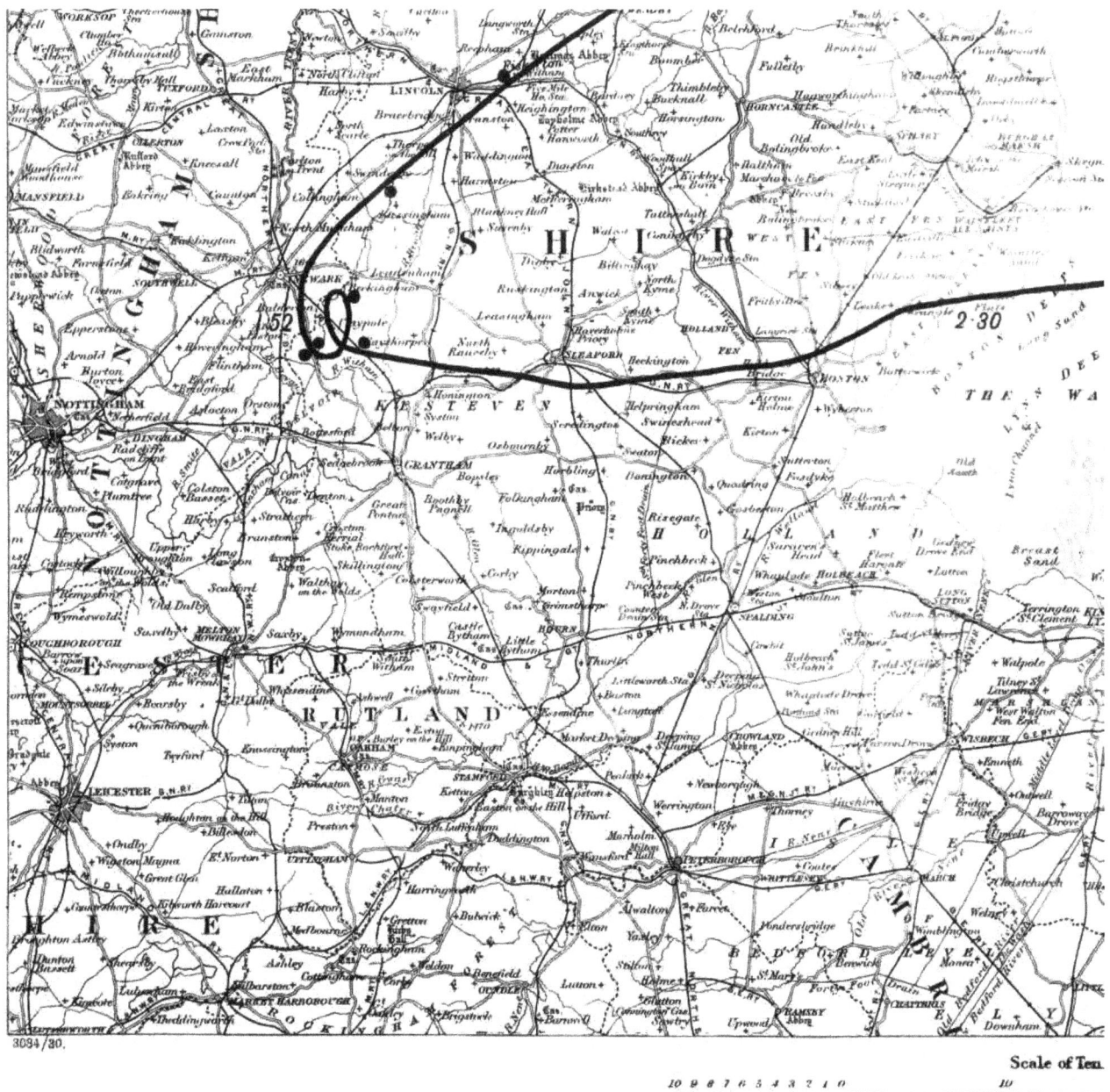

Spread 2

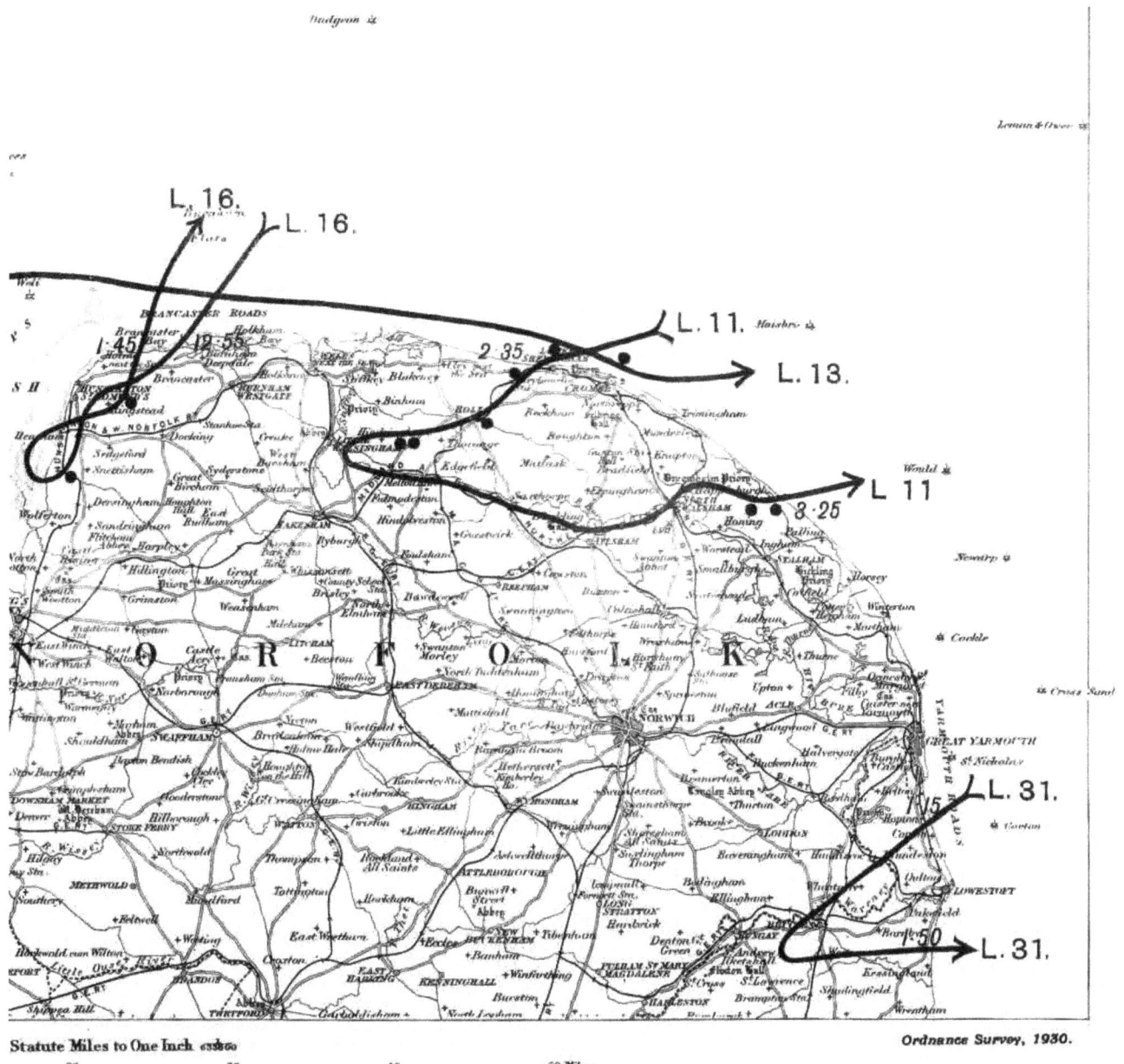

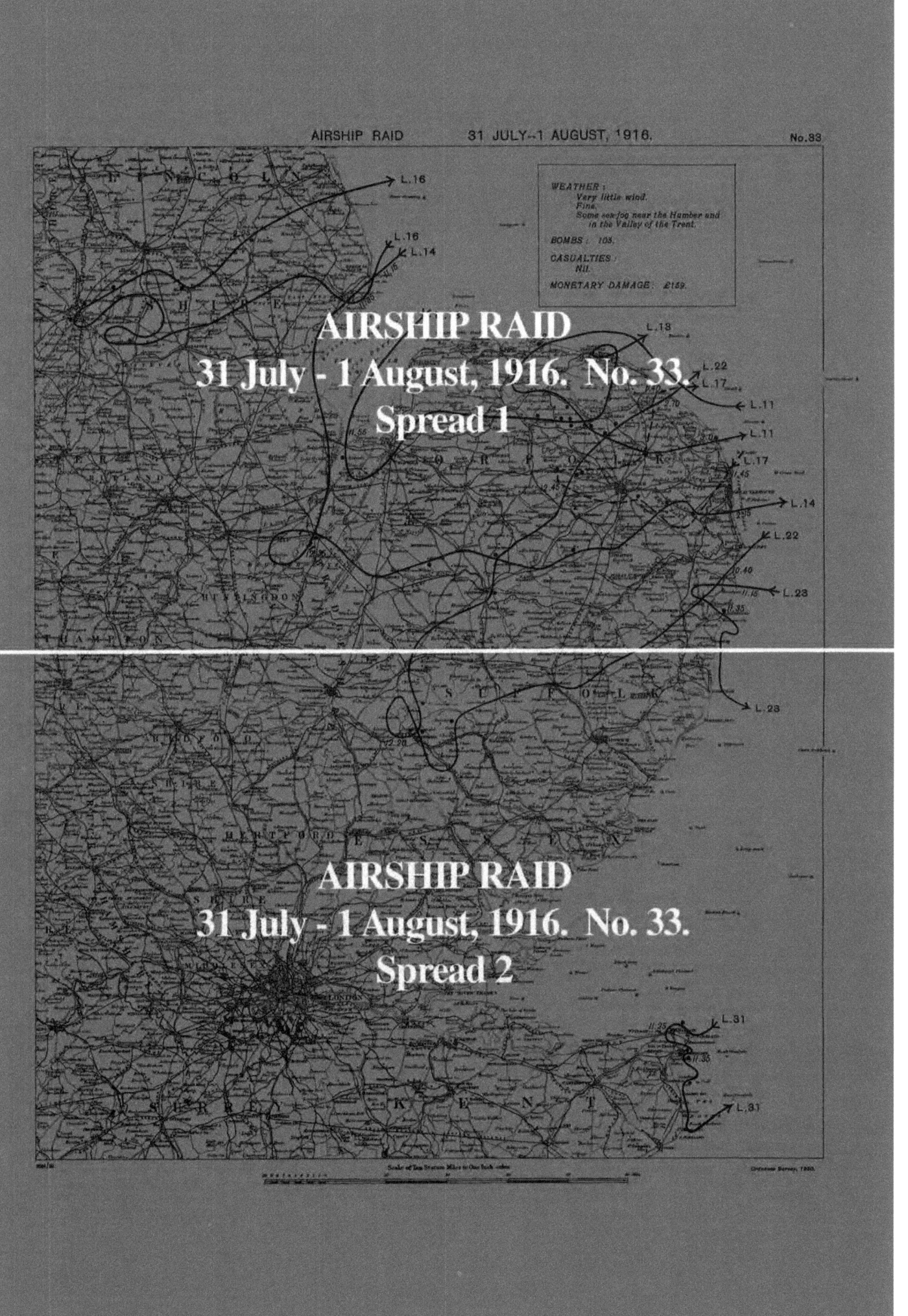

Spread 1

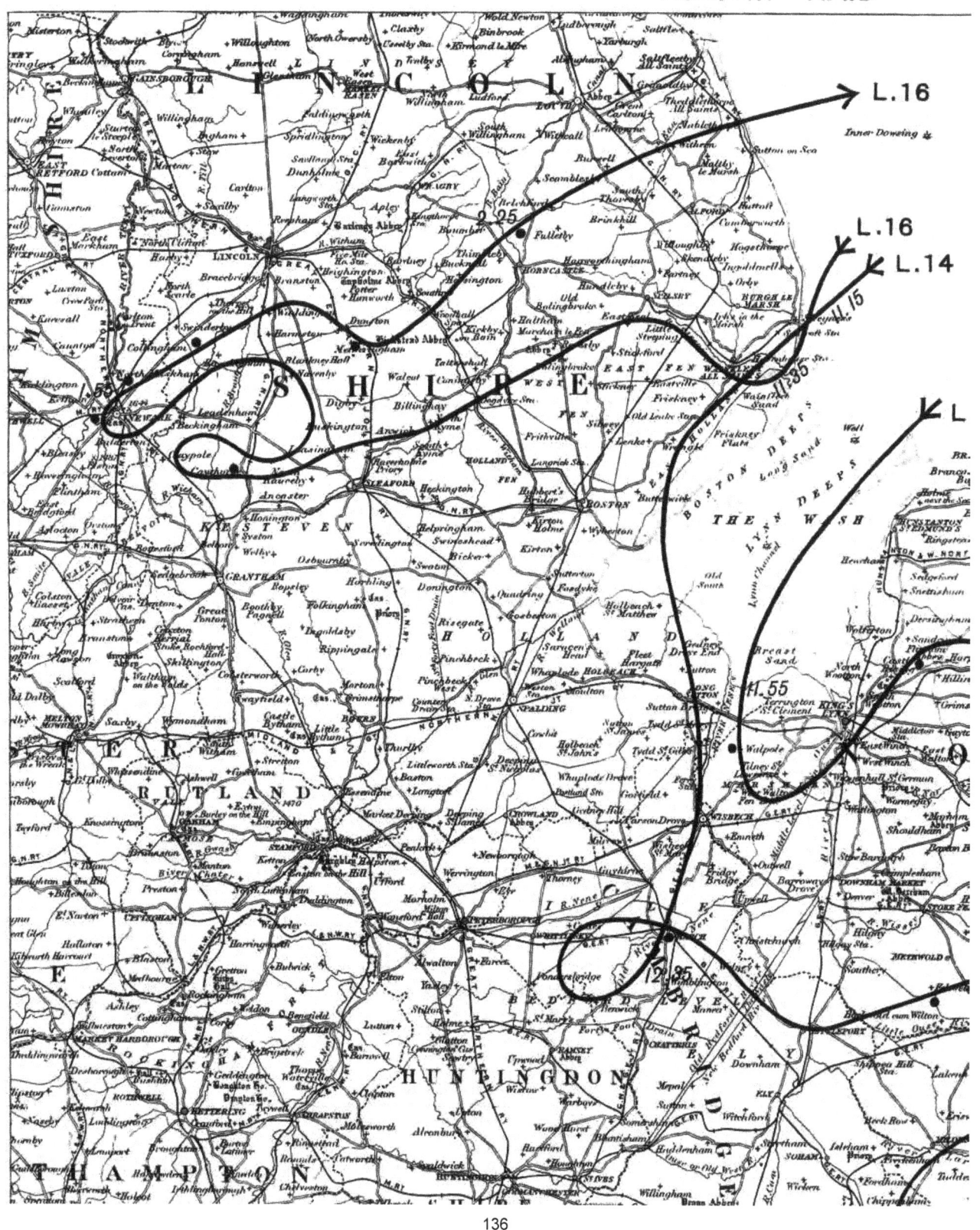

31 JULY--1 AUGUST, 1916.

No. 33

WEATHER:
   Very little wind.
   Fine.
   Some sea-fog near the Humber and in the Valley of the Trent.

BOMBS: 103.

CASUALTIES:
   Nil.

MONETARY DAMAGE: £139.

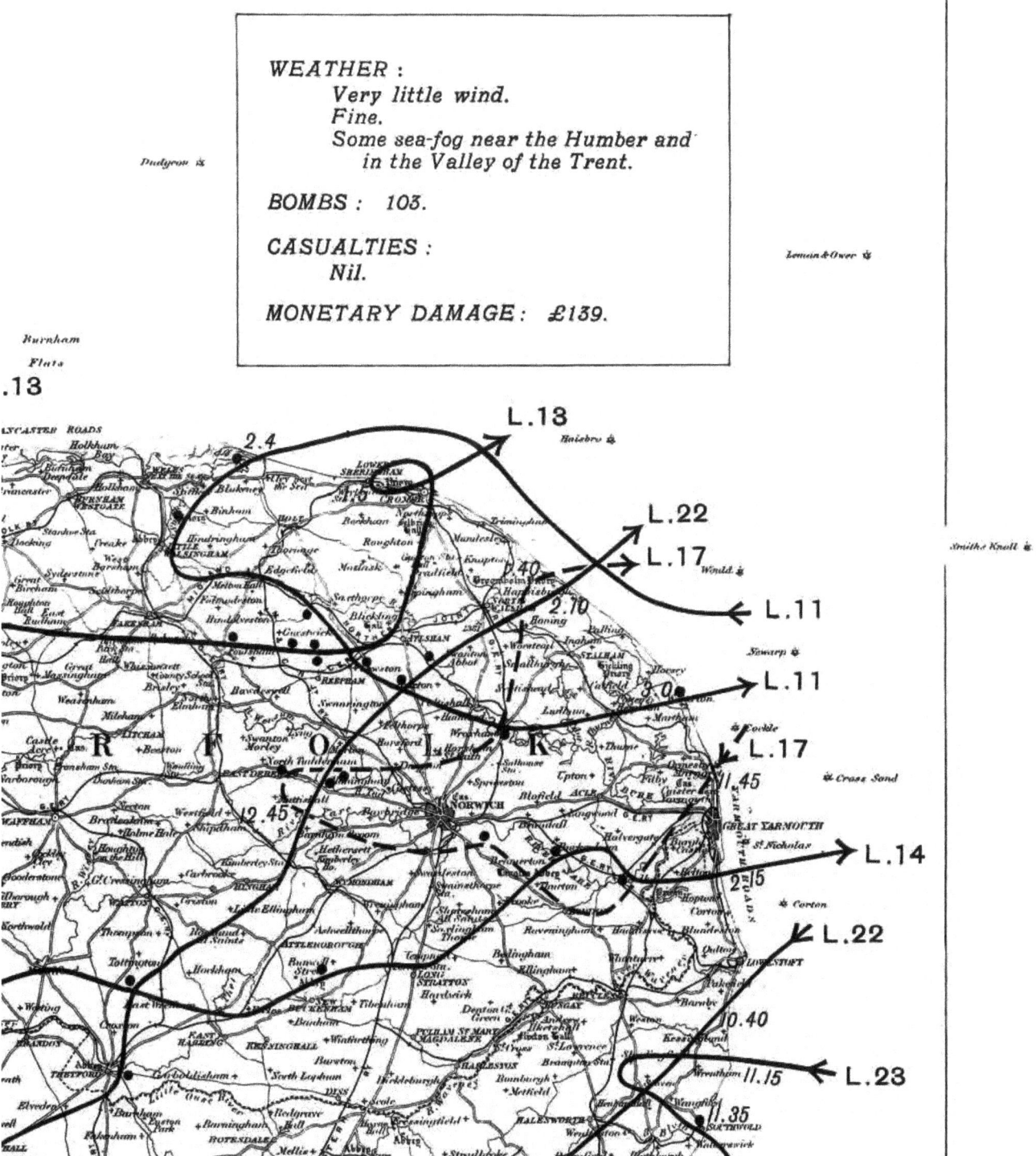

Spread 2

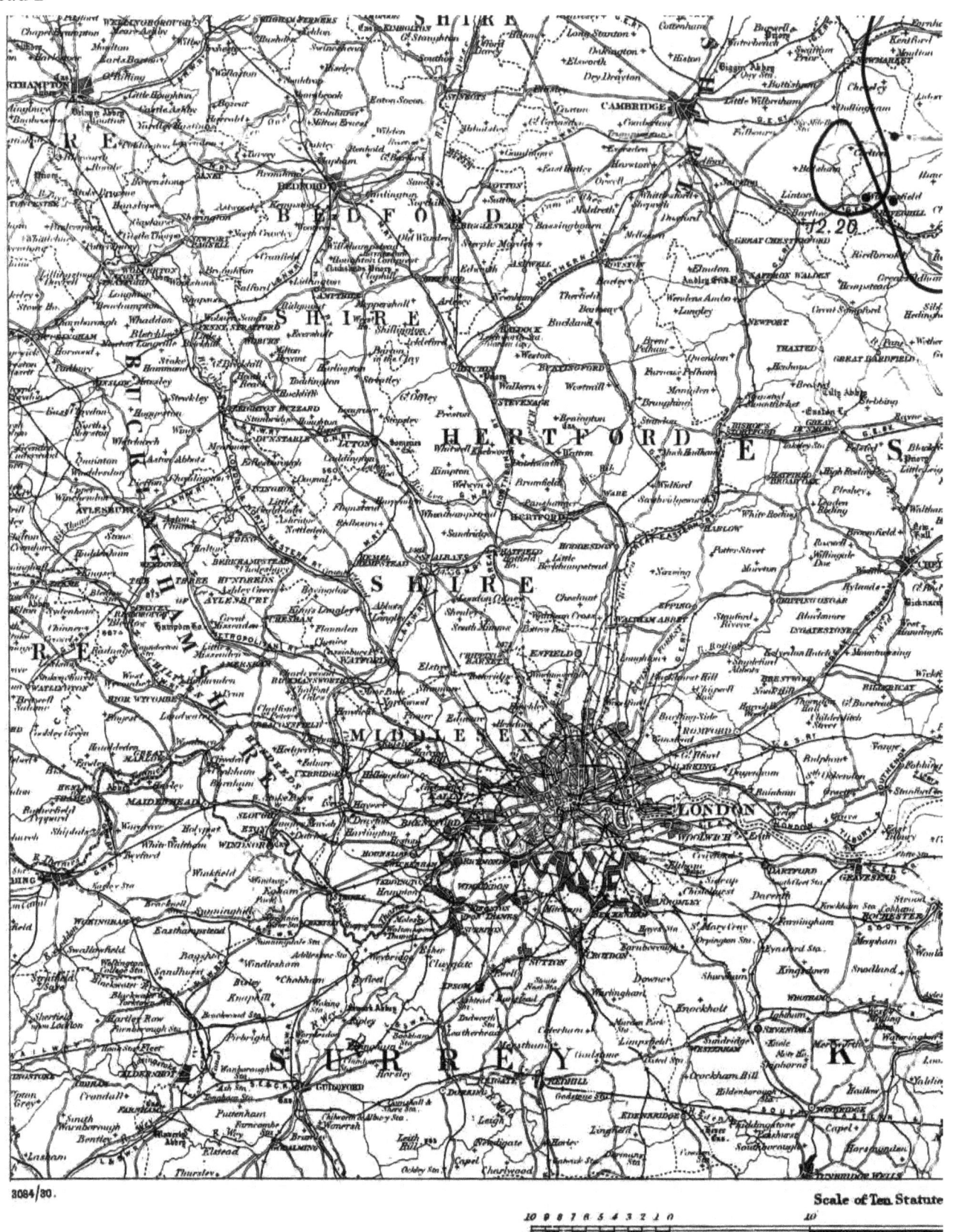

Spread 2

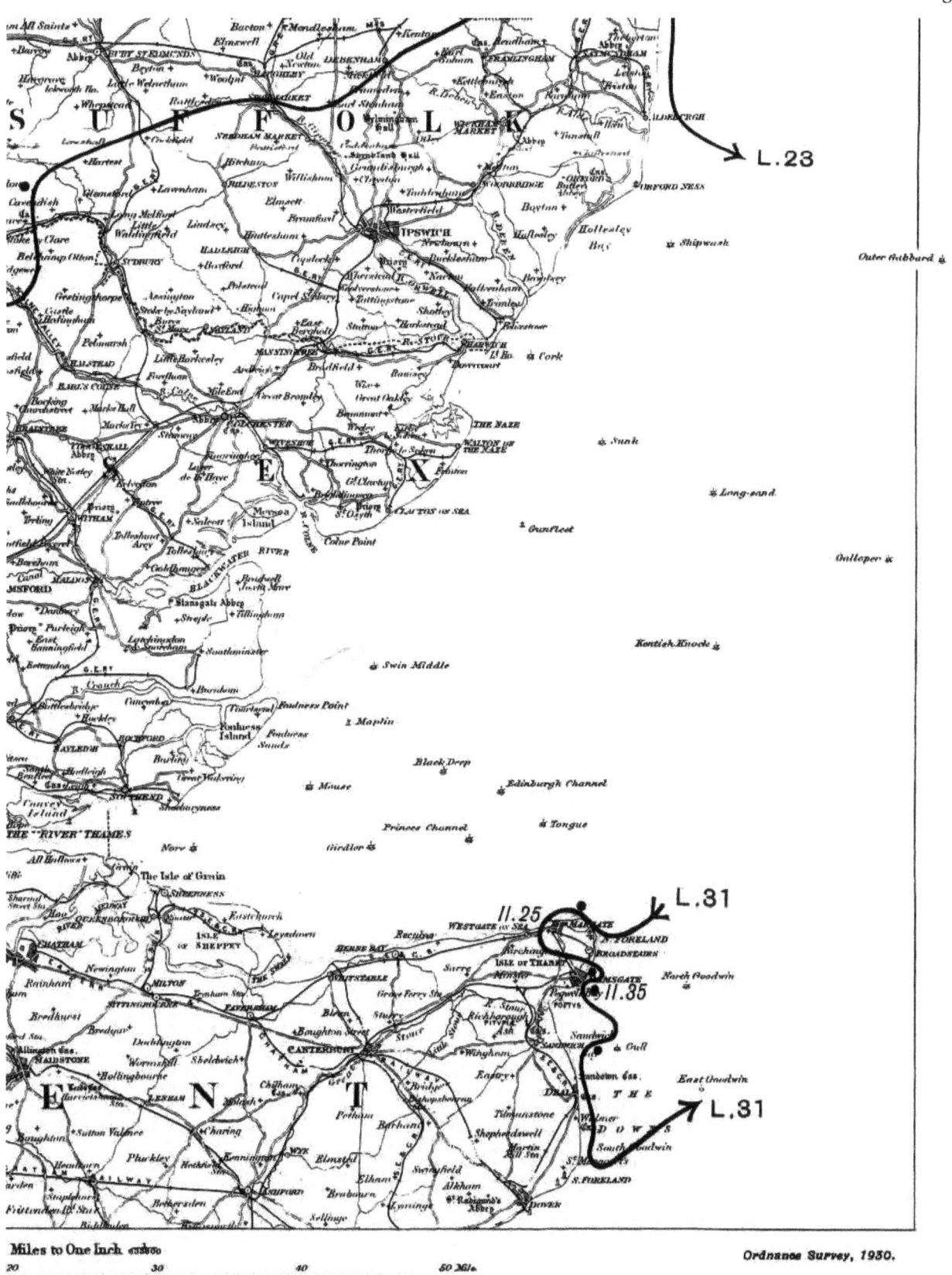

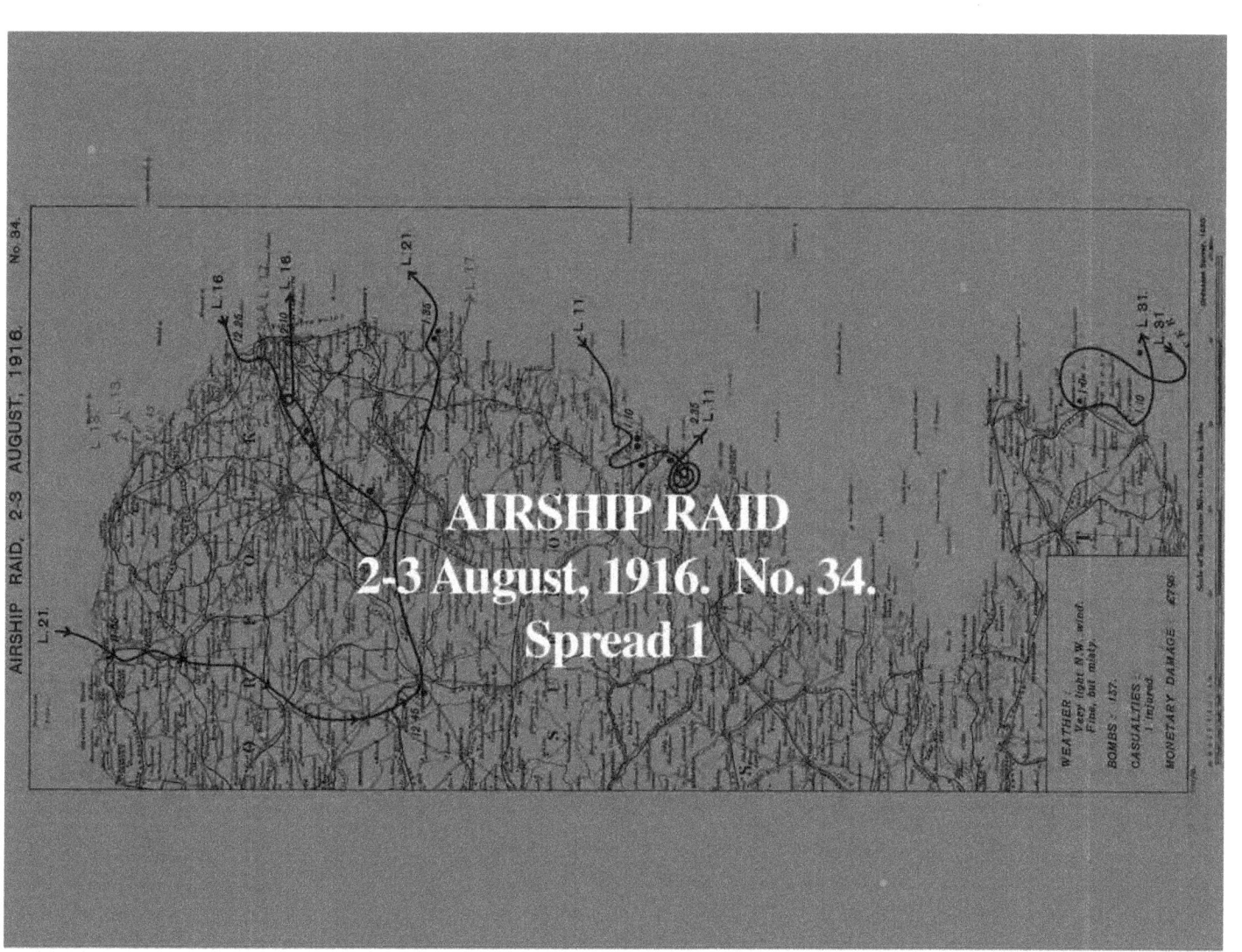

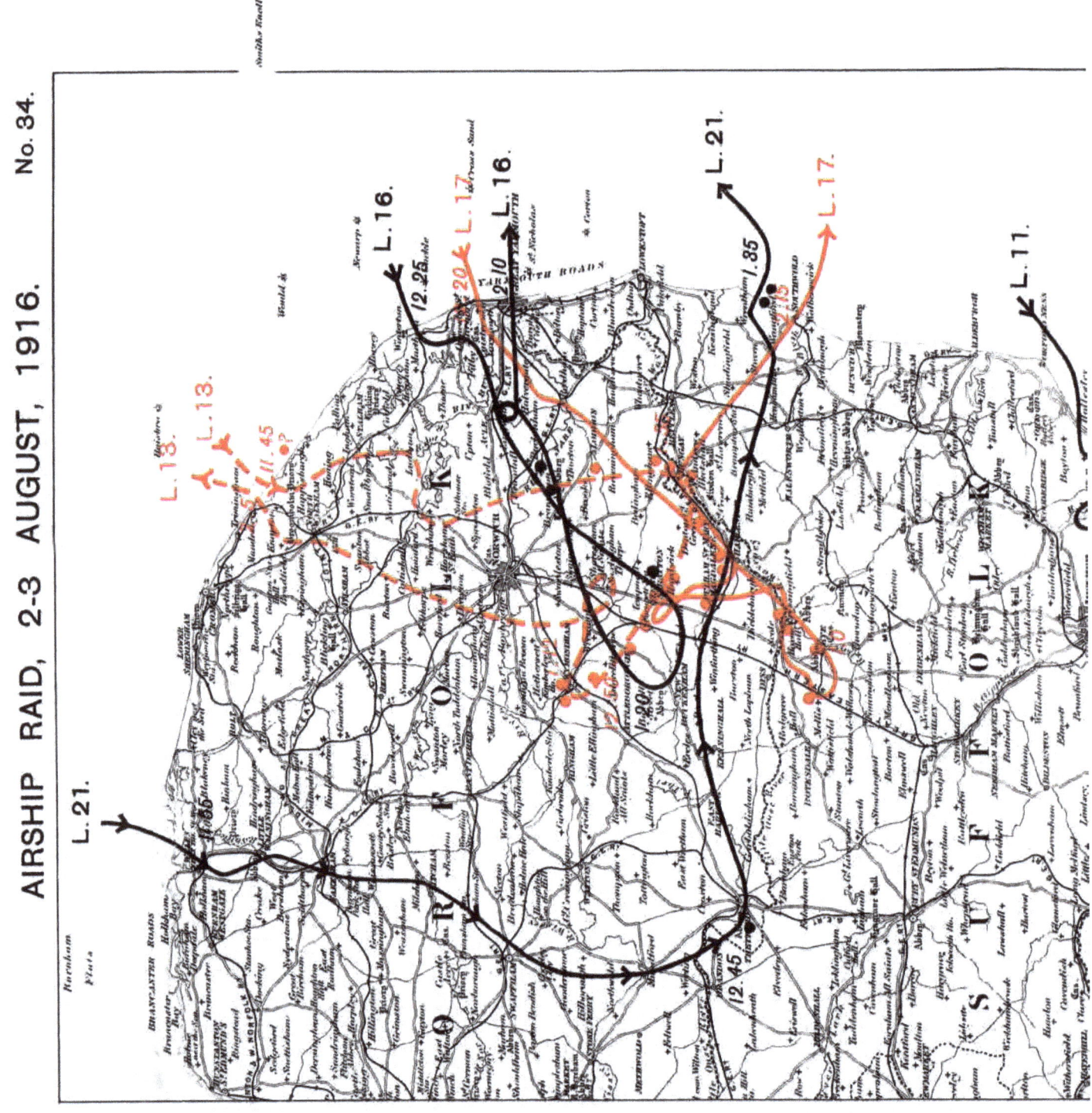

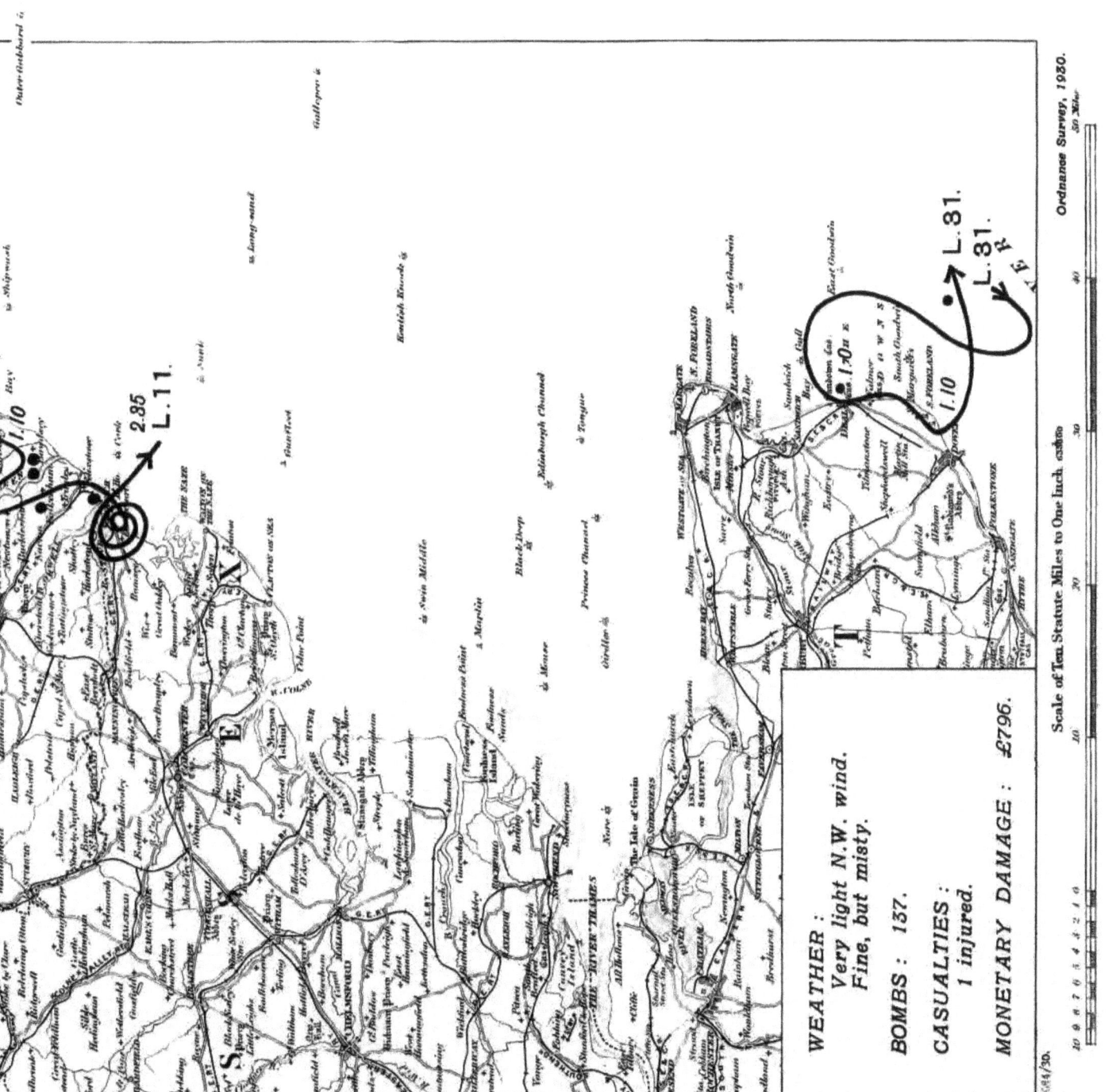

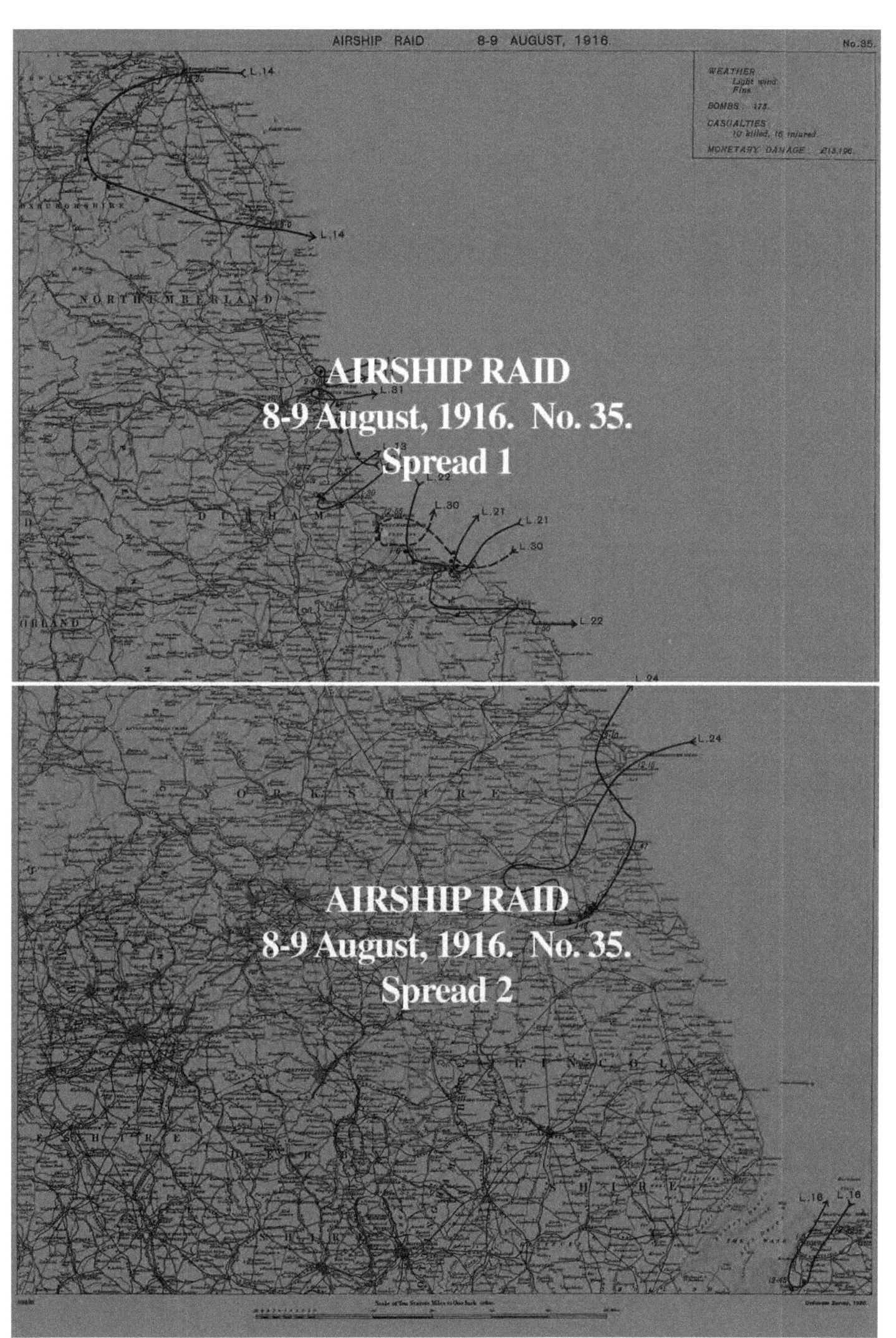

Spread 1

AIRSHIP RAID

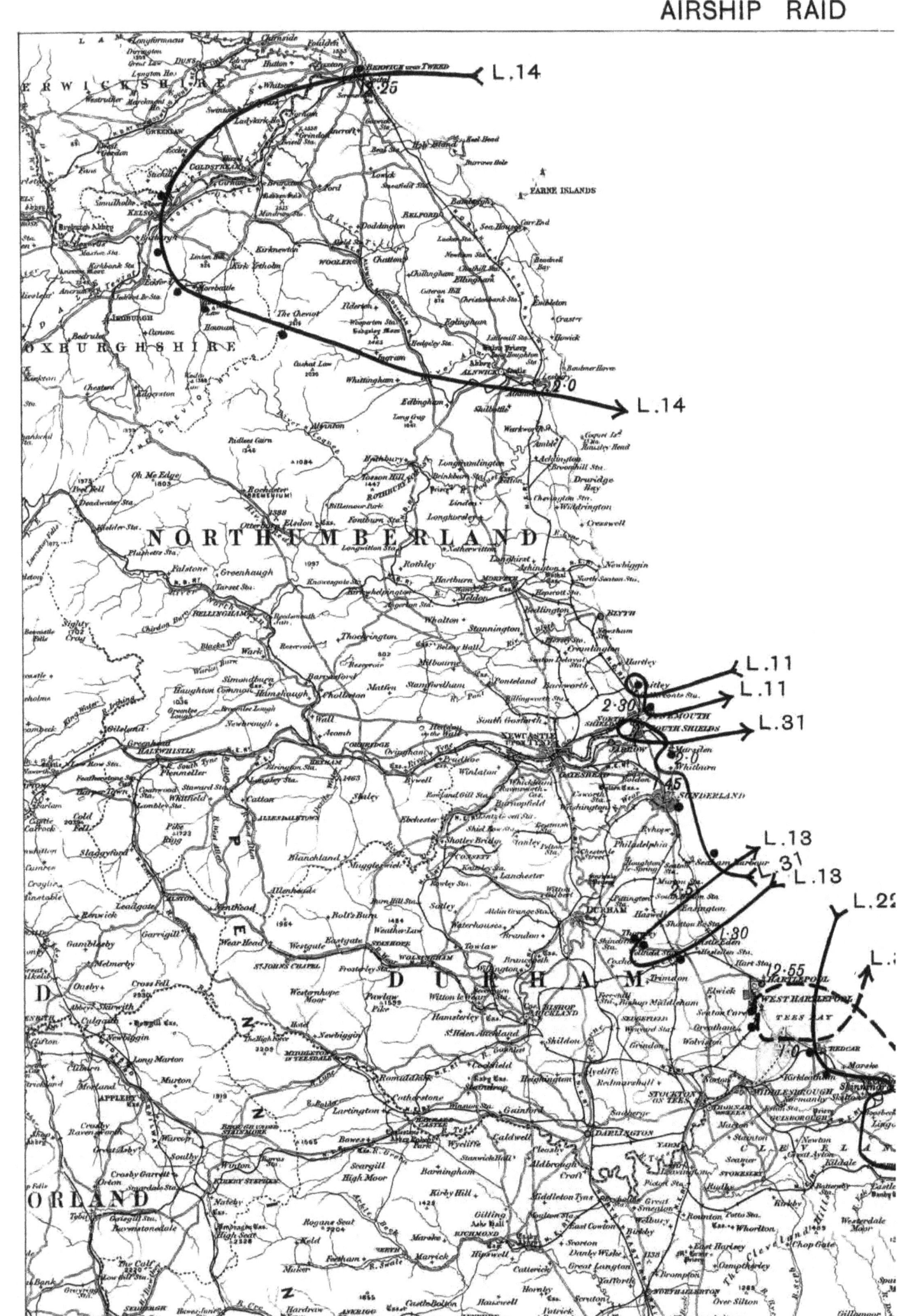

8-9 AUGUST, 1916.

No. 35.

> WEATHER :
>   Light wind.
>   Fine.
>
> BOMBS : 173.
>
> CASUALTIES :
>   10 killed, 16 injured.
>
> MONETARY DAMAGE : £13,196.

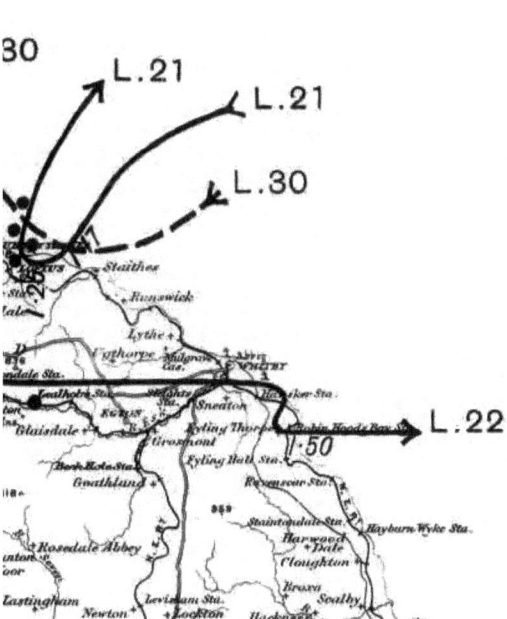

Spread 2

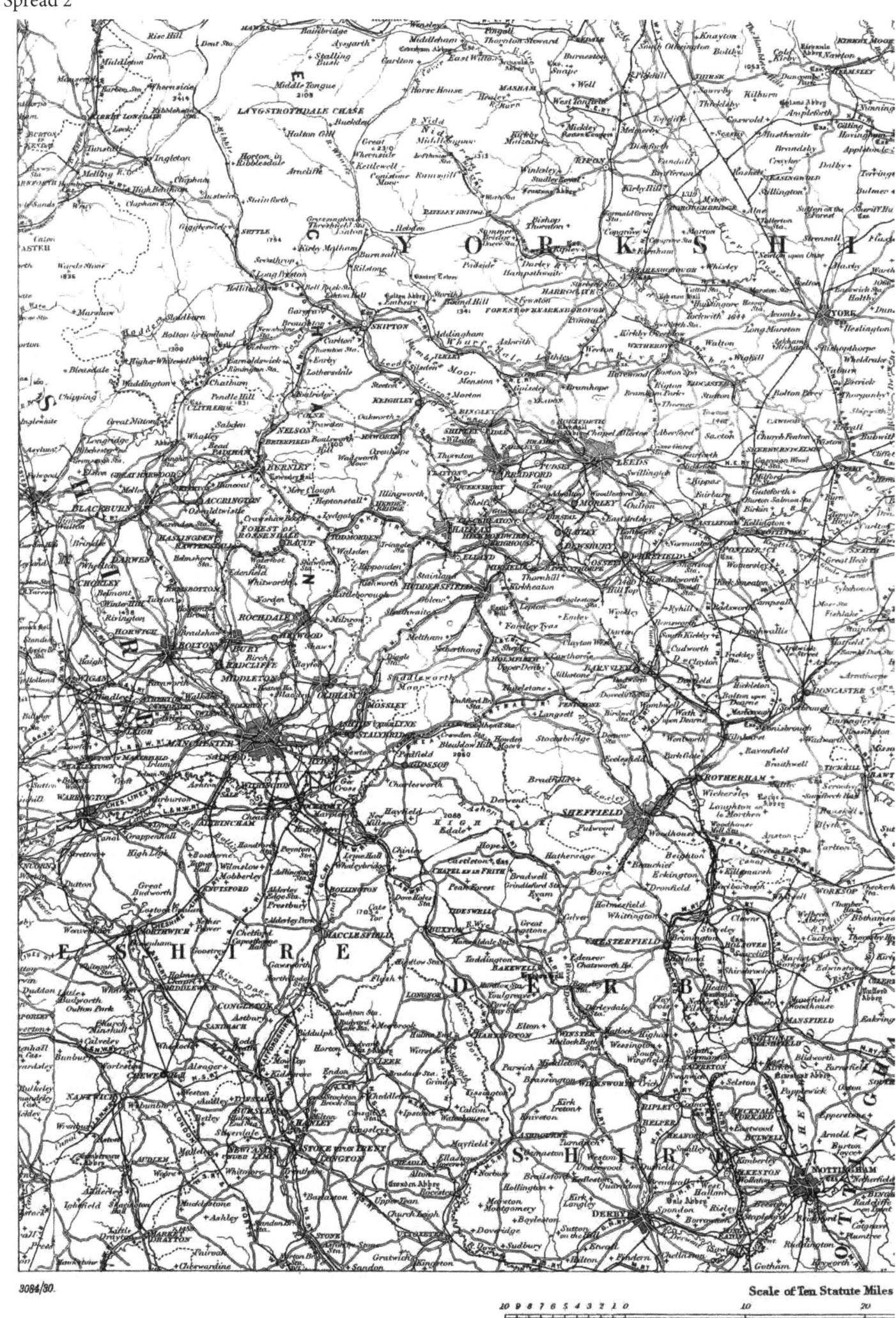

Spread 2

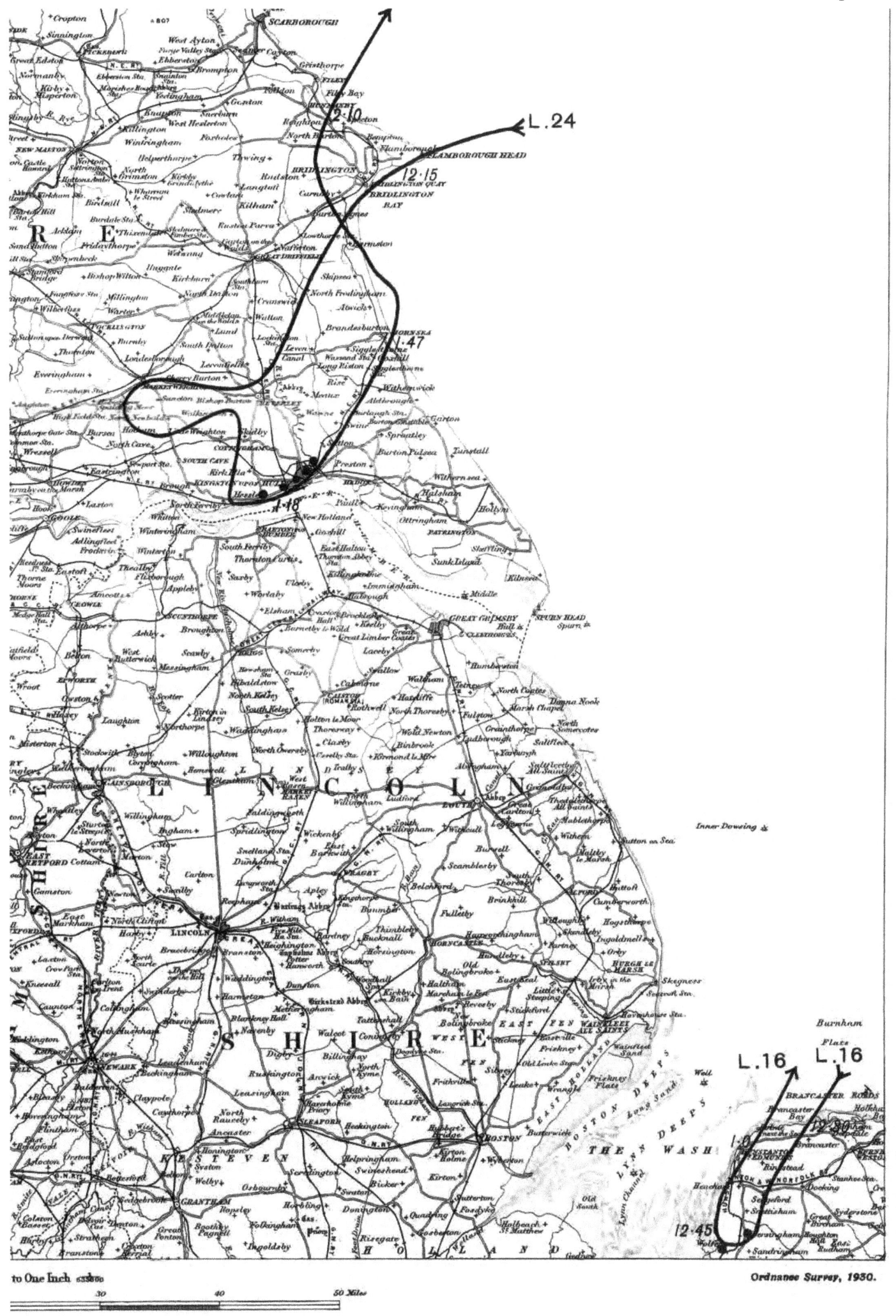

AIRSHIP RAID, 23-24 AUGUST, 1916.

No. 36

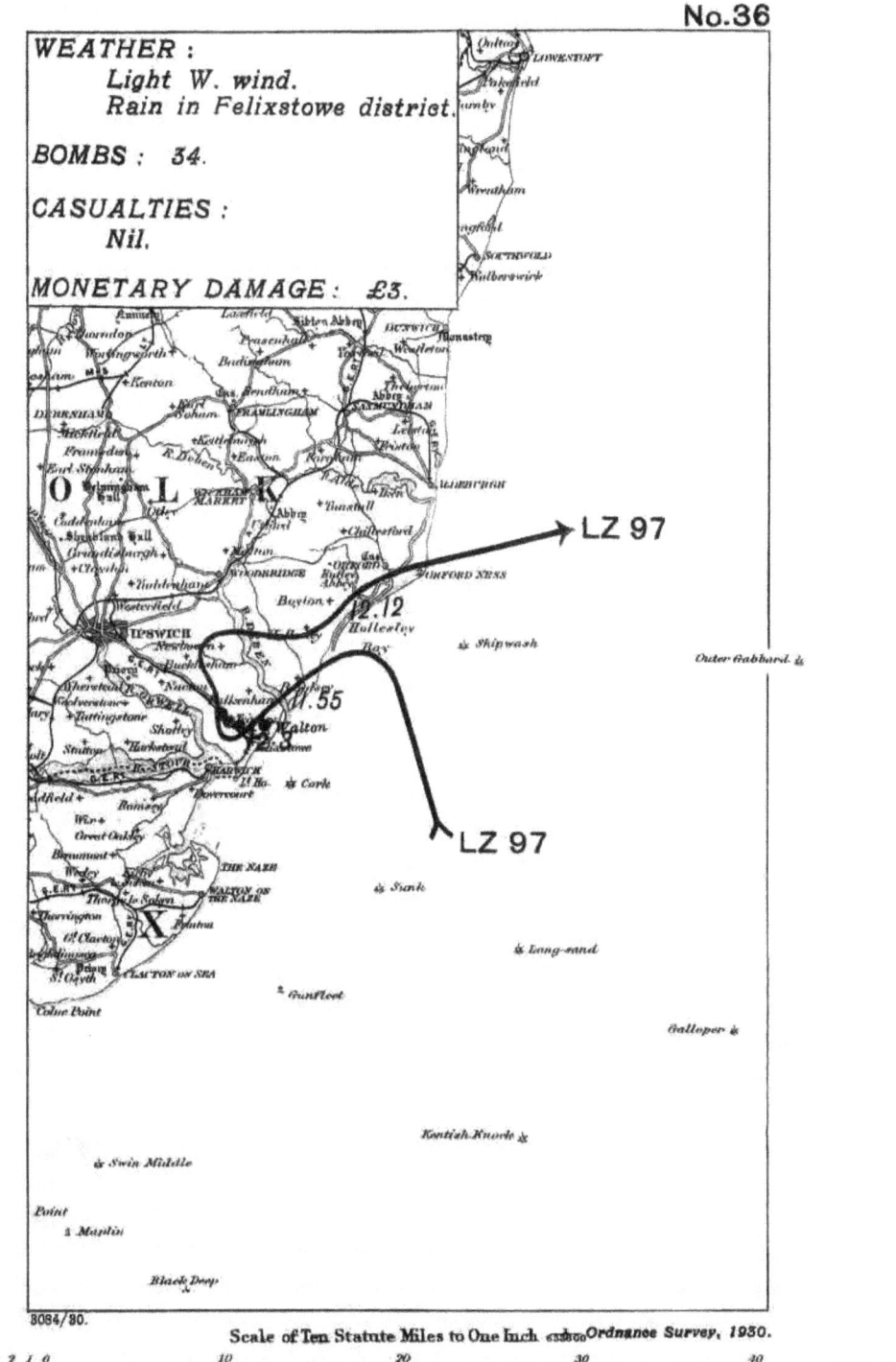

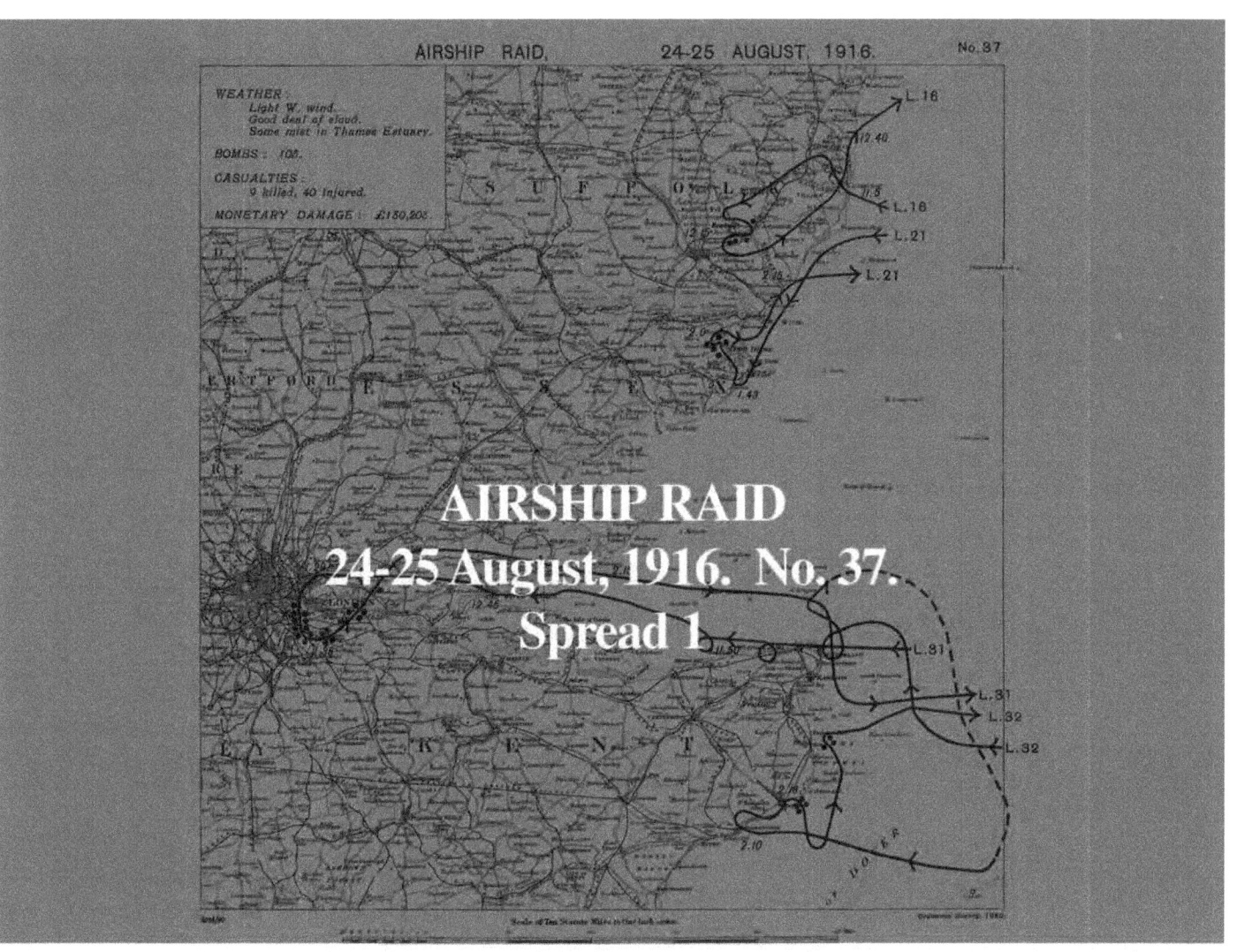

Spread 1

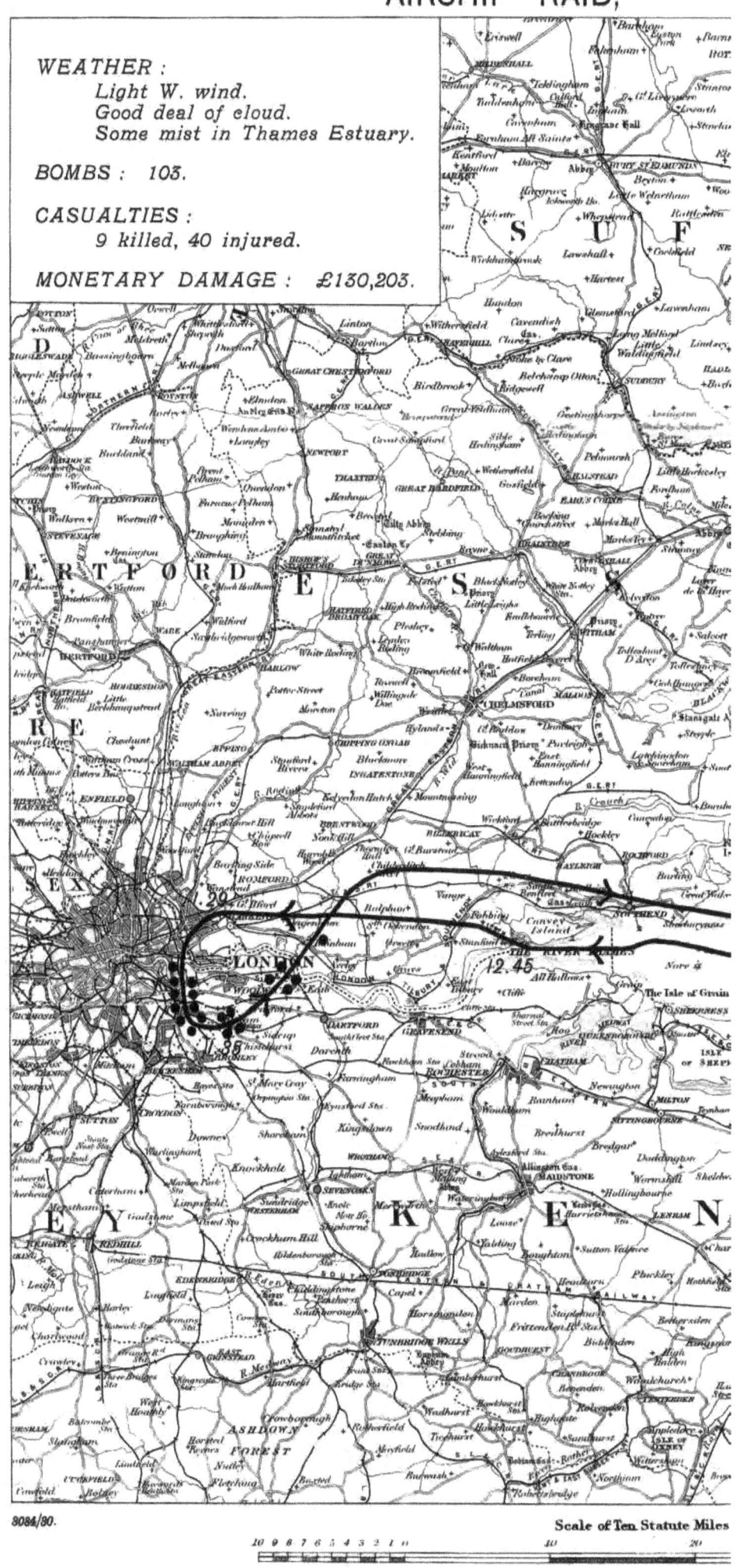

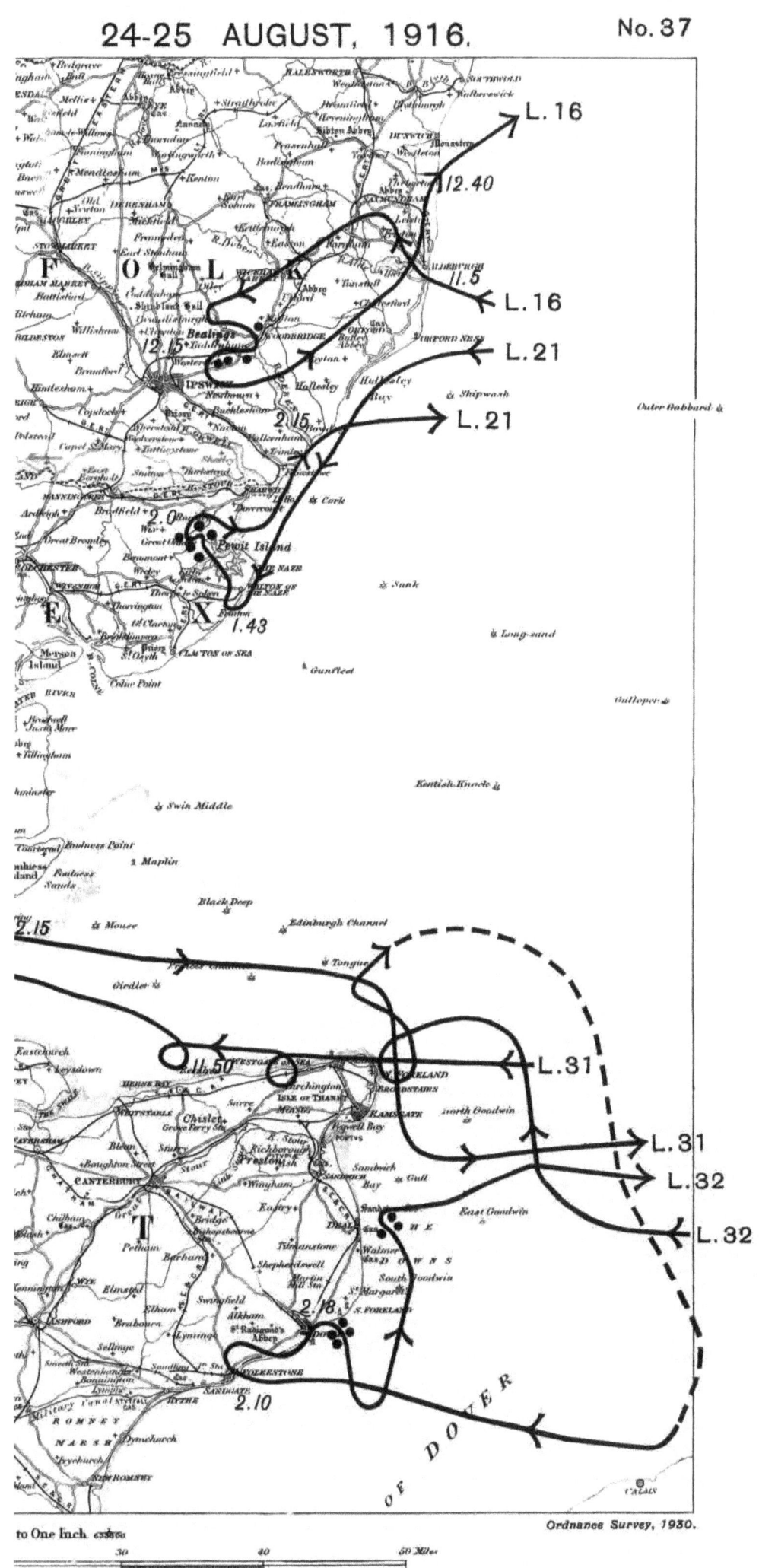

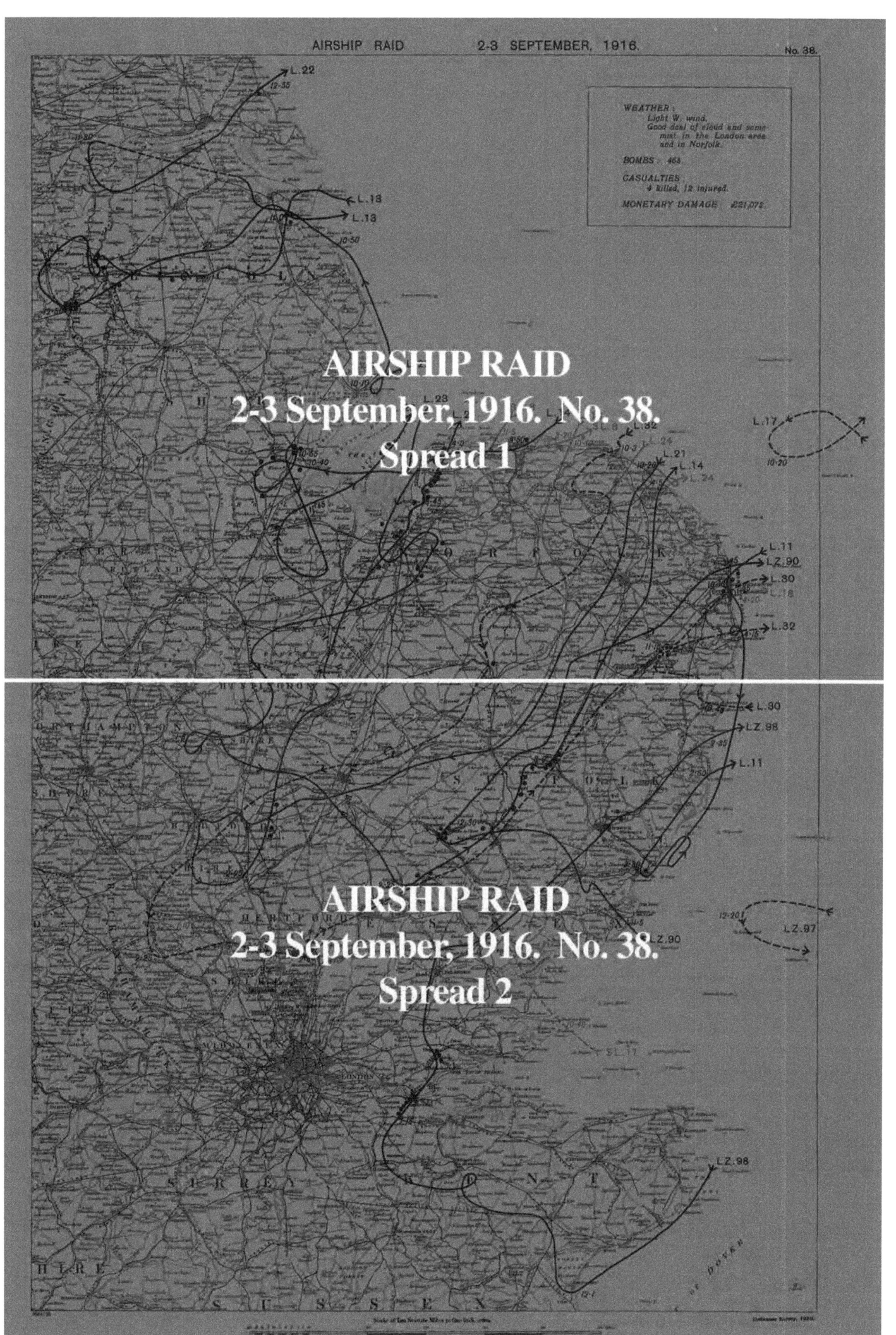

Spread 1

AIRSHIP RAID

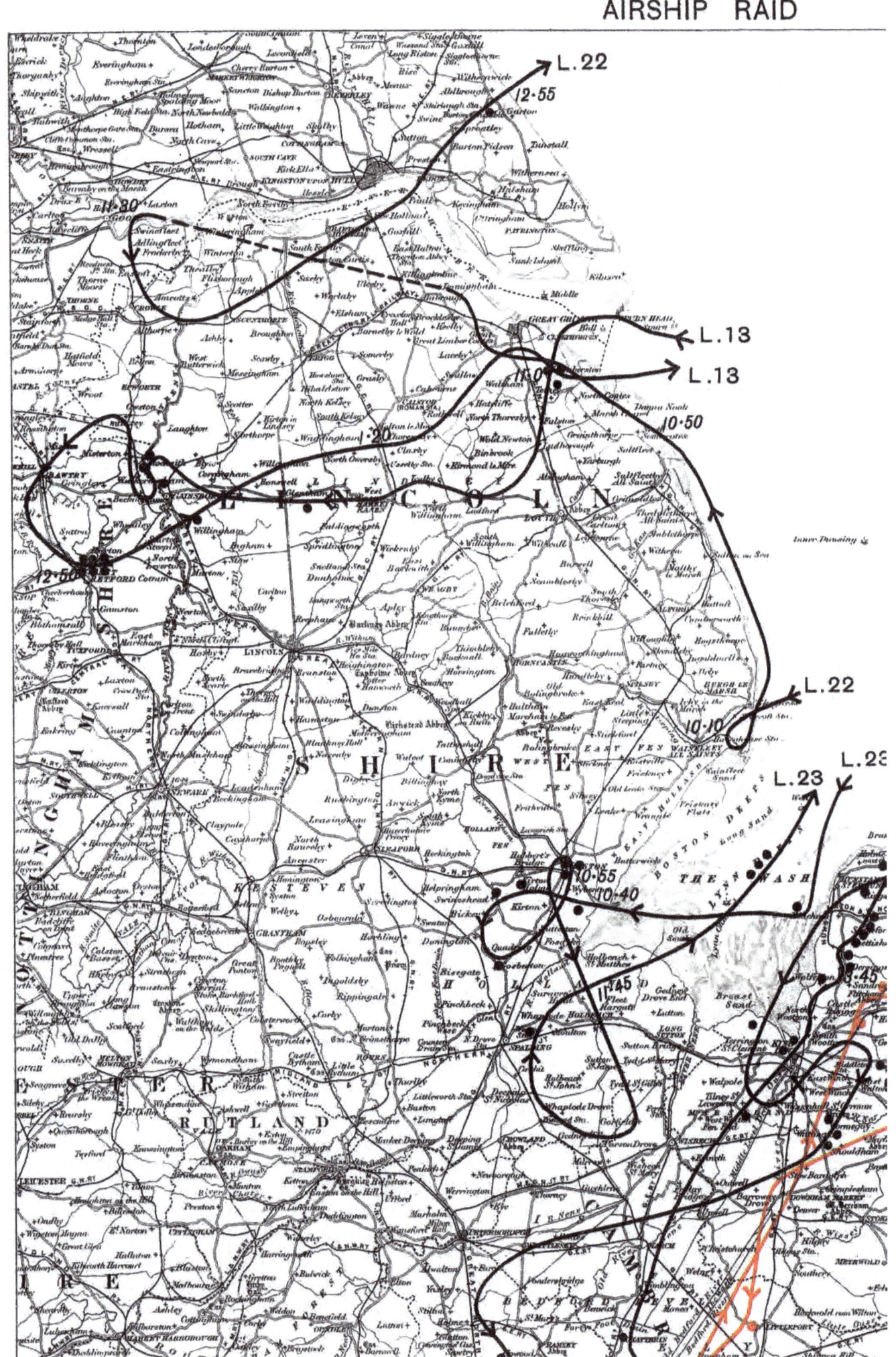

2-3 SEPTEMBER, 1916.   No. 38.

> **WEATHER:**
>   Light W. wind.
>   Good deal of cloud and some mist in the London area and in Norfolk.
>
> **BOMBS:** 463.
>
> **CASUALTIES:**
>   4 killed, 12 injured.
>
> **MONETARY DAMAGE:** £21,072.

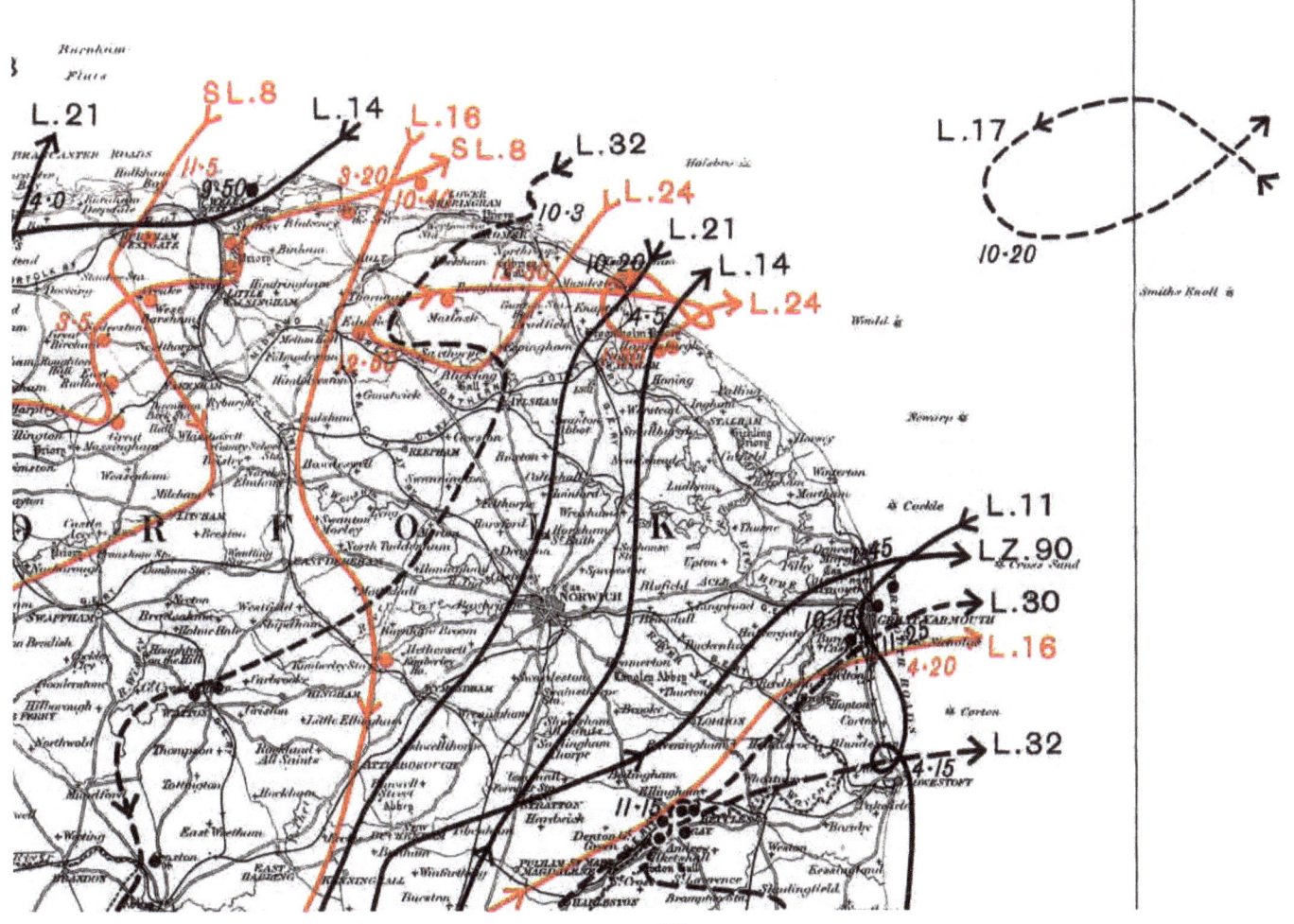

Spread 2

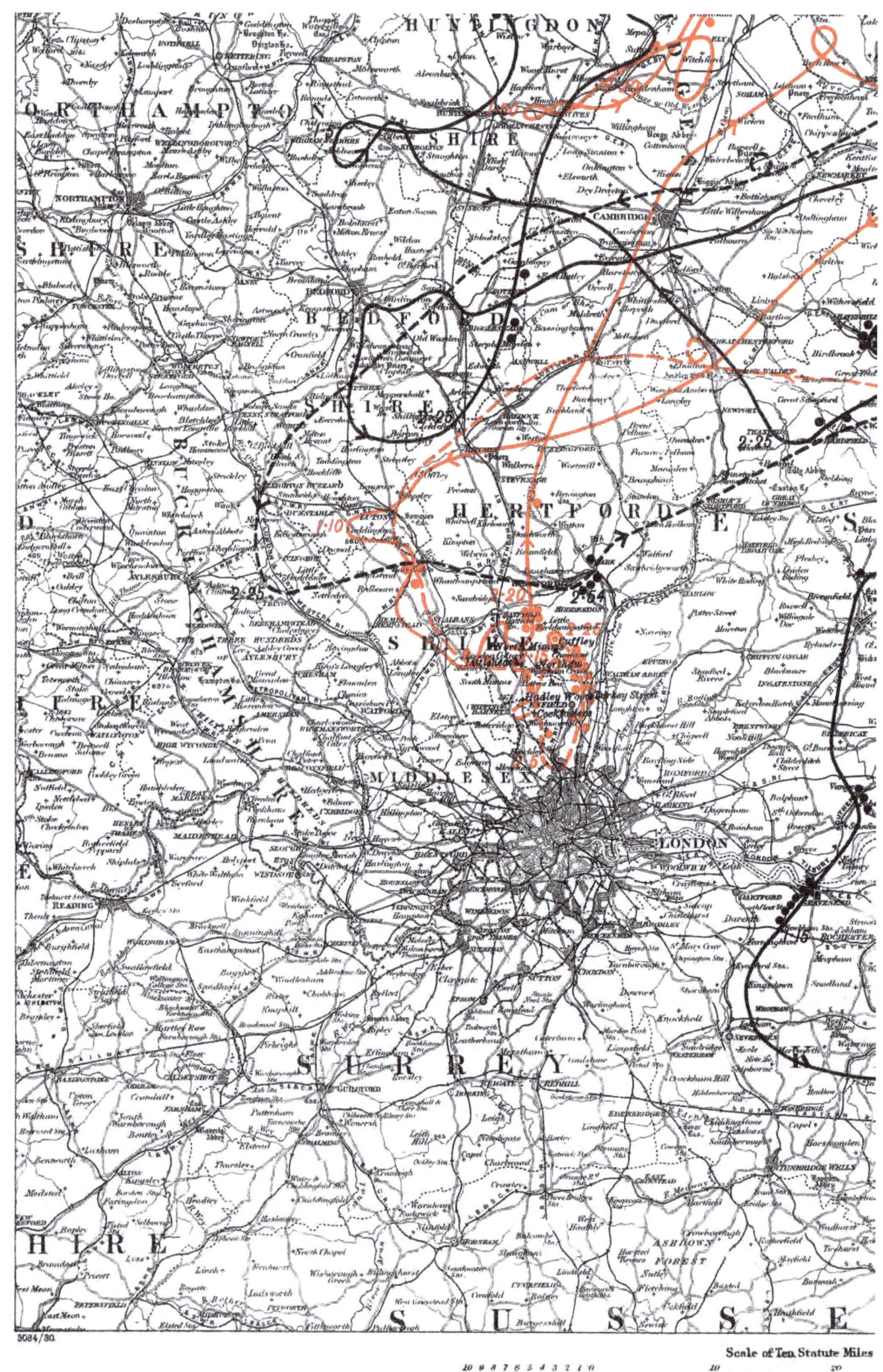

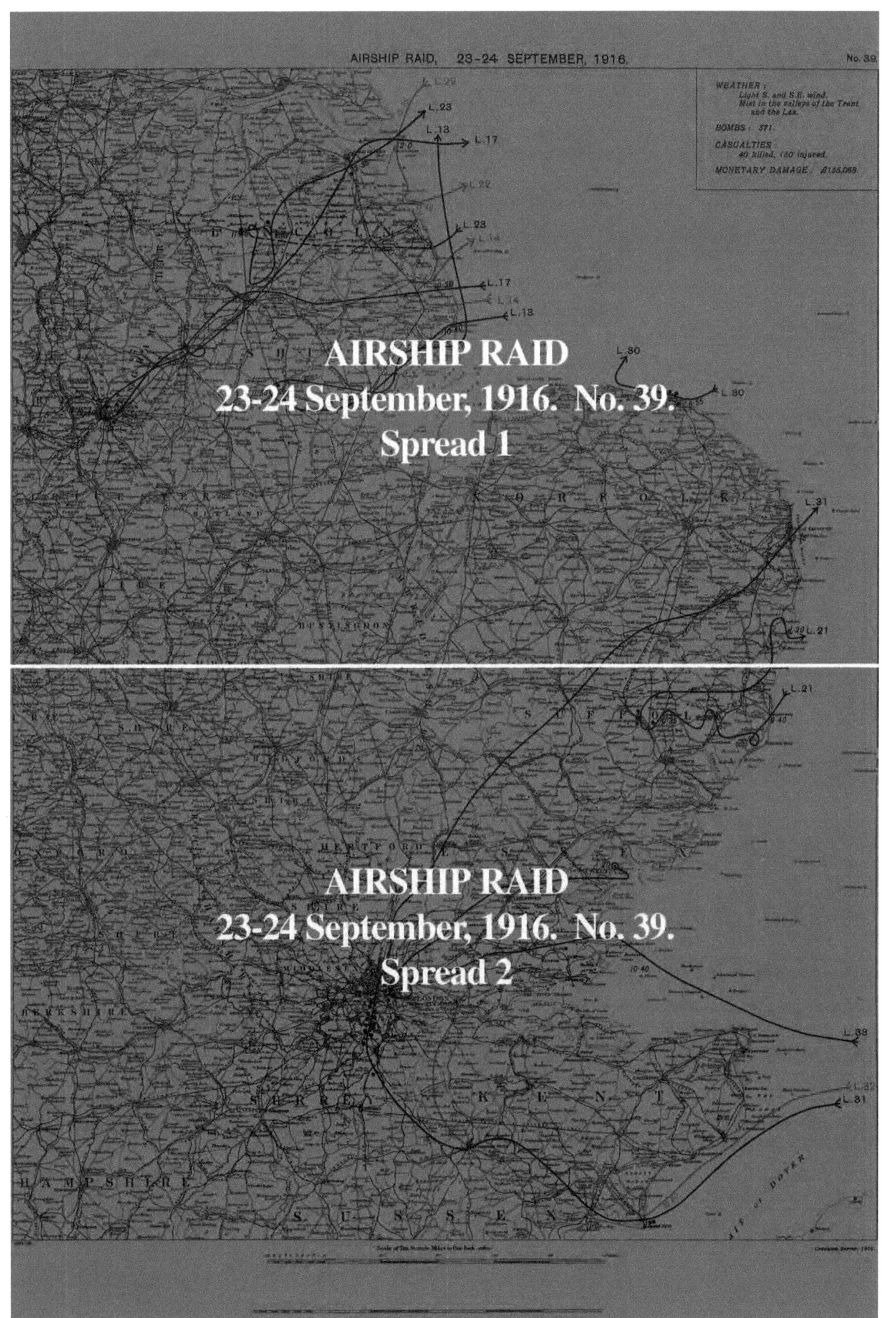

Spread 1

AIRSHIP RAID,

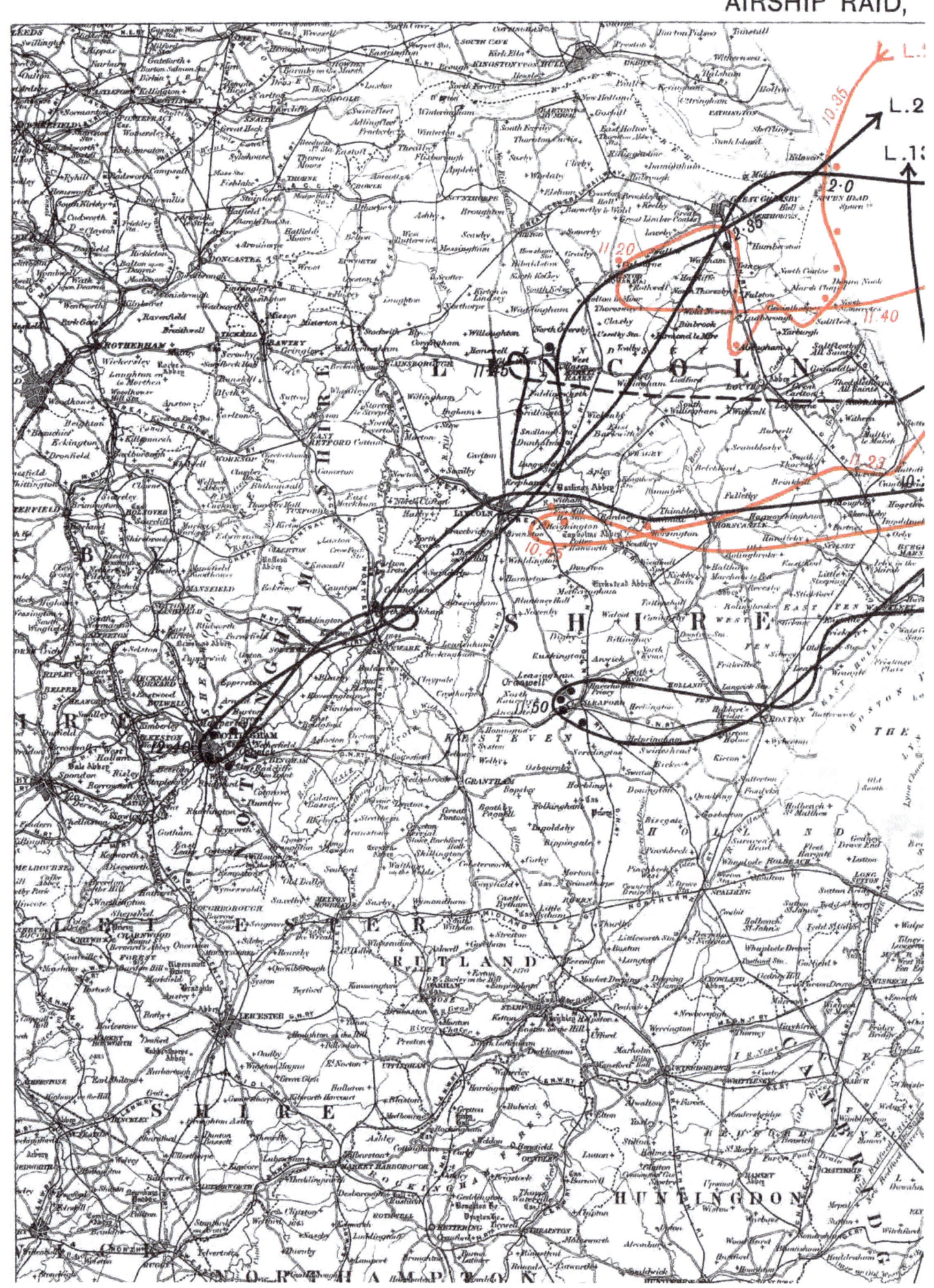

23-24 SEPTEMBER, 1916.

No. 39.

WEATHER:
Light S. and S.E. wind.
Mist in the valleys of the Trent and the Lea.

BOMBS: 371.

CASUALTIES:
40 killed, 130 injured.

MONETARY DAMAGE: £135,068.

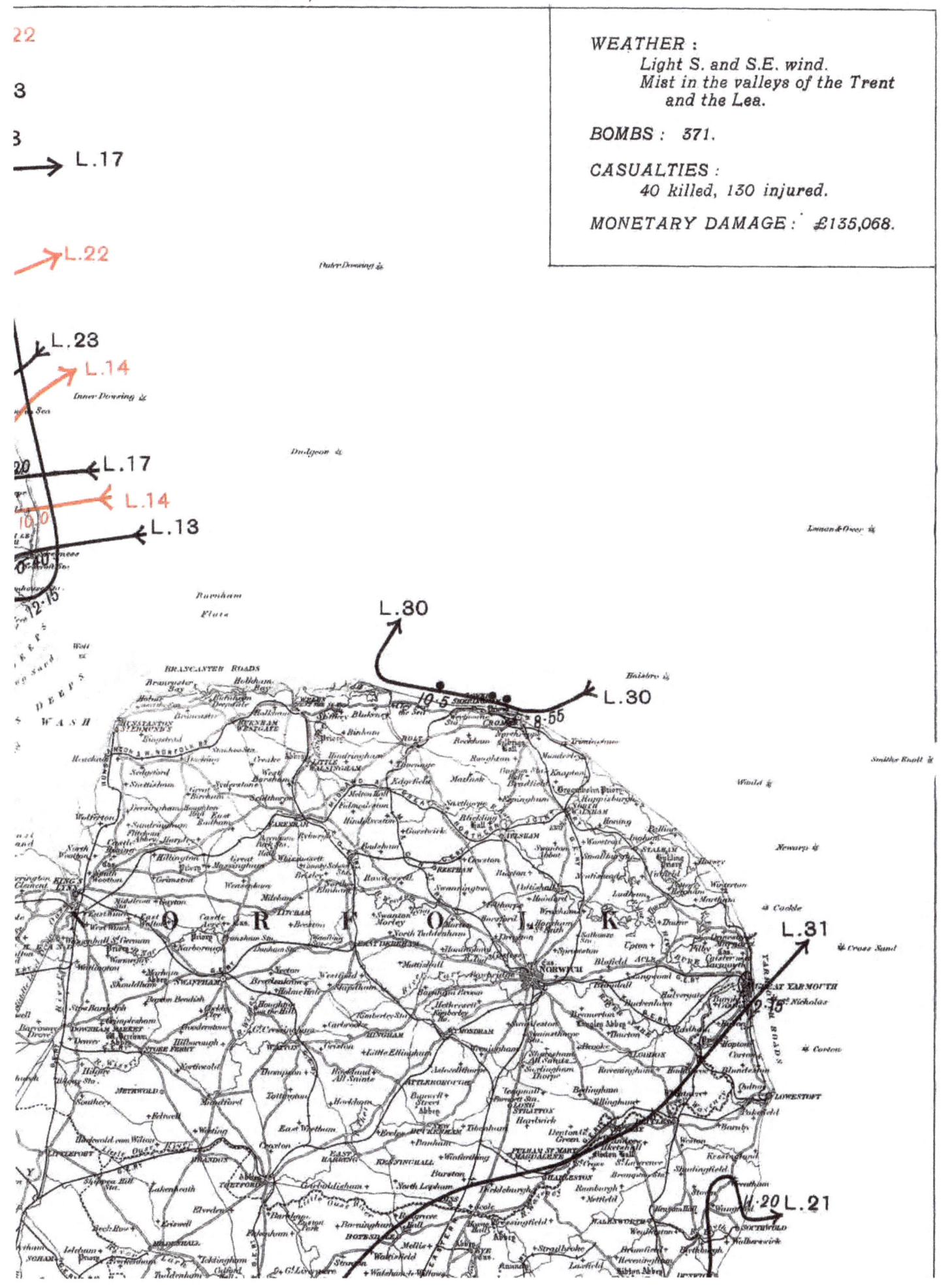

Spread 2

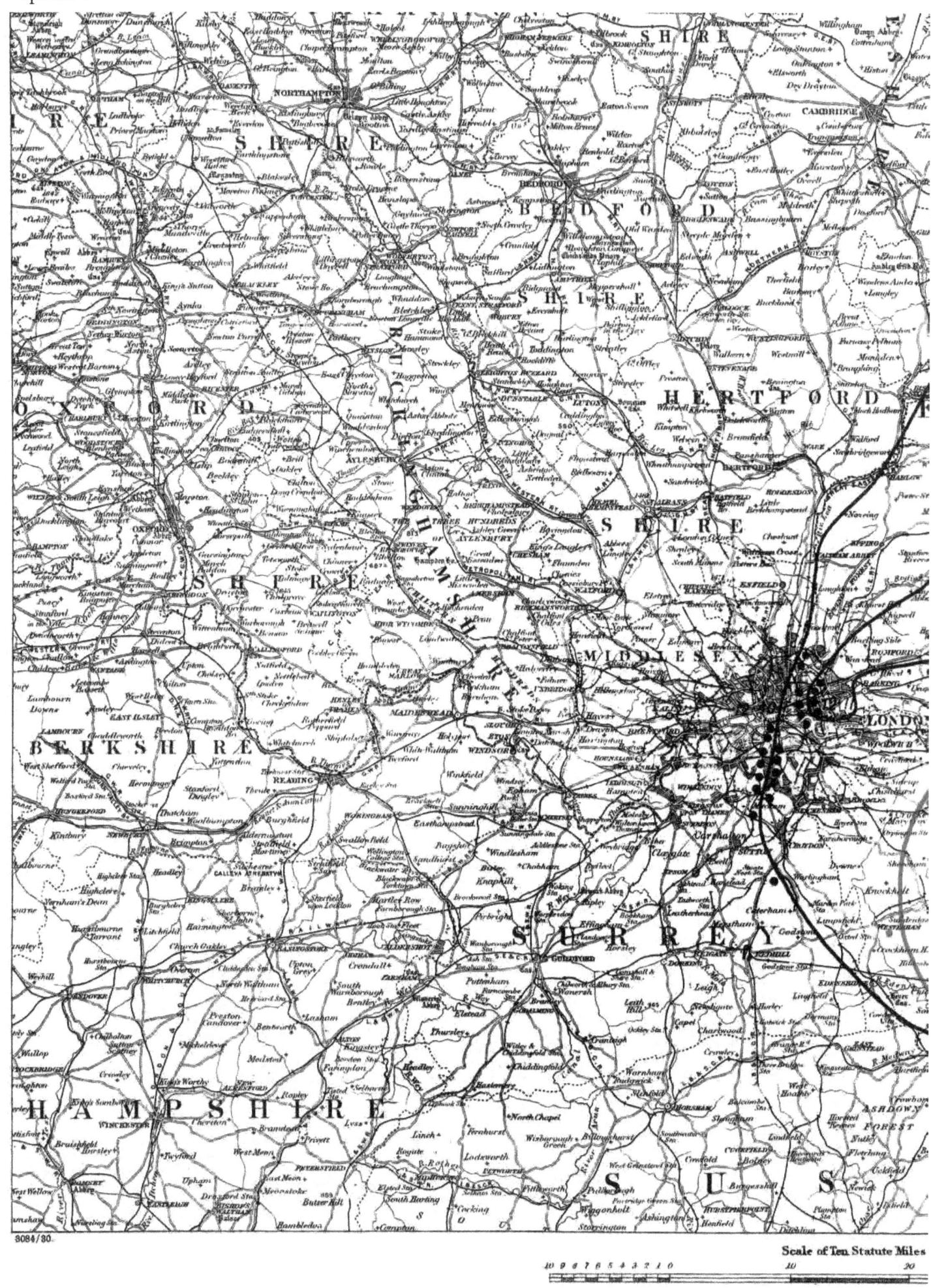

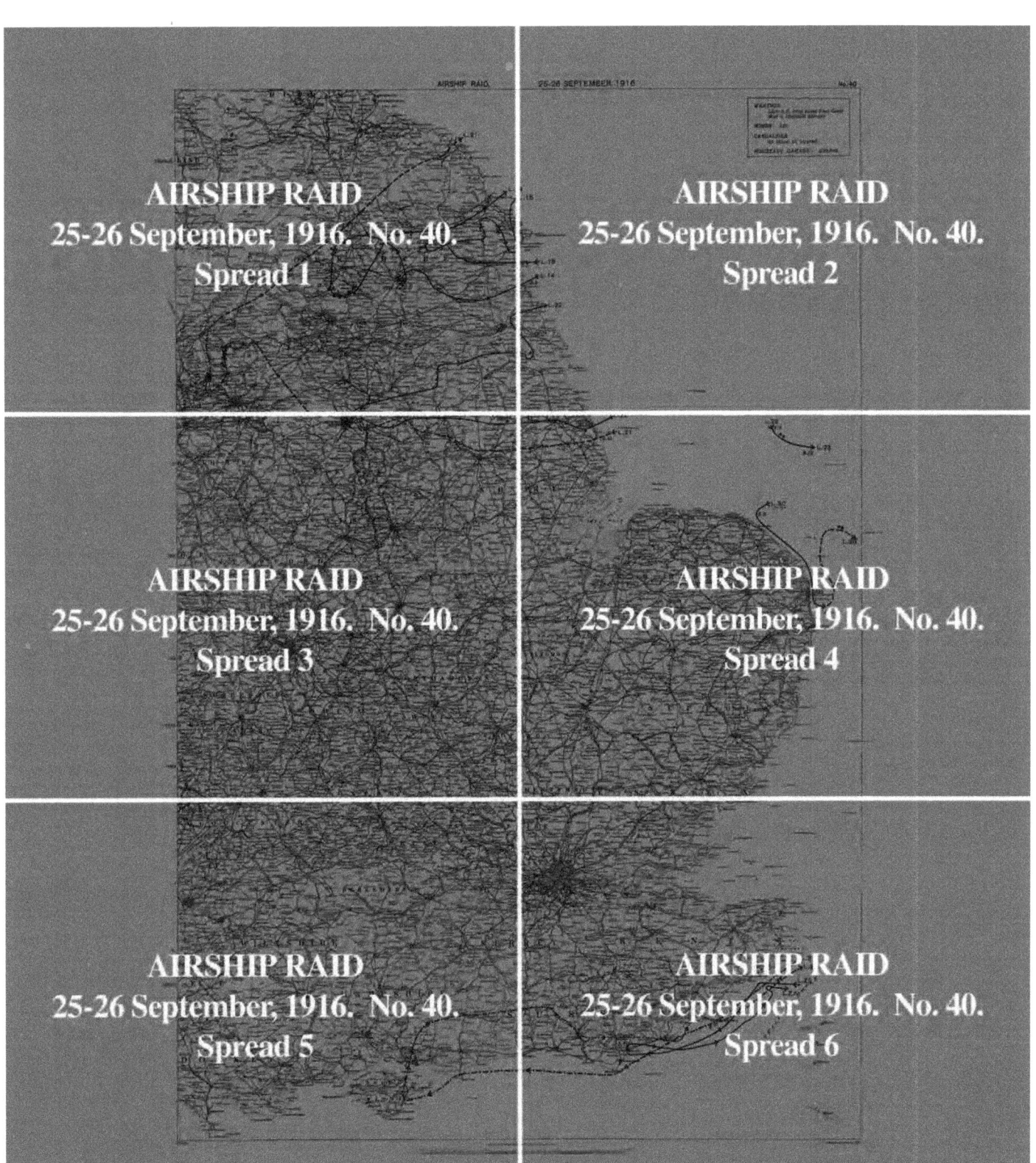

Spread 1

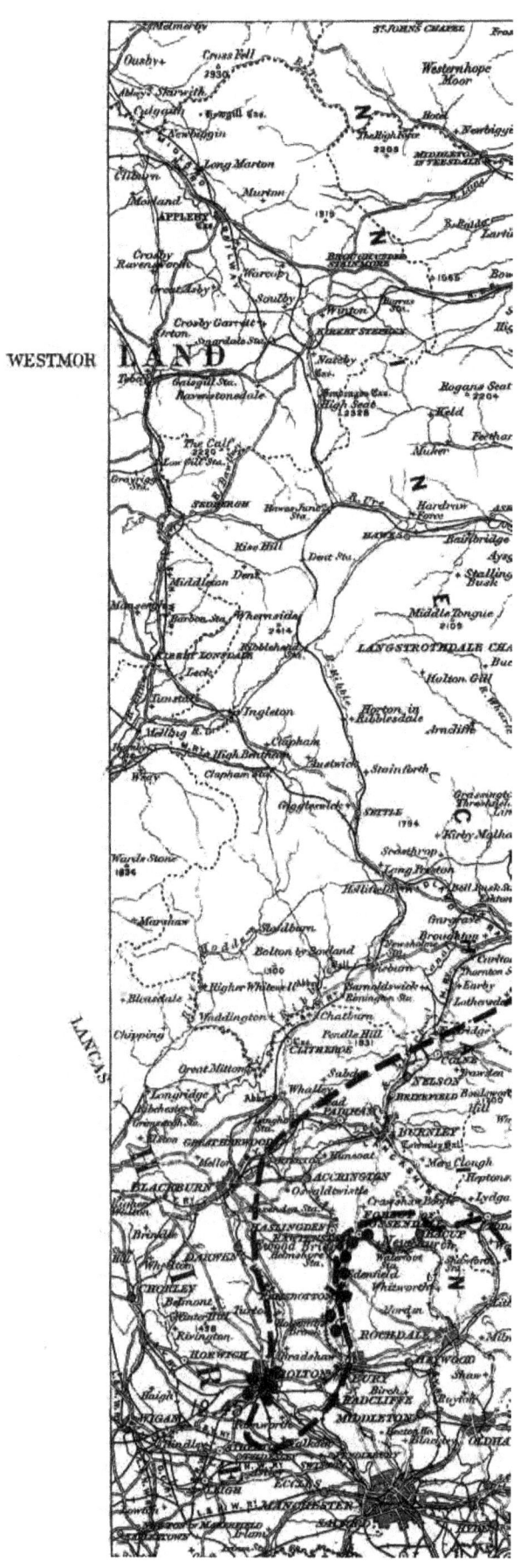

Spread 1

AIRSHIP RAID,

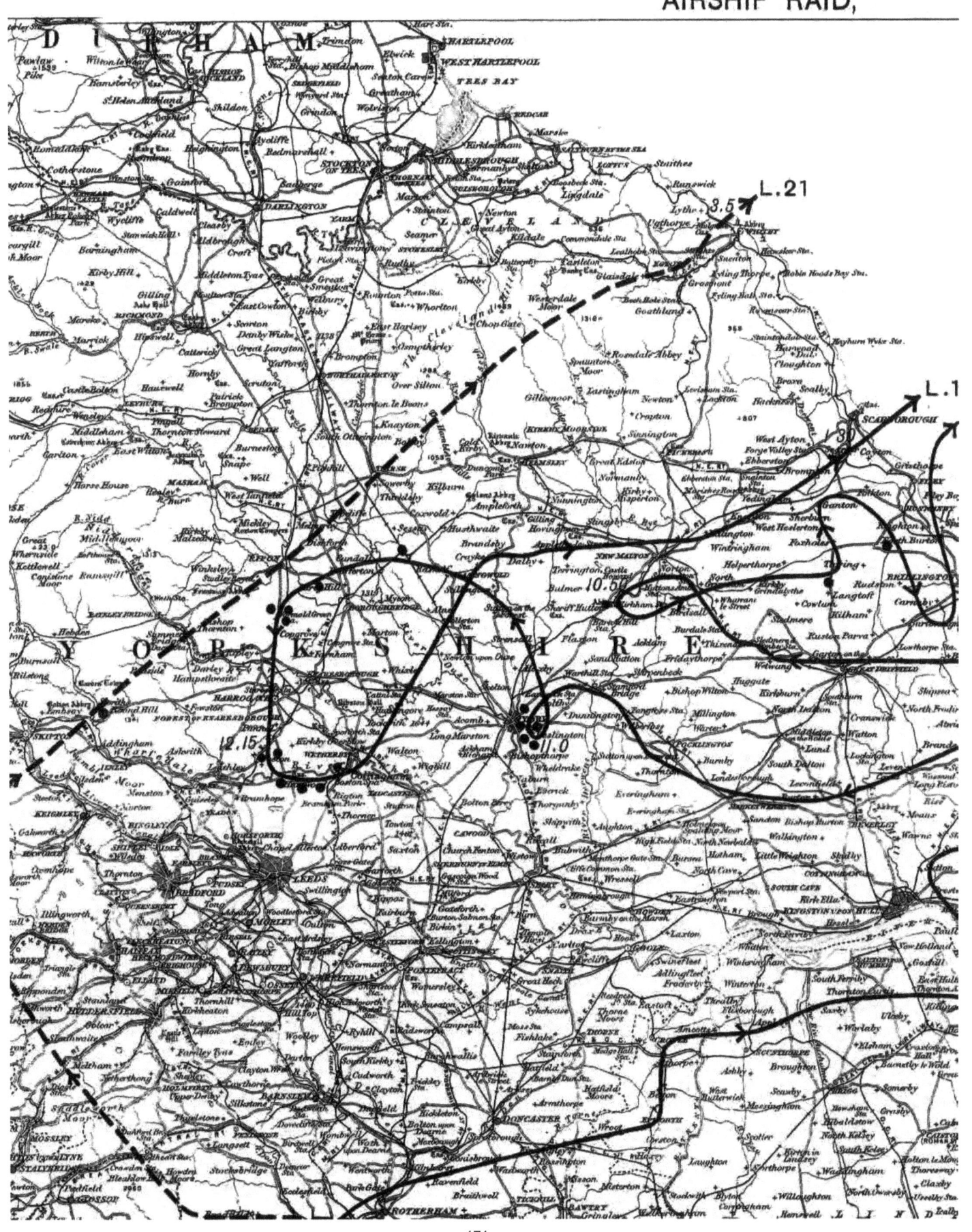

25-26 SEPTEMBER, 1916.

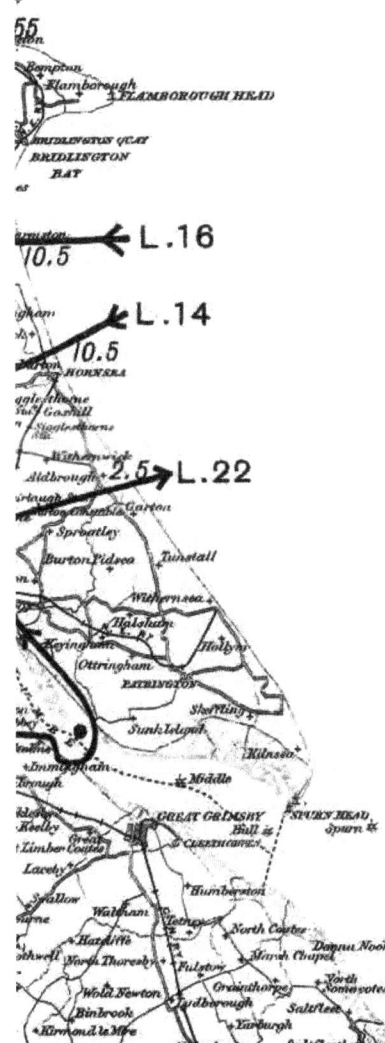

No. 40

WEATHER :
    Light S.E. wind along East Coast.
    Mist in Sheffield district.

BOMBS : 127.

CASUALTIES :
    43 killed, 31 injured.

MONETARY DAMAGE : £39,698.

Spread 3

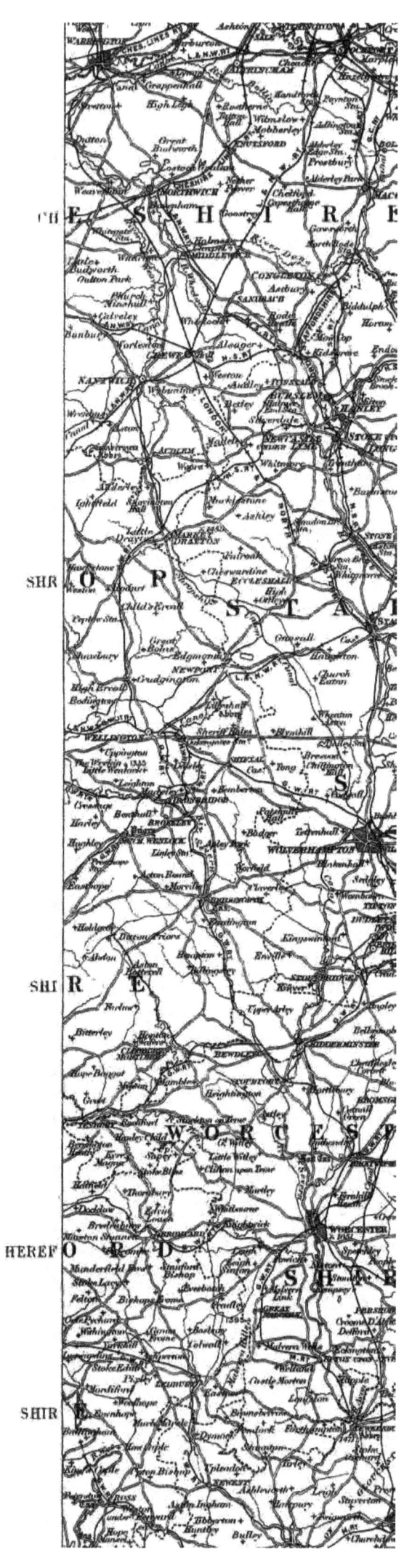

Spread 3

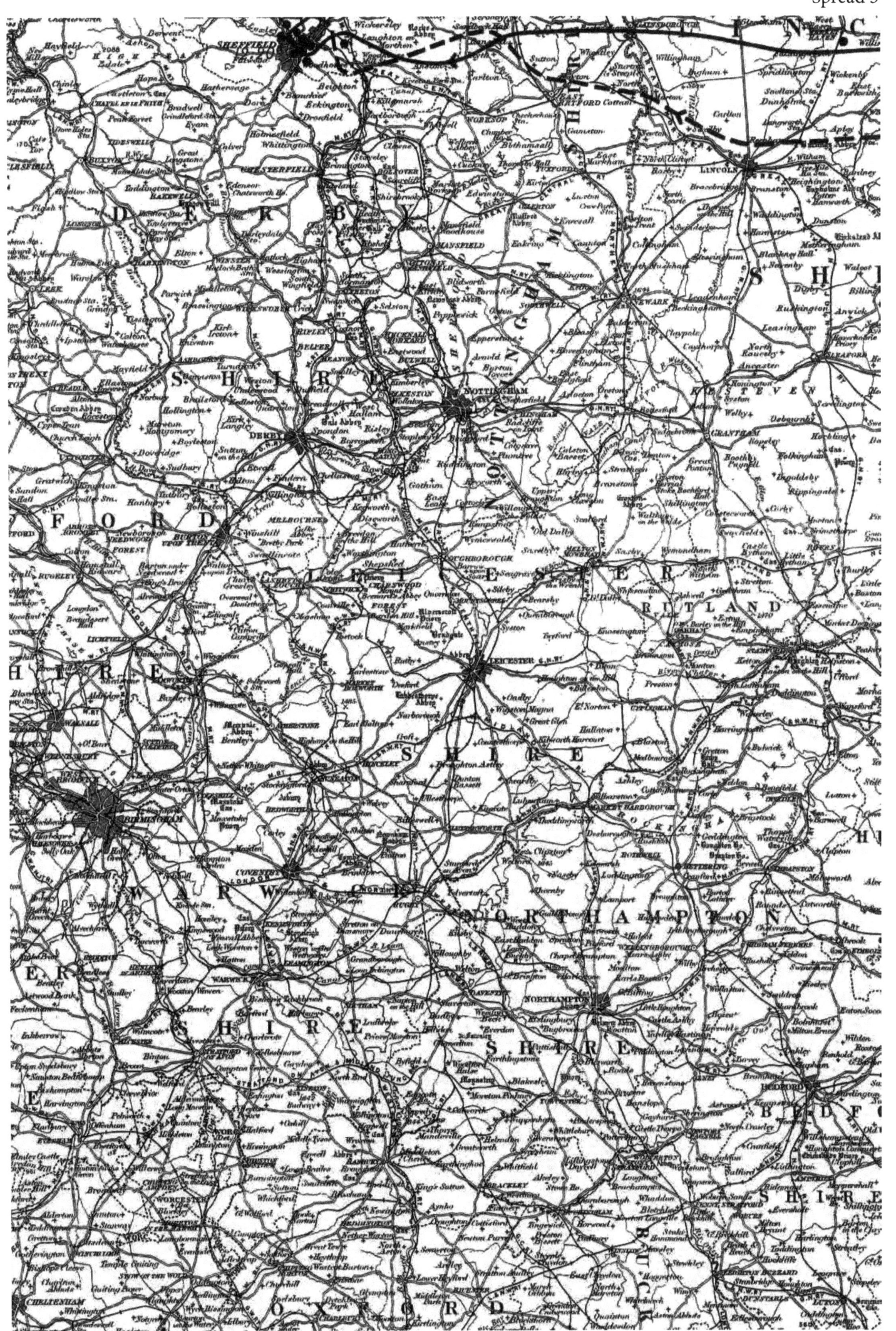

Spread 4

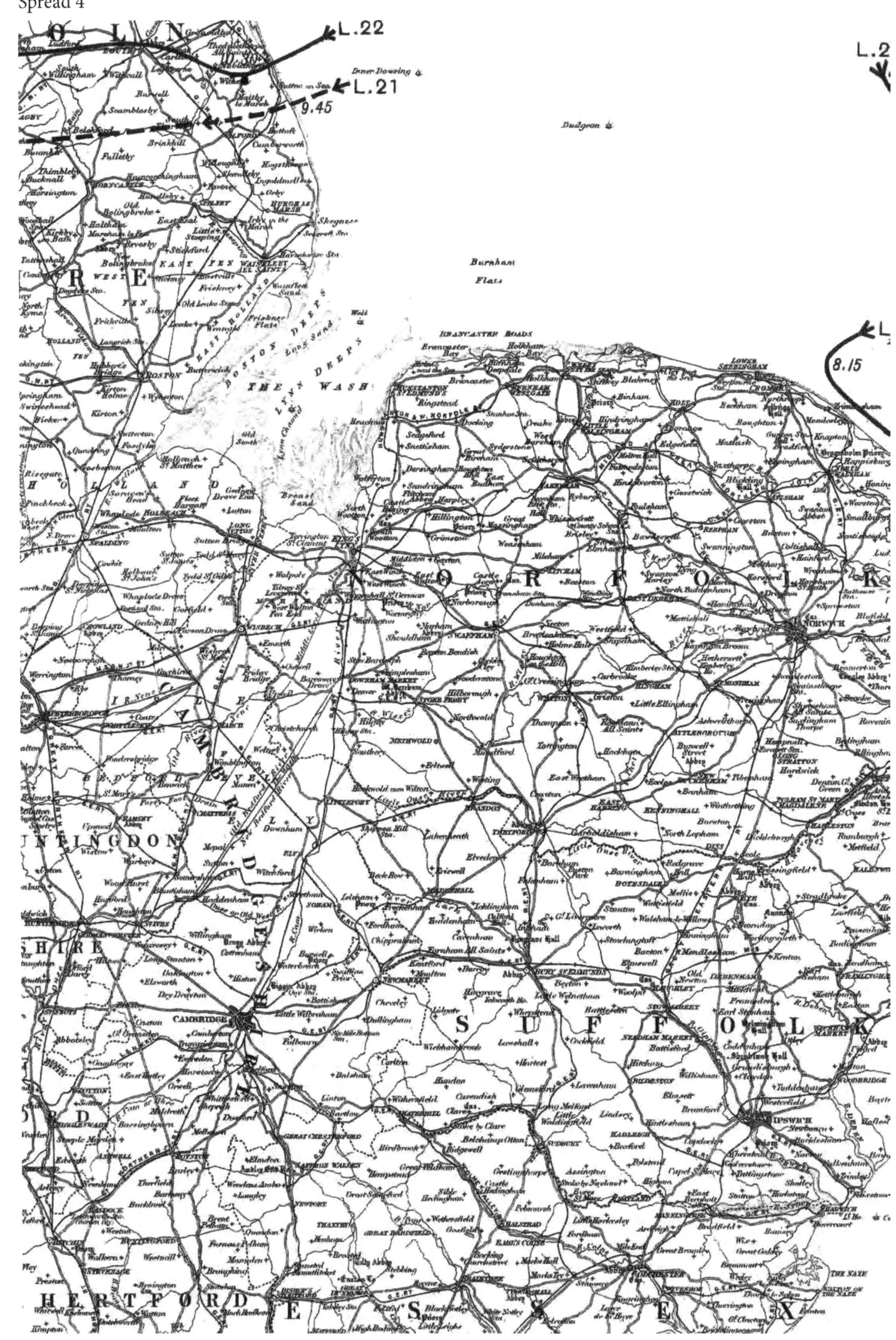

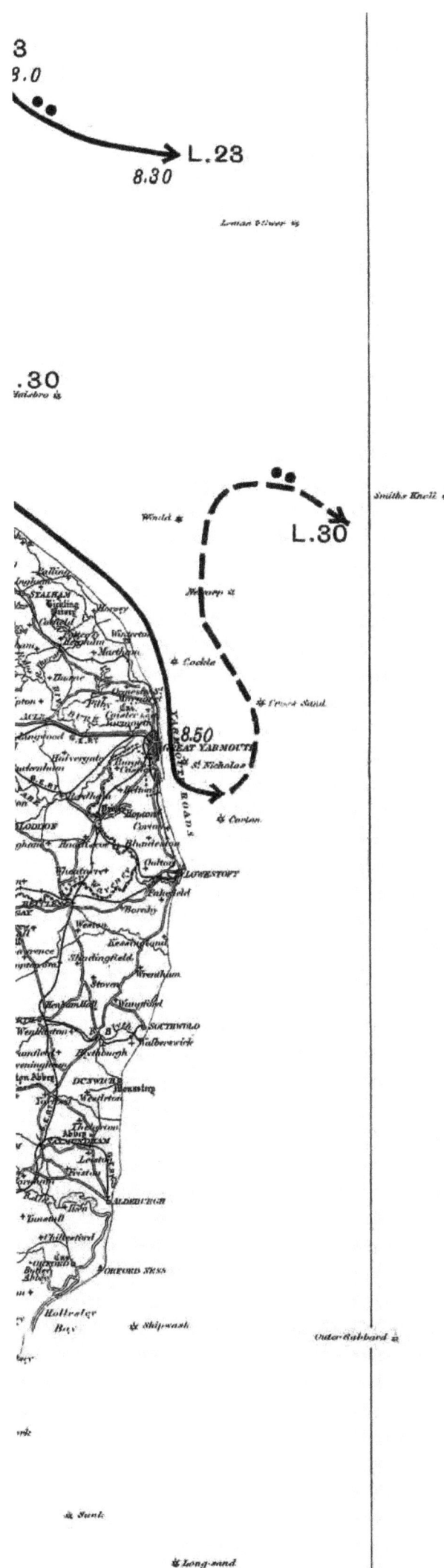

Spread 5

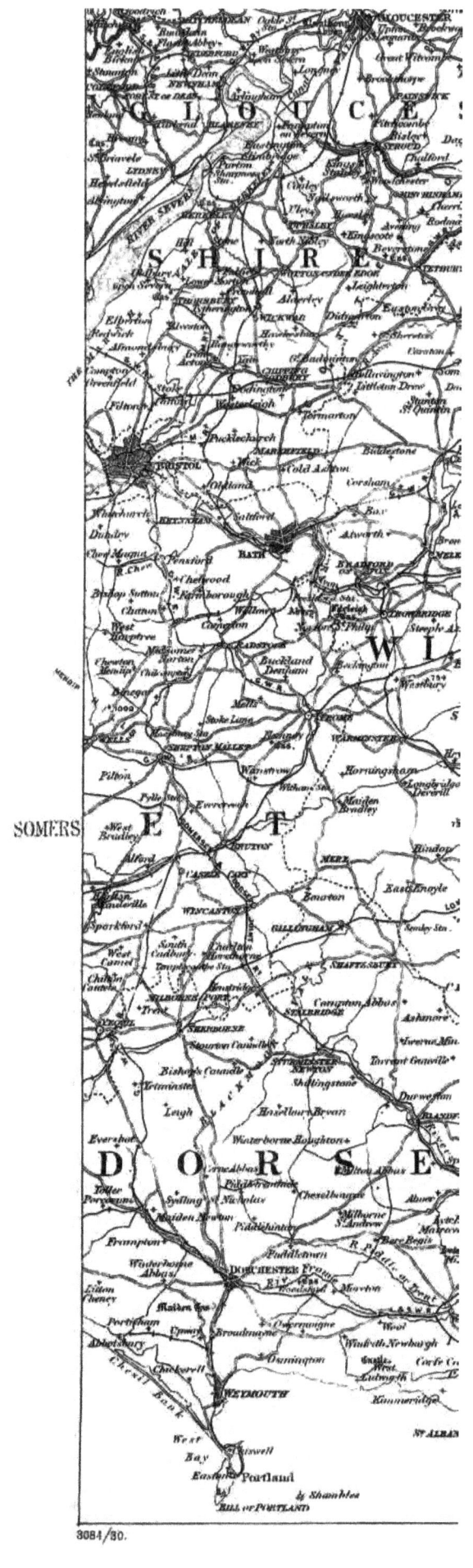

Spread 5

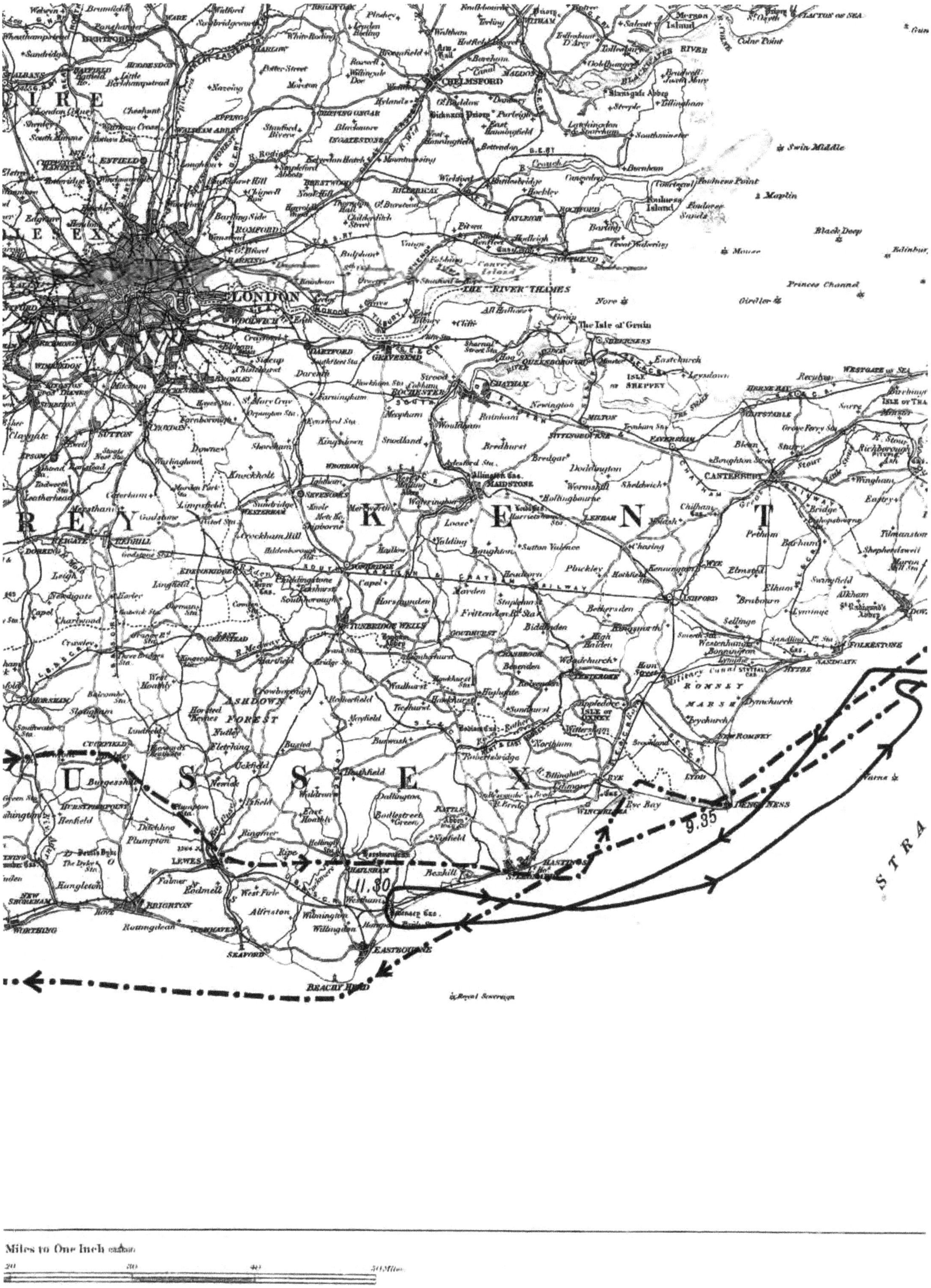
CHELMSFORD
MALDON
ROMFORD
LONDON
WOOLWICH
DARTFORD
GRAVESEND
ROCHESTER
CHATHAM
SHEERNESS
The Isle of Grain
THE RIVER THAMES
SOUTHEND
MAIDSTONE
CANTERBURY
ASHFORD
FOLKESTONE
HYTHE
TONBRIDGE
TUNBRIDGE WELLS
ASHDOWN FOREST
LEWES
BRIGHTON
WORTHING
HAILSHAM
EASTBOURNE
BEACHY HEAD
HASTINGS
RYE
Rye Bay
DUNGENESS
NEW ROMNEY
ROMNEY MARSH
K E N T
S U S S E X
11.30
9.35
Miles to One Inch
20
30
40
50 Miles

Spread 6

Ordnance Survey, 1930.

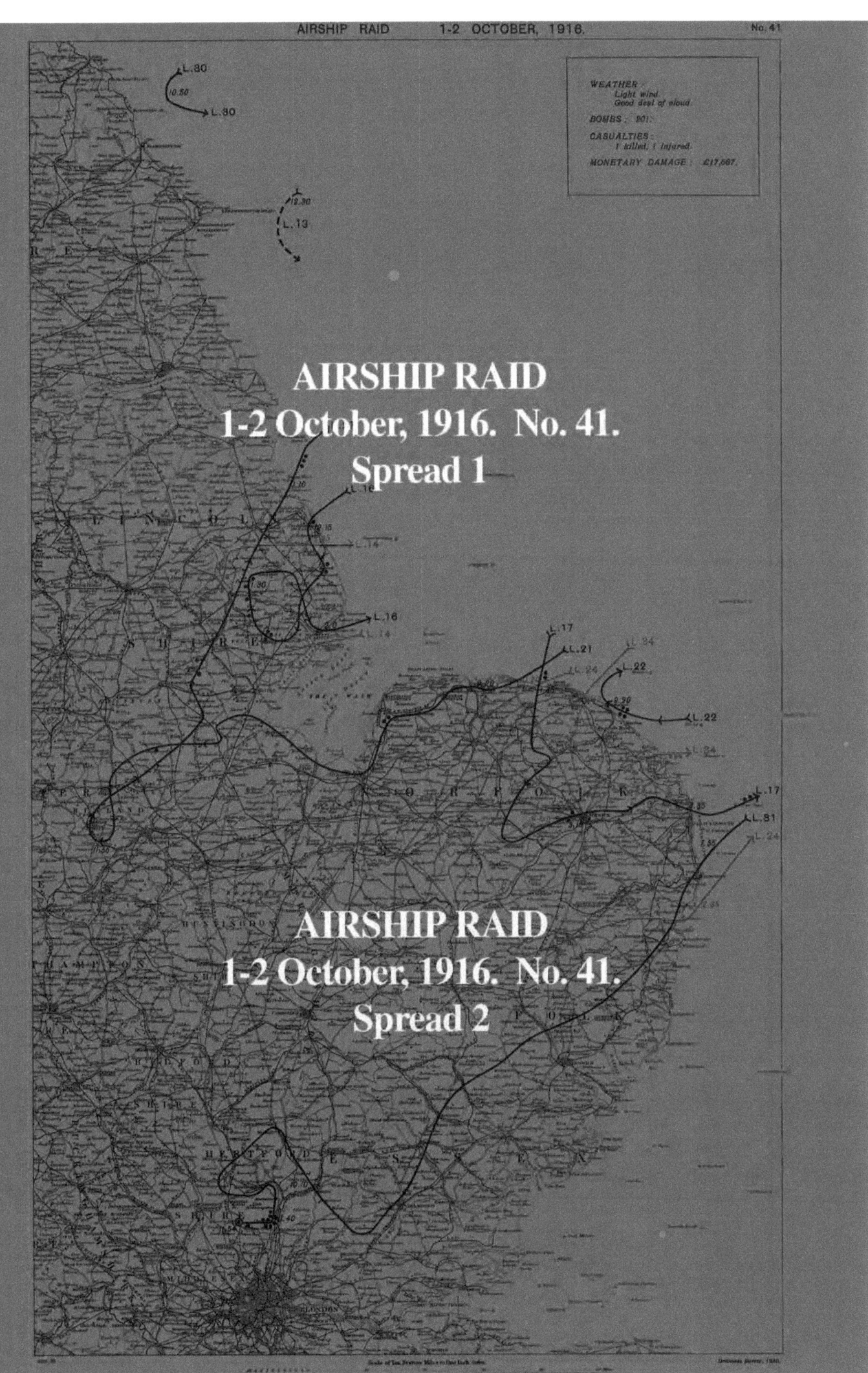

AIRSHIP RAID

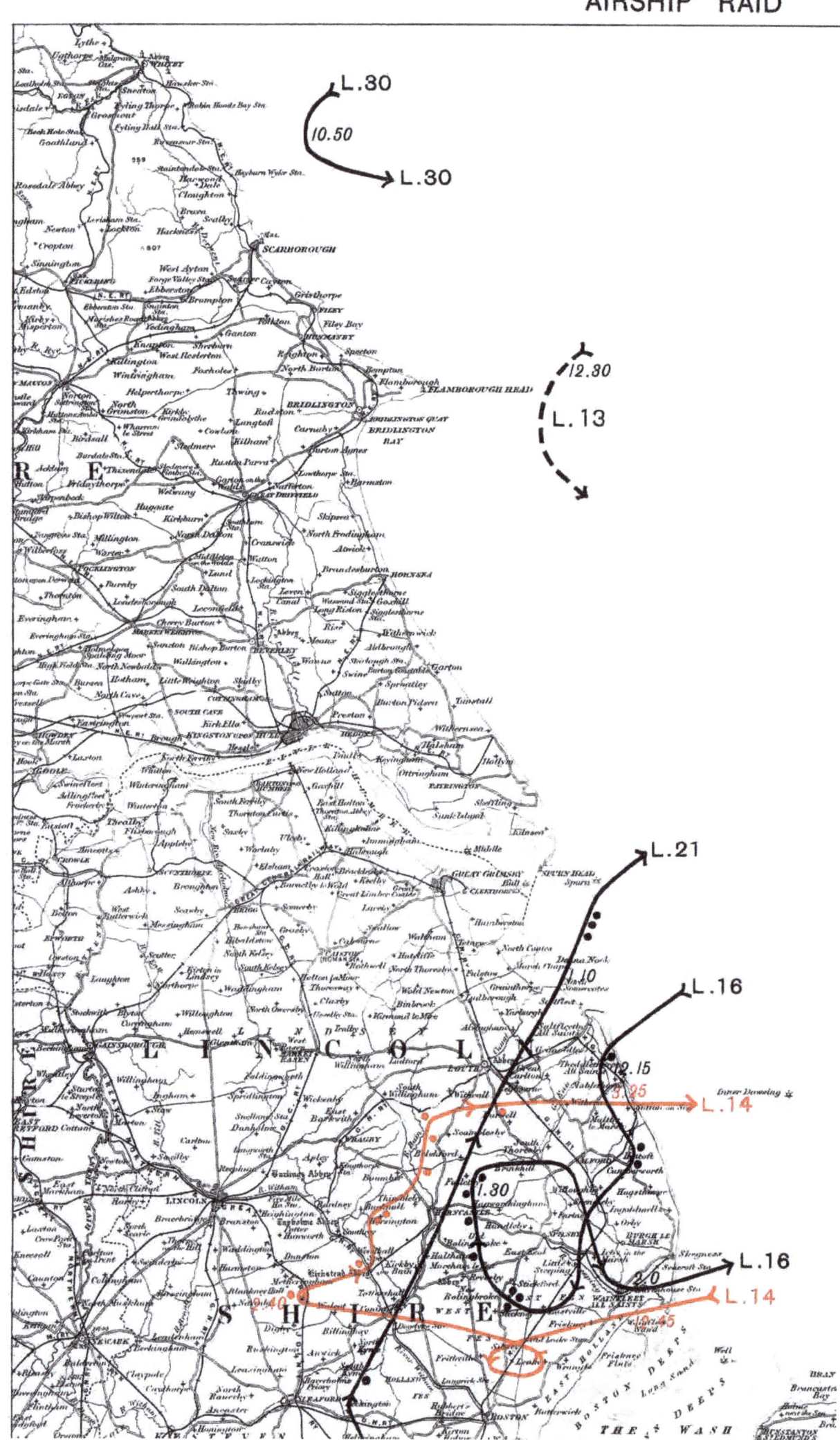

1-2 OCTOBER, 1916.   No. 41

> WEATHER :
>   Light wind.
>   Good deal of cloud.
>
> BOMBS : 201.
>
> CASUALTIES :
>   1 killed, 1 injured.
>
> MONETARY DAMAGE :   £17,687.

Spread 2

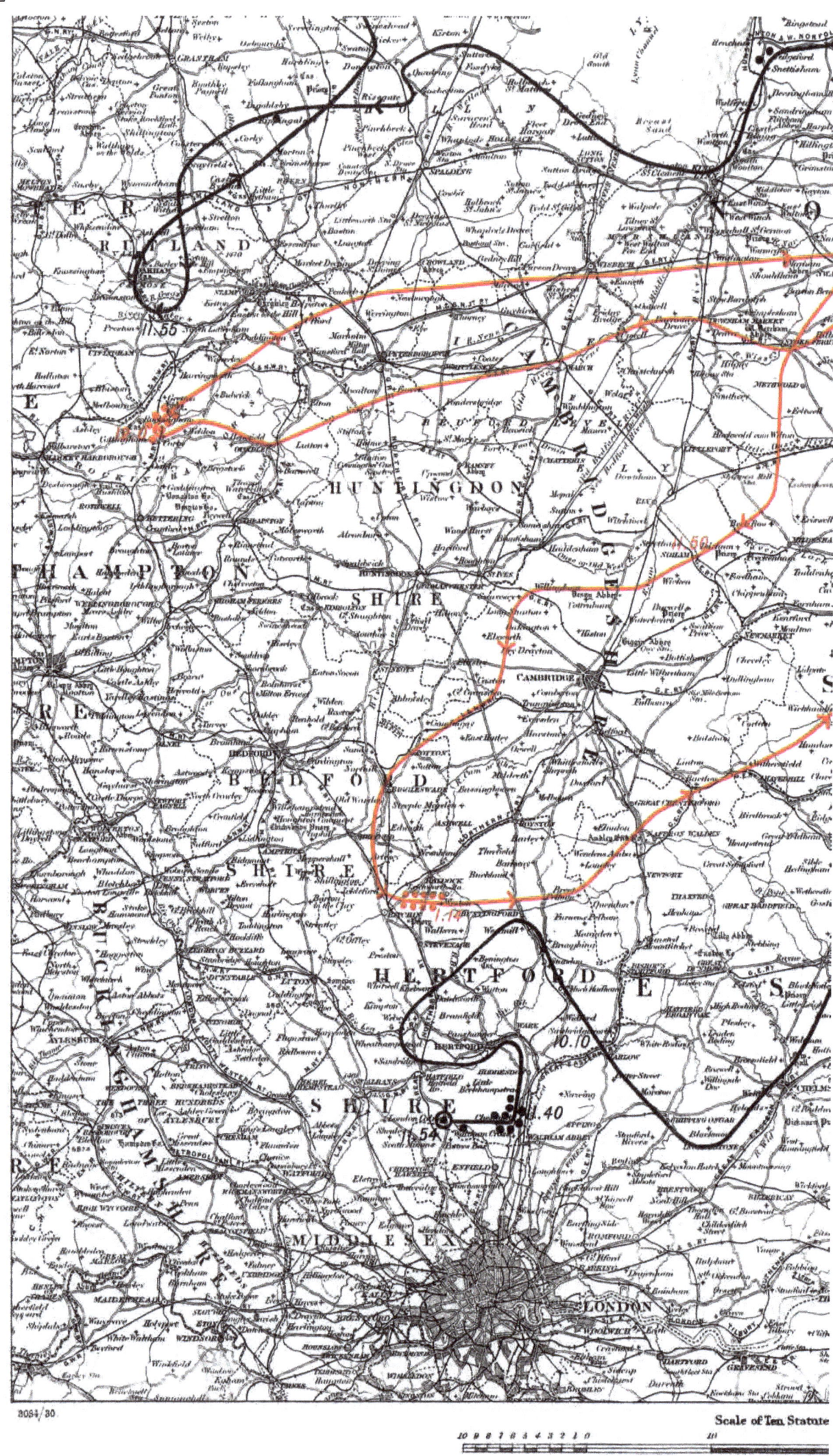

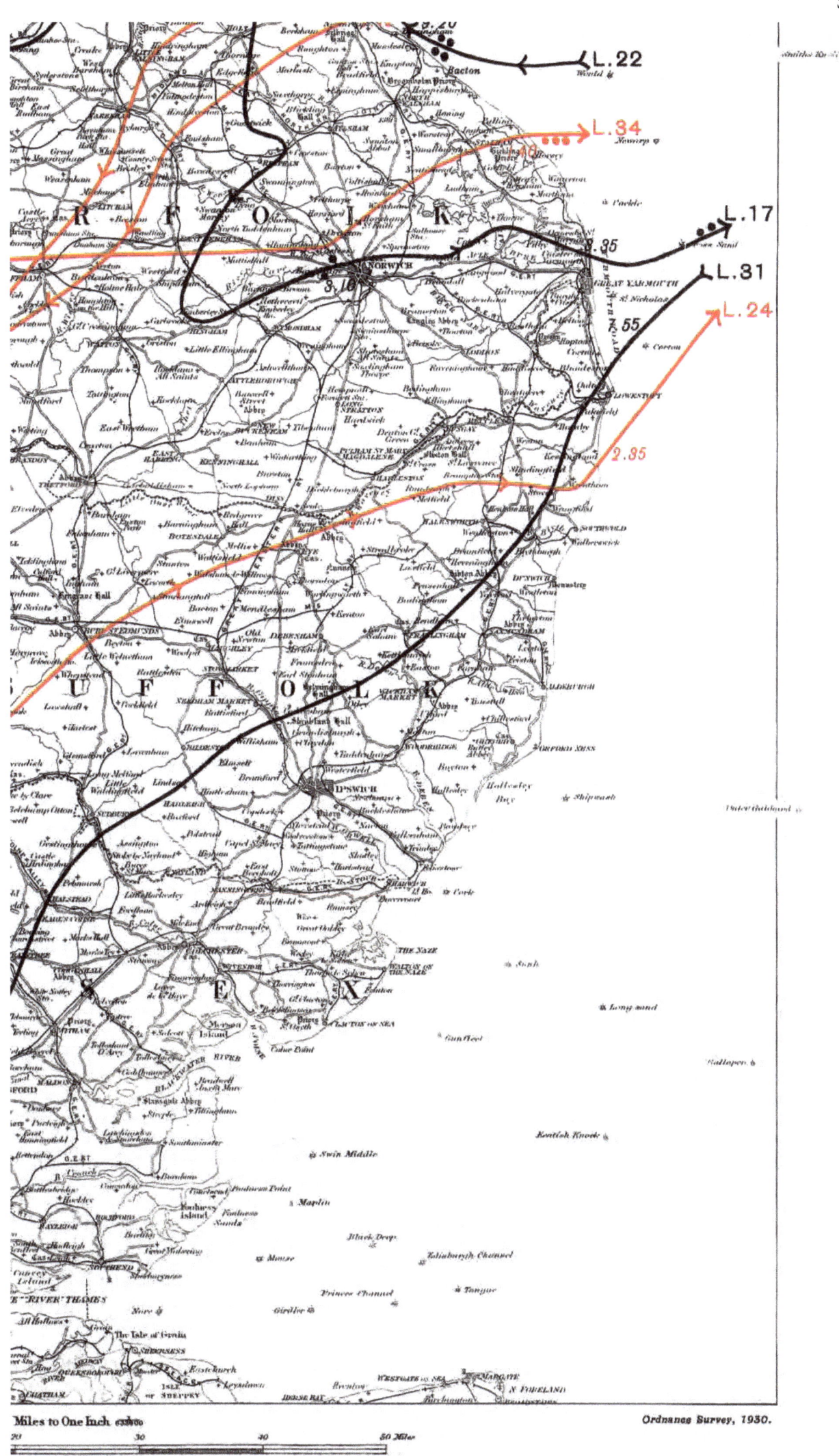

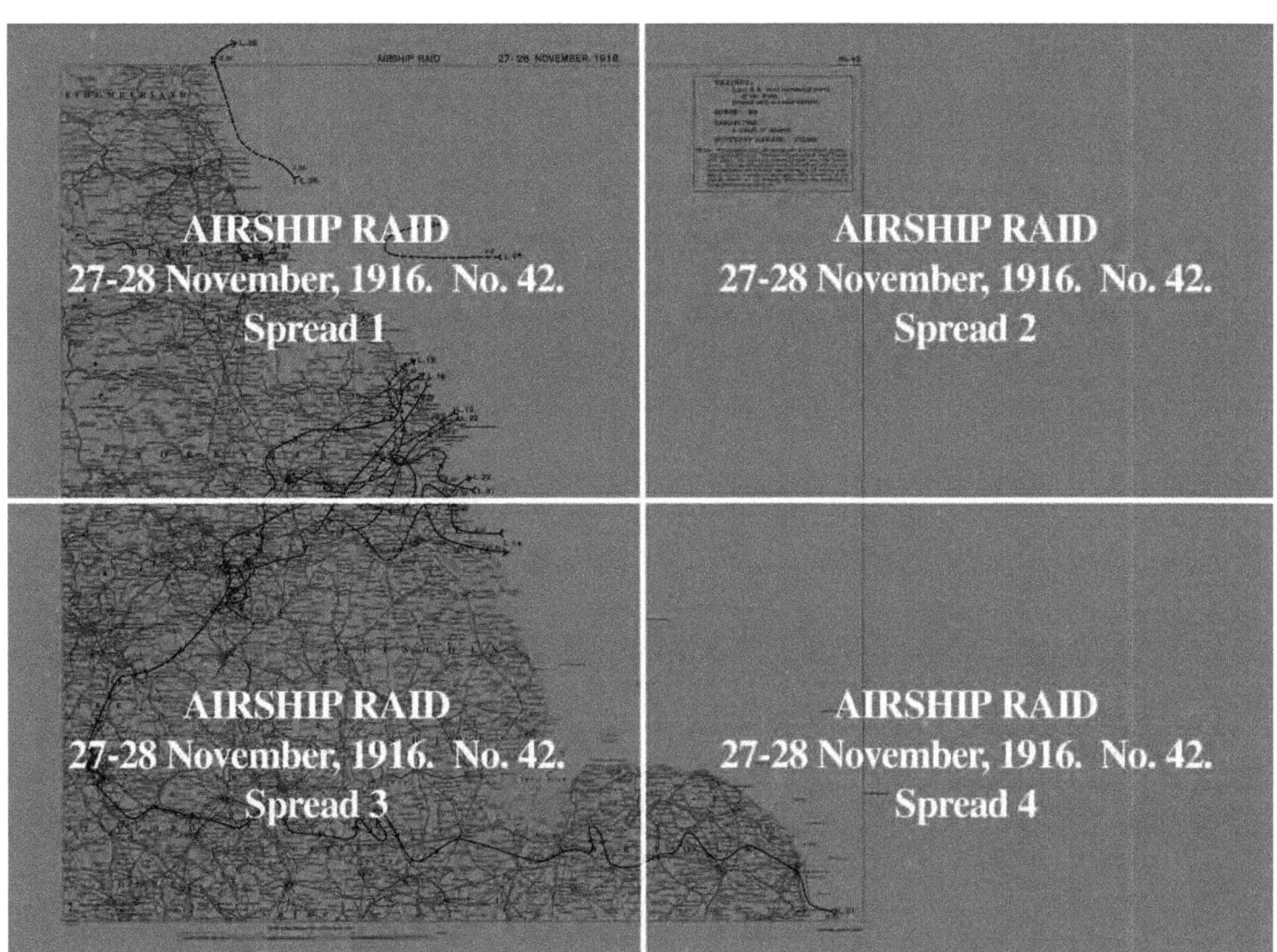

Spread 1

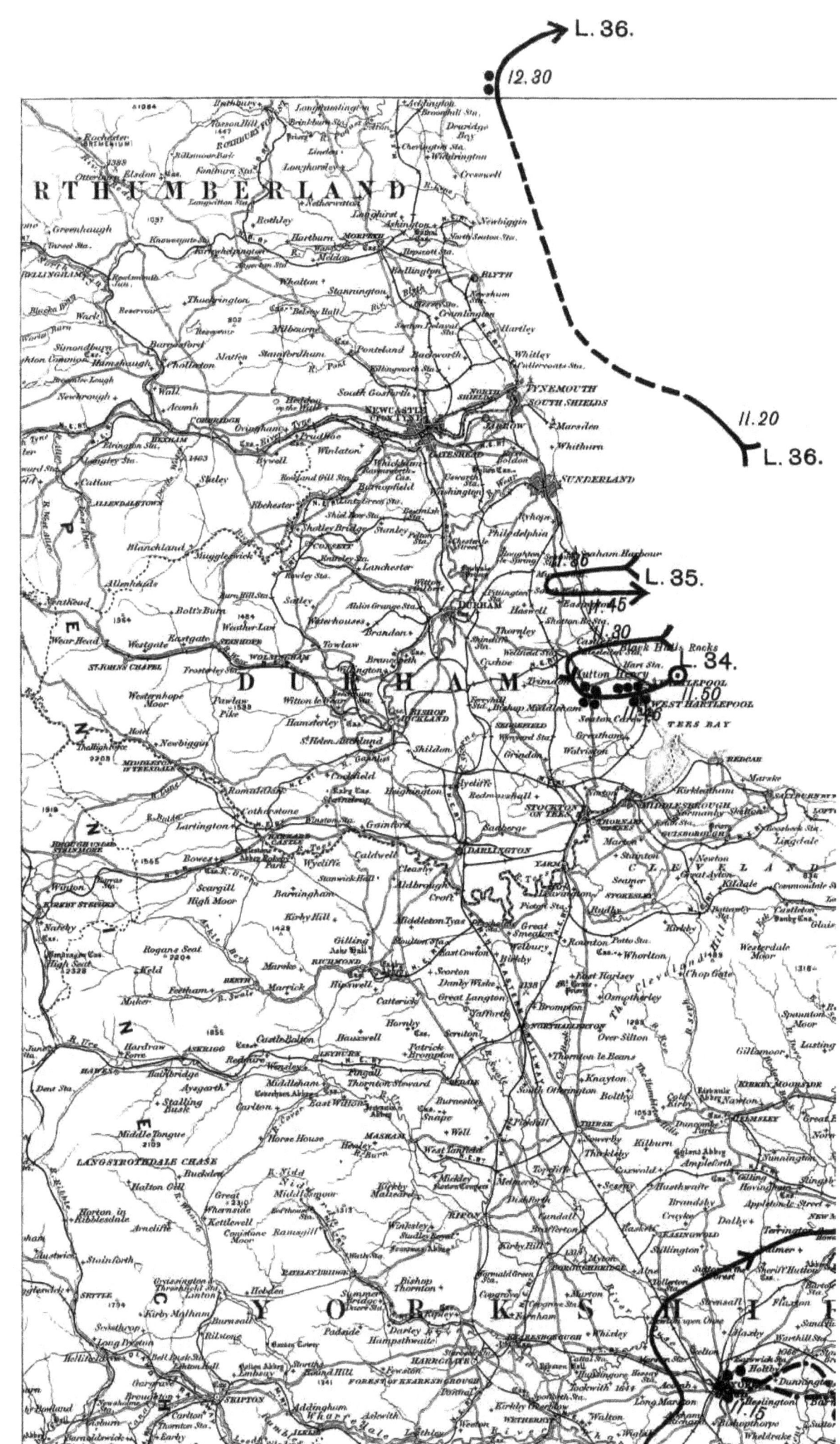

AIRSHIP RAID 27- 28 NOVEMBER, 1916.

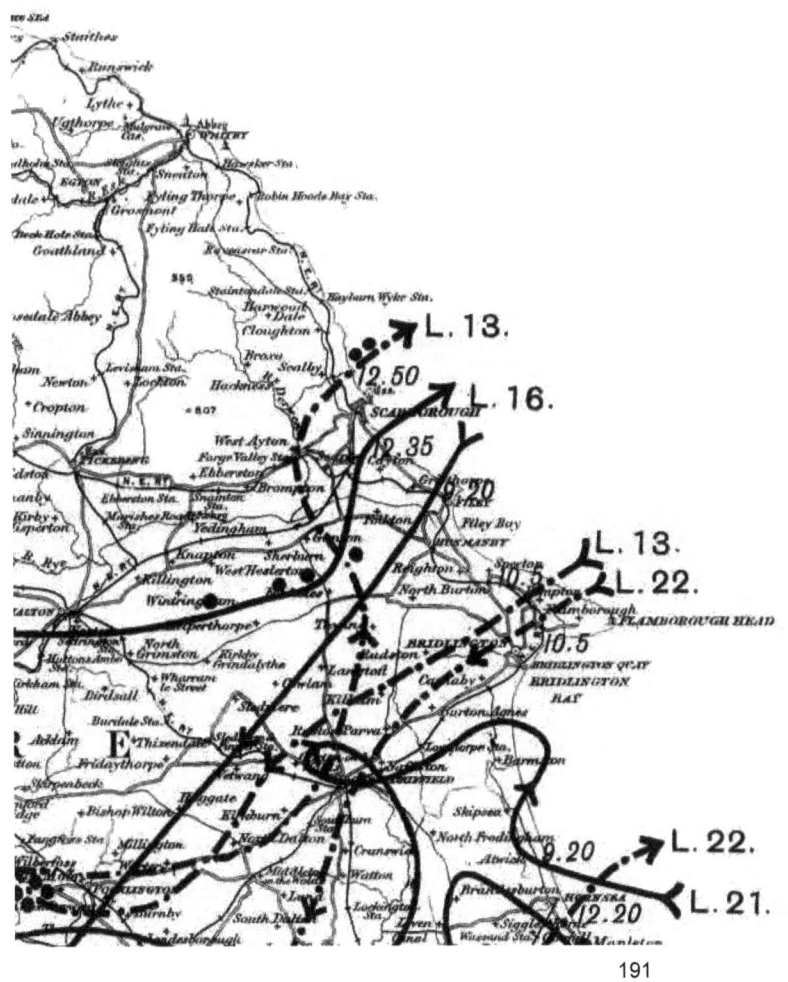

No. 42.

WEATHER:
    Light N.W. wind increasing North of the Wash.
    Ground mist in Leeds district.

BOMBS: 206.

CASUALTIES:
    4 killed, 37 injured.

MONETARY DAMAGE: £12,482.

NOTE: We followed the L.22 during part of her inland journey, with some difficulty. She claimed attacks on New Malton and York. No incoming airship passed near the former town. We traced no bombs from the L.22 on land, but it is not impossible she followed close behind L.13 (as her navigating officer stated) and was responsible for some of the bombs which fell on Barmby Moor and the outskirts of York attributed to the L.13.

Spread 3

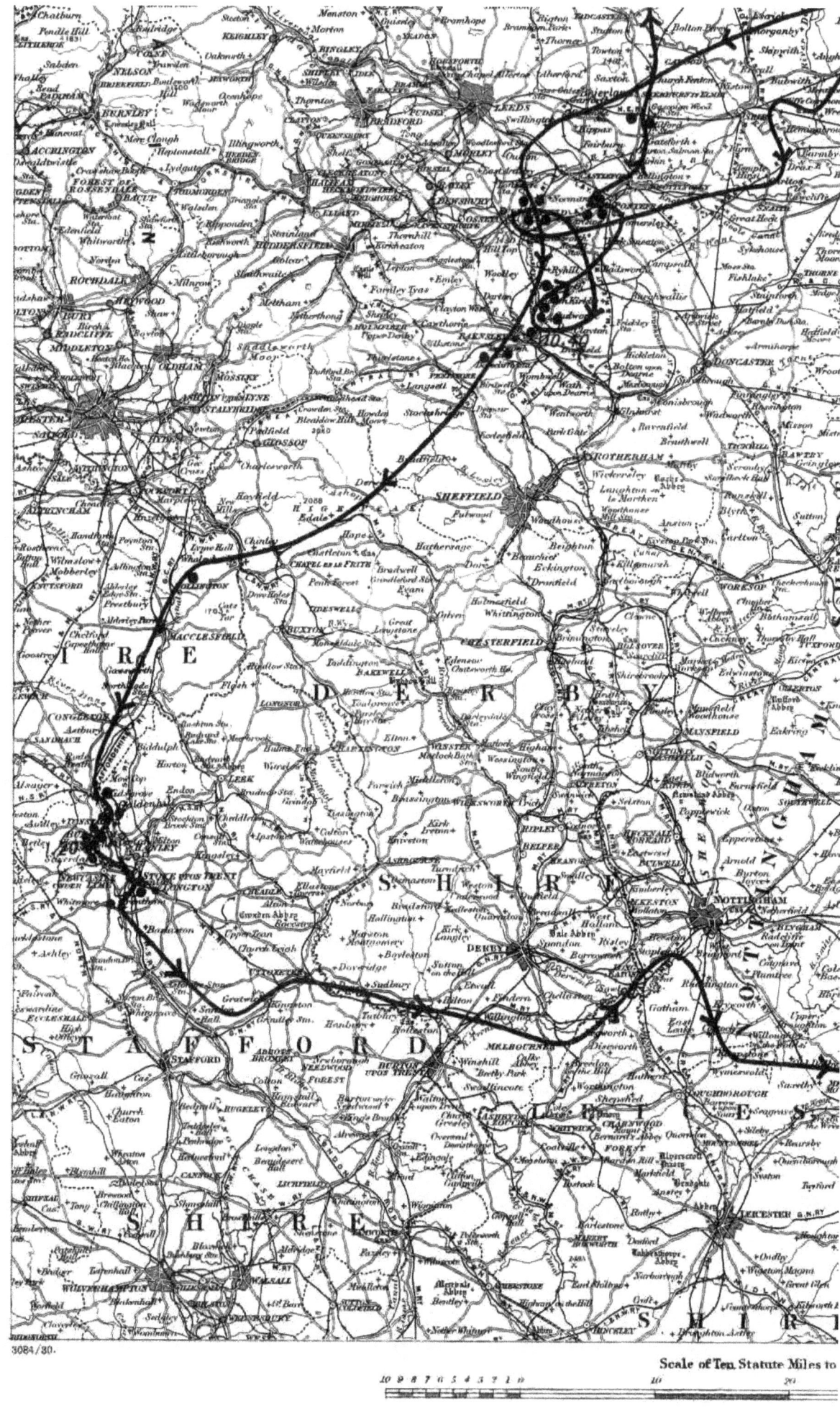

Spread 3

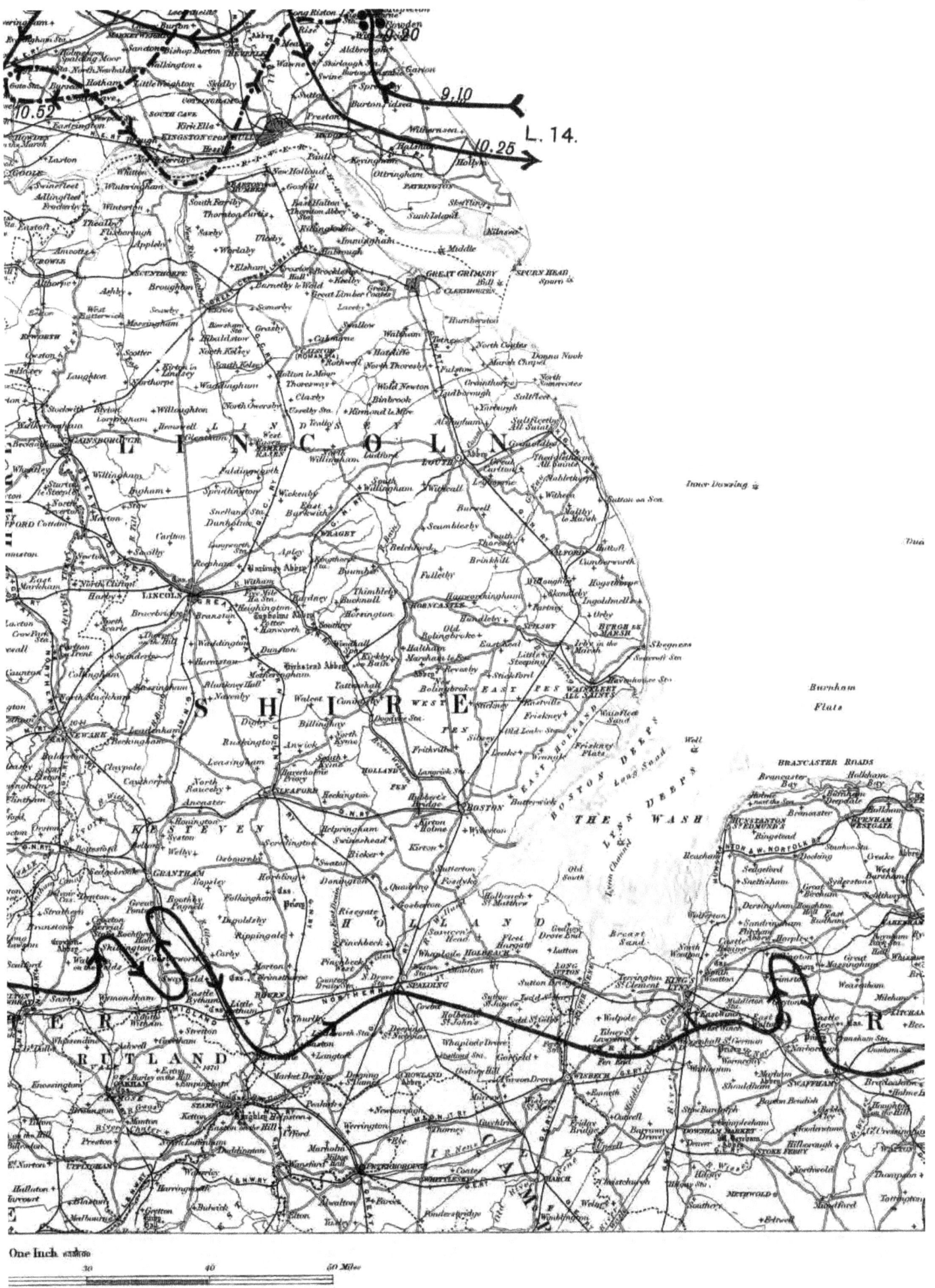

Spread 4

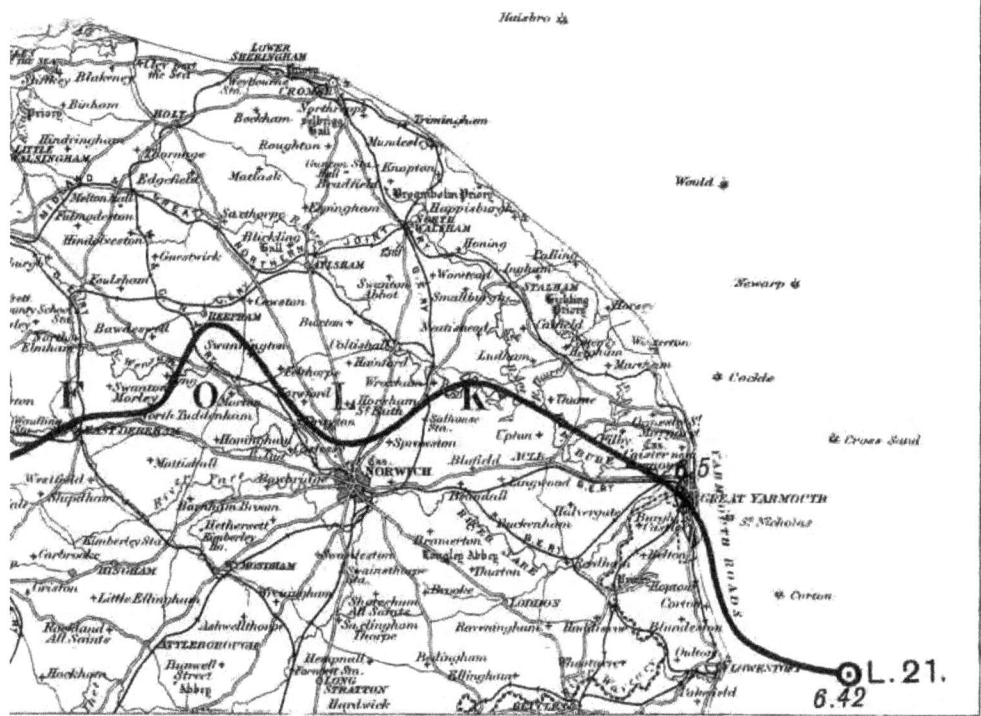

Ordnance Survey, 1930.

Spread 4